NOTHING FEELS GOOD

NOTHING FEELS GOOD

PUNK ROCK, TEENAGERS, AND EMO

Andy Greenwald

 st. martin's griffin ❧ new york

www.stmartins.com

Book design by Jonathan Bennett

Song permissions appear on page 321.

Library of Congress Cataloging-in-Publication Data

Greenwald, Andy.
    Nothing feels good : punk rock, teenagers, and emo / Andy Greenwald.
        p. cm.
    ISBN 0-312-30863-9
    1. Punk rock music—History and criticism. 2. Music and teenagers. 3. Emo (Music)—History and criticism. I. Title.

ML3534.G75 2003
781.66—dc22

                                                                    2003058543

10   9   8   7   6

For my parents, Anne and Michael Greenwald, and for Rachel Bien.
Out of love, respect, gratitude, and necessity.

CONTENTS

PREFACE

On a warm fall night in Manhattan, kids are buzzing around CBGB. From across the Bowery, it could be any night, any fall from the last twenty years—young discontents and their older, slightly mellowed fore-bears jacked up on caffeine/nicotine/alcohol/other waiting to get their collective rocks off at the seediest, oldest, and best punk club in New York City. But there's something different about this night, noticeable from the median and then rapidly more so as one approaches the entrance. These aren't the violently pierced, mohawked, leathered, pleathered, and glassy-eyed punks of yesteryear—there isn't a single Ramones jacket or safety pin in sight. Nor are they the dirty-jeaned, big-booted collection of indie-rockers, diehards, and straight-edgers of punk's more recent milieu. The kids here are different. Shockingly, bizarrely so. The kids, it appears, are all right.

There are young girls in powder blue, midriff-baring tank tops embla-zoned with the word "rockstar" emerging from idling SUVs, waving goodbye to their parents behind the wheel with a dismissive nod. There are clean-cut high school boys wearing baseball hats and overly long shorts and khakis. Serious-looking fifteen-year-olds smile awkwardly and switch off their cell phones. There is backslapping. There are high-pitched giggles.

It's a young and different crowd, in from the suburbs and out in the big city tonight for a concert. Here to watch their version of punk ascend triumphantly and not notice the differences. To sing along wide-eyed and happy. To feel better at the end of the night instead of bruised.

It's November 2001 and I'm attending my very first Dashboard Con-fessional concert. The city is unseasonably warm and wary—what hap-pened two months before still hangs heavy, but not heavy enough to weigh down the enormous anticipation that's building inside CB's scarred innards. Before the show, I run into a friend who attends NYU. She laughs when she sees me. "I never figured you for an emo kid," she says. "I didn't either," I answer. She's just there to keep her friend company—her friend who, at twenty-one is a good three years above the room's median age. She seems embarrassed to be there—or at the very least to be asked about it.

"Are you a big fan?" I ask the friend.

"I think he's really good," she says.

Just then, the lights dim and the girls recede into the crowd. Some fellows in white T-shirts to my left climb on the back of chairs and start hooting. I catch a glimpse of a small Asian-American teen in glasses standing just below the stage furiously scribbling in her journal, oblivious to the diminishing light. Nervous applause ripples through the crowd. It's the awkward hum of a classroom when the teacher leaves to get help resetting the fraying film reel. Just before the juvenile boiling point is reached, a surprisingly short and compact dark-haired man walks out onto the stage alone. He musses with his collapsed black pompadour hairdo, swings his acoustic guitar to the front, squints into the expectant crowd, and flashes a rabbity, nervous smile.

"OK," Chris Carrabba says, "are you guys ready to try one?"

The crowd erupts, and, as the first few notes are plucked, what was once a disparate collection of homework-dodgers is transformed into a head-nodding choir. Carrabba's voice is a bit yelpy in spots, chasing the high notes like an affection-starved pet nipping at the heels of its owner. He has two full sleeves of tattoos on his arms, one of which strums out chunky acoustic chords. "You look cute in your blue jeans / but you're plastic just like the rest . . . dying to look smooth with your tattoos / but you're searching just like everyone." And the audience sings with him. Every single word, with some lingering behind and some charging forward. It's like an extremely successful bout of responsive reading, except the hypercharged and ecstatic look on the kids' faces says they're not just echoing—they're *emoting*. When the song ends, everyone screams, as much for themselves as for the shy-looking fellow on stage. The guys next to me are practically falling all over themselves. One of them, baseball hat perfectly molded to his head, arms thrown around his friends' shoulders, screams out, "We love you, Chris!"

The songs go on and on—and the crowd's voices never diminish. Halfway through, some of the guys are doing harmonies. It's hard to tell whether it's CB's notoriously low stage or Carrabba's small stature, but with each successive number the crowd seems to surge up higher and higher—both in volume and mass—until by the end the two sides are meeting each other full-on from the start of each song. Occasionally, Carrabba builds to a refrain and then merely steps away from the mic, letting the devotees fill in the blank. Someone walks past me towards the back, retreating from the stage, crying. But there is no moshing, no physical injuries. I've never seen such well-behaved teenagers in a rock club. Song after song with titles like "Again I Go Unnoticed" and "This Ruined Puzzle" have the kids around me glassy-eyed with glee and reverence.

After a few more rousing choruses, it's over.

As the lights—or what passes for lights in the cramped dankness of CB's—rise, taking away the equalizing darkness and any possible chance of a second encore, the kids file out, bouncing into chairs, jazzed up from the music, the scene, the experience, their hearts and other muscles sore from a bout of heavy emoting. The guys to my left continue to paw at each other—high-fiving, singing fragments of Dashboard songs, laughing over private jokes. Gritting my teeth; I turn to approach them. Though this night hasn't even flirted with the typical, I'm still wary. Usually, approaching kids in punk clubs and telling them that you write for *Spin* is roughly equivalent to tapping a bunch of starving wolves on the shoulder and casually mentioning that you're a rabbit.

"Excuse me," I try. The three boys are in mid-celebration, their arms thrown around each other's shoulders like they're doing the Superbowl Shuffle. They look up at me expectantly. "Hi. I'm a writer for *Spin* magazine doing a story about Dash—"

"Wow!" says the boy in the middle with the white baseball hat. This is slightly better than the slap I was pessimistically expecting.

"You guys seem like big fans. . . ."

"We are!"

"That's great. I was wondering if you'd be willing to talk to me about him sometime this week, over the phone or maybe even over email?"

The boys give me a look like they've just won the lottery.

"We'd love to!" gushes the one with spiky, wet-looking hair.

"Yeah, we'd be honored," says the broad-faced one, deadly serious for a second.

"We love Chris," says the white hat. "We'd do anything to help him out."

"That's great," I say, handing them business cards. "Please get in touch with me sometime next week, if you can."

"We sure will!"

They continue on their way, still high-fiving as if they'd just been given one more reason to celebrate. Watching them recede towards the exit, I imagine their broad, T-shirted backs would be equally plausible, if not more so, stumbling around the parking lots of Giants Stadium, desperately in search of nitrous balloons or a cheap, illicit beer before the Dave Matthews concert begins. But these kids weren't high. They were *polite*.

This wasn't normal to me. Not yet.

NOTHING FEELS GOOD

INTRODUCTION

Emo means different things to different people. Actually, that's a massive understatement. Emo seems *solely* to mean different things to different people—like pig latin or books by Thomas Pynchon, confusion is one of its hallmark traits. Casting back from its current status as the necessary name-dropping accoutrement in all music reporting, a general, wary-eyed consensus seems to date the term to 1984 (or thereabouts) and suburban Washington, D.C. (or thereabouts). Once there (or thereabouts), though, things begin to get sticky.

There are 47,150 matches for an "emo" search on MP3.com, 403,000 for a search on Google. On Amazon.com, dozens and dozens of user-made lists promise to aid the consumer in the purchase of only the finest in emo recordings. It's been used as a cover line (repeatedly) in magazines such as *Spin, NME, Rolling Stone, Alternative Press, College Music Journal,* and *Blender.* Stories have been written about it in every major daily newspaper, in *Time, Newsweek,* and by the Associated Press. Online, there are the websites emotionalpunk.com, emocore.com, and emoporn.com. The main page at emomusic.com once read, "Fuck You MTV: We Love Sellouts!" Another site, emo.com, is selling an obscure computer application called Writer's Workbench, and emopunk.com, apropos of nothing, has links to naughty pictures of ravers. There have been style guides in *Seventeen* and the *Honolulu Register.* There are even subgenres, like screamo and nuemo.

The word has survived and flourished in three decades, two millenniums, and two Bush administrations. It's older than four baseball teams, six basketball teams, four football teams, and two soccer leagues. It's older than five former Yugoslav republics, the last seven national spelling champions, and Avril Lavigne. It's older than most of its fans.

It's been a source of pride, a target of derision, a mark of confusion, and a sign of the times.

It's been the next big thing twice, the current big thing once, and so totally over millions of times.

And yet, not only can no one agree on what it means, there is not now, nor has there ever been, a single major band that admits to being emo. Not one.

That's pretty impressive. And contentious. And ridiculous. Good thing too—because so is emo.

Emo is short for emotional. But isn't all music emotional? Well, yes, or at least it should be. Originally, emo was short for "emocore," a strain of hardcore punk that was notable for its obsession with feelings (as opposed to politics, anger, and smashing stuff up). Then it started to be applied to bands that weren't punk, to fashion trends, to sad-eyed kids in the back of class. It's always been mildly derisive, a term used by haters and critics to dismiss something that's overly weepy, self-indulgent, or unironic. Every generation that loves emo bands simultaneously rejects the term while claiming ownership of it—meaning even if they won't admit that they love emo, they certainly will say how much they hate everything that's been called emo since them. But still, no one knows what it is.

This total confusion was best displayed in a simple questionnaire I sent out to friends and colleagues of different backgrounds, locations, and ages. The email itself was simple—I asked for help writing this book and asked four questions to work towards a definition of "emo." The questions were: What is emo?, When did you first hear the term?, What is an example of an emo band?, and Have you ever encountered a band that actually referred to themselves as emo? As with most things regarding emo, the answers proved to be more trouble than the original questions.

Andrew Beaujon, a thirty-four-year-old writer and musician, is originally from the D.C. area and first encountered the term in 1985, "when it was a joke." Perhaps a little jaded, he defines emo as "an unnatural attraction to the Smiths that continues after high school and mates with a love of power chords" and goes on to say that "the term seems to make people who actually fit emo's classic definition (e.g., the Promise Ring) violently angry." Thirty-two-year-old Darren Walters, co-owner of the independent Jade Tree record label, has a more serious definition: "Originally it was a genre of hardcore punk that was less focused on politics and heavy music and more on personal politics and melody. It looked to address issues of a personal nature that were being overlooked in the extremely political punk landscape of the Reagan era." Tristin Laughter, a thirty-one-year-old publicist, agrees with Edwards: "Emo is a subgenre of punk rock. Its roots are found in the mid-eighties D.C. scene, but many other contemporary American punk bands echoed its characteristic frantic, wailing, big-guitar sound and its eschewing of pop sensibility in favor of an emotional and musical rawness." Tristin has devoted her life to punk, so she's more than a little prickly about today's music being lumped in with her emo heroes of yesteryear: "In 2002 emo is just a term used to mean poppy punk with intense fans." To hear Tristin tell it, emo was the last great artistic movement of the millennium. She claims that "emo clearly shows the connection between twentieth-century American punk and nineteenth-century French romanticism." One would think that the respondents' age would correspond to the gravitas of their feelings, but the reverse was often true. Thirty-two-year-old Jason Roth, a major-label record publicist, claims he never heard the term until the late '90s, even though he was listening to lots of D.C. punk as it was happening.

For those over thirty, emo is a fixed, definite thing that has been sullied, confused, and lost. For those under twenty, it's as all-encompassing, elusive, and powerful as a deity. Eighteen-year-old Utah-born Whitney Borup enthuses, "Emo is emotion. Music charged with emotions that people can relate to. Music that makes people feel they're not alone in their sadness . . . or even in their happiness." Texan Taylor Stolly, sixteen, claims that, "to me, all music is emotional. The word emo is just a word that people use these days for bands that write songs about girls and life and stuff—which is cool because that's my cup of tea." Seventeen-year-old Jesse Williamson is more specific: "I would say that a song is emo based on the lyrics; they need to be very deep, insightful, and poetic." Eighteen-year-old Ian Bauer combines elements of his peers' observations to make his own, writing that, "emo is 'punkish' music with lyrics that allow you to connect both musically and emotionally with yourself, the band, other people listening to the music, and pretty much everything. It's music aimed for the heart of the listeners—like all music—but based on things people experience in daily life."

The one thing everyone agrees on is that they've never encountered a band that claimed to be emo. Not one of them. Throughout 2002, while researching this book, I asked dozens—if not hundreds—of people this question and never once received a "yes." Being called emo is a scarlet E across your guitar strap—a mark of shame or a reason to beg off and plead ignorance. Being an emo band is kinda like being in the KGB— everyone knows who they are, but no one admits anything and no one likes talking about it in public. Why is this? I can provide three reasons.

1. EMO IS A LAME WORD. Why would anyone in their right mind choose to be called something so silly, reductive, and confusing? As Andrew Beaujon put it in his response to the above questionnaire: "Only artists who'd be just as happy selling shoes don't mind labels."

2. HEARD ANY GOOD GRUNGE BANDS LATELY? The last time there was a media buzzword thrown at bands, many of them didn't survive the impact. Before *Nevermind* was released, Nirvana was a punk band, mining the grooves of old Pixies and Hüsker Dü records for inspiration. Afterwards, it was the preeminent grunge band, a musical style known more for its flannel shirts than its stylistic consistency. It's the marketers, the publicists, and the radio formatters who refer to music by genre, certainly not the bands themselves. (When was the last time you heard the Red Hot Chili Peppers refer to themselves as a "modern rock" act or, even better, the Dixie Chicks professing their solidarity with the "Triple A" scene?) Nobody wants to hitch their careers to a bandwagon. Unless, of course, they wouldn't mind selling shoes.

3. READ THE FINE PRINT. Or, how can you agree to be something if no one knows what it is? Which takes us back to square one, or the beginning of this chapter. (Note: please don't actually go back to the beginning of the chapter—if you do we'll never get through this.)

The truth is, the thread that connects the D.C. hardcore bands of the '80s with the lovelorn, clean-cut pop-rockers of the '00s doesn't lie in the music at all; it's in the fans. Emo isn't a genre—it's far too messy and contentious for that. What the term does signify is a particular relationship between a fan and a band. It's the desire to turn a monologue into a dialogue, to be a part of the art that affects you and to connect to it on every possible level—sentiments particularly relevant in an increasingly corporate, suburban, and diffuse culture such as ours. Emo is a specific sort of teenage longing, a romantic and ultimately self-centered need to understand the bigness of the world in relation to *you*. It takes its cues from the world-changing slap of community-oriented punk, the heart-swollen pomp of power ballads, and the gee-whiz nostalgia of guitar pop. Emo is as specific as adolescence and lasts about as long.

In short, everyone has their own emo. It's too contentious, too stylistically and generationally diverse to be a genre, too far-reaching to be a subculture. Emo is an essential element of being a teenager. It is the sound of self-making. Emo—or whatever you call it—doesn't happen on the stage and it doesn't happen in the diary. It happens somewhere between the two. It is the act of reaching out towards something larger to better know yourself. It's the desire to make yourself bigger by making yourself part of something bigger.

And so, by rights, emo could be anything. But for those reading who don't know a Promise Ring from a Makeoutclub, please relax and think of it this way: Emo is seeking a tangible connection out of intangible things. It's the painting that you stare at because it makes you calm; it's the book you read and re-read every year because it reminds you of childhood. Emo is Fitzgerald's eternal green light and emo is Salinger hoping beyond hope that Jane Gallagher will keep all her kings safely in the back row, even while he knows that for her to do so would be impossible.

Emo is the music you carry with you—it's why your parents cry at *The Big Chill,* why your older sister tears up at *Say Anything* or *Singles.* Except in emo's case, we're talking about soundtracks to real life, not a movie.

As long as there are feelings, teenagers will claim that they had them first. And as long as there are teenagers, music will get labeled emo.

PART ONE

EMOTIVATIONS

ONE

The one fact no one seems to debate—or at least debate that loudly—is that emo emerged from hardcore.

As author Stephen Blush puts it in his *American Hardcore: A Tribal History* (2001), "hardcore was the suburban American response to the late-seventies punk revolution." At the beginning of the '80s, the first wave of punk rock had shot its bolt. It had been replaced in the natural consciousness by its artier stepson, New Wave, co-opted by big business and major labels, and flattened by disco. It may have been the beginning of "morning in America," but night still fell occasionally, and there was a generation of disaffected kids on the outskirts of the country's cultural capitals seething with resentment and untapped creative energy. Hardcore pushed punk's intensity to the breaking point—far, far past style, convention, and, oftentimes, past melody. The godfathers of hardcore were California's Black Flag, a raggedy group of self-loathing outsiders from the surf towns south of Los Angeles. Rejected by the mainstream and the hipper-than-thou underground, Black Flag's music bubbled with resentment and self-doubt.

But it would be in the even less cool town of Washington, D.C., that hardcore would unleash its most definitive act: Minor Threat. Formed in 1980 by a bunch of furious teenage outcasts from D.C.'s Wilson High School and led by the infernally charismatic Ian MacKaye, Minor Threat found artistry in economy, pumping the bottomless teenaged well of rage—against the establishment, against the cops, against apathy and each other—to fuel blistering, ferociously short sharp sonic shocks in the form of songs. The beats were monochromatic and the instruments were raced as fast as they possibly could go—the goal was catharsis through the passionate expenditure of energy. MacKaye's lyrics were didactic and instructive, battering against the audience like a shoulder

against a locked door. On "Seeing Red," MacKaye railed against getting picked on ("you taunt me from safe inside your crowd") and when he voiced his anger in the chorus those in the crowd, knowing exactly what he was talking about, would scream the words back at him, pointing their fists, testifying. This interaction was the key to the performance.

Some found MacKaye's stridently political hollering overly preachy; others were leery of hardcore's propensity for violence. Despite the rage, however, hardcore, at its racing heart, was about community. On the song "Minor Threat," MacKaye voices a very sweet and simple plea to hold onto youth. Ever prescient, MacKaye knew that this band, this particular form of expression, was equally fleeting: "'cause we're all heading for that adult crash / the time is so little, the time belongs to us / why is everybody in such a fucking rush?" Minor Threat—the band—rode a wave of localized frustration and made entire rooms sing out the stress. Taking this one step further, MacKaye would often pass the mic into the crowd, sharing the power of the stage, transforming a republic into a true democracy. Near the end of the band's two-year life span, the other members grew sick of MacKaye's encouragement of the audience to rush the stage and become part of the performance. As MacKaye told Michael Azerrad in *Our Band Could Be Your Life* (2001), "I love hearing people sing along with bands—I think it's incredible. There's few things that affect me more powerfully than a room full of people singing with a band."

MacKaye used this dedication to community to foster one in his hometown of D.C. He and Minor Threat drummer Jeff Nelson founded a record label, Dischord, in their basement that thrives to this day, and MacKaye fought just as hard to support bands started by his friends and family as he did to keep ticket prices low. But by the end of two years together Minor Threat's outward anger had begun to dim slightly. As with all rebels, it becomes harder to work up the requisite rage when more and more people are finding what you have to say persuasive. So, as their numbers grew, the hardcore kids began turning their anger in on themselves. Divisions appeared within Minor Threat—some band members became fans of the chiming guitars of U2 and wanted to expand the group's sound, others wanted to consider signing to a major label. While MacKaye sang about topics ranging from failed friendships to racial politics, his most influential anthem was "Straight Edge," a punishing song

excoriating those who sought strength in the weakness of drugs or drink. What had started as a community was slowly being brought back to the individual, to, in a very real sense, the only thing that each of us is truly able to change. "Ian made this decision in the mid-eighties to not drink or do drugs, and then he started singing about it," Jawbox/Burning Airlines guitarist J. Robbins told *Spin* in 1998. "And soon after that, people started examining their politics. Up until that point, you could just say 'Fuck the system! Fuck the system!' but then we were like, 'What does that mean?' Maybe we need to stop being so negative and leave behind some of the overt trappings of punk rock, like the mosh pit, which had just turned into this ritual where people got hurt."

Minor Threat broke up in 1983, leaving a perfect legacy of twenty-six songs. Those songs would, over the following two decades, inspire countless bands to adopt the hardcore sound, image, and politics, and countless more to misappropriate the spirit of the music as an excuse for wanton violence. But to those who made it, the music was over. "When I started hearing bands who were just playing the same thing . . . that's where it lost its soul to me," MacKaye told Azerrad. Hardcore is statement, a thrown punch. Once delivered, it can't be undone, and repetition is often pointless.

It is often after the rage dissipates when the possibility for real change begins. Minor Threat hadn't transformed the world, but it had put the world on notice. While many of his imitators imagined hardcore as an end to a means, to MacKaye it was always about articulating a means to an end. The band had gotten that far. Something had to come next.

Guy Picciotto, a tall, wiry, handsome student at the elite Georgetown Day School, was a huge Minor Threat fan and, though he had little musical training or inclination, he fervently believed in the power of music. Harnessing all of the anger, disillusionment, paranoia, and fear to which MacKaye had given a voice, he turned every last drop of it in on himself. The name of the band he formed, Rites of Spring, was cannily chosen—it echoed the riot-inducing Stravinsky piece that had shocked the world seventy years before, a true example of artistic expression fomenting a cultural and political shift.

With Rites of Spring, the goal was no longer to shake your fist at the injustices of the world, it was to shake yourself, to push down, "Deeper

Than Inside," as one song put it, to confront and break down the limitations of the self. "To hurt yourself playing guitar while falling around onstage is far more noble than to be sitting weeping to yourself somewhere," Picciotto said at the time. There was a certain nobility about the music that Rites performed—breaking free of the rigid, self-imposed bonds of hardcore, the guitars careened dramatically and melodically across the songs like paintbrushes on canvas, the rhythms enlivening and varied. Yet it was Picciotto himself who made the band what it was, taking to the microphone like Van Gogh took to his own ear; he was heroically, desperately impassioned, screaming and moaning, often refusing to sing at band practice so that he could more fully unload onstage. "The world is my fuse," he screamed wildly on one song, waving his body like a lit match. Even though the band members were dirt poor, they destroyed their instruments with abandon.

Picciotto's lyrics were like nothing ever heard before in punk rock: majestic, poetic, indulgent, ecstatic. At times he would swoon like a punch-drunk Rimbaud ("drink deep, it's just a taste / and it might not come this way again"), but mostly he would lead the charge against his own limitations: "once inside, gonna tear till there's nothing left to find," he sang, "and from inside, outside just can fall apart." On one song, the frustration was romantic: "I read somewhere that every wall's a door to something new / well if that's true—why can't I get through . . . / it feels like I'm falling through a hole in my heart . . . / I could walk around—fall in love with a face or two / but it wouldn't be you." On another, morbid: "hope's just a rope to hang myself with." But again and again, Picciotto was stymied by a lack of true communication, an inability to connect with another like-minded soul: "if I started crying would you start crying? / now I started crying—why are you not crying?" he wailed on "Theme." On "In Silence/Words Away" he sang, "I am not living—in someone else's eyes I am lived," and on "Patience" he was "wanting to understand . . . a hand that's not my hand . . . wanting a heart and hearts that won't just beat on their own."

Though his themes and artistic references—including numerous echoes of T. S. Eliot—were far more rarified and driven than much of the emo that was to come, Picciotto's lyrics do contain a number of images and tropes that would become familiar: nostalgia ("caught in time so far away from where our hearts really wanted to be / reaching out to find a way to get back to where we'd been"), romantic bitterness ("I was the champion of forgive forget / but I haven't found a way to forgive you yet"), and general poetic desperation ("it's so hard /'cause the night can fill my eyes").

Somewhat perversely, Picciotto's relentless lyrical self-mutilation became a rallying cry for a community. Whereas Minor Threat's fury transformed disparate outcasts into a unified, extroverted force, Rites of Spring brought together an inspired hodgepodge of individuals eager to convert private pain into public purging. At Rites of Spring shows, audience members would weep among strangers; hardened cynics would rock and sway like born-agains. On what may be Rites of Spring's most definitive song, "Remainder," Picciotto martyrs himself for his own sins, but therein glimpses a world of redemption:

> *We are all trapped in prisons of the mind, it's a hard*
> *sensibility but we'll see it through in time, but when*
> *words come between us noiseless in the air, believe me*
> *I know it's easy to despair—don't.*
> *Tonight I'm talking to myself—there's no one that I*
> *know as well, thoughts collide without a sound,*
> *frantic, fighting to be found.*
> *And I've found things in this life that still are real*
> *A remainder refusing to be concealed.*
> *And I've found the answer lies in real emotion*
> *Not the self-indulgence of a self-devotion.*

In 1984, Jenny Toomey was a high school junior in suburban Chevy Chase, Maryland. Politically active from a young age, Jenny spent far more time participating in protests at the South African Embassy than she did collecting records. "I came sort of reluctantly to punk, music-wise," she says. "The first punk records I heard left me a little flat—it just didn't seem like there was that much going on." But one day in school, two friends of hers couldn't stop talking about a band they had seen the night before—it was Rites of Spring's first show and it had left them breathless. Intrigued, Jenny went to check the band out when they next played. She was blown away.

"Once you saw them . . ." she trails off, awe creeping into her voice even now. "They just didn't hold back at all. They were completely charismatic. There wasn't any real distinction from the role of the audience and the role of the band. There was this insane connection; as soon as you saw it, you wanted it. I think for a lot of people of a young age, where you're finding yourself and your peers, it was hard not to feel that this wasn't the coolest thing in the entire world."

From that point on, Jenny says, she "lived from show to show." The D.C. scene was, at that time, incredibly small and incestuous, but, simultaneously, wide open to newcomers. "When a scene is that small," Jenny says, "you don't have the luxury of saying people aren't punk. You don't have the numbers to define it. So there was a lot of diversity and a lot of women around. Honestly, at that time it barely went beyond twenty-five people who lived in group houses and worked at six jobs and had twelve bands between them. Half of them had the same tattoo and were best, best friends. It had the same function as people who try to suck you into a cult might have. To be eighteen and surrounded by all those stupid eighteen-year-old things—keg parties and the like—and then all of a sudden to be presented with a charismatic group of thinking people offering not only cooler things to be doing but also numbers. So at a Rites show you could actually be in the majority because you didn't drink, weren't an idiot, and cared about emotions. It was great, like flipping a coin, reversing the norms. When you went to a show you felt like you could be who you liked to be."

Rites of Spring may have been the most important band in D.C. of its time, but it certainly wasn't alone. Ian MacKaye was such a huge Rites fan that he not only recorded what was to be the band's only album in 1985 and served as a roadie for them while on tour, but his own new band, Embrace, explored similar themes of self-searching and emotional release. Other peers followed suit, including Grey Matter, the archly political and arty Beefeater, and Fire Party, whom Jenny termed "the world's first female-fronted emo band."

The origins of the term "emo" are shrouded in mystery—Jenny states that both a guy named Mike and one named Dan claim to be its inventors—but it first came into common practice in 1985. If Minor Threat was hardcore, then Rites of Spring, with its altered focus, was emotional hardcore, or emocore. "It didn't mean anything then and it doesn't to me now," says Jenny. "The only people that used it at first were the ones that were jealous over how big and fanatical a scene it was. The band existed well before the term did and they hated it. But there was this weird moment, like when people started calling music 'grunge,' where you were using the term even though you hated it."

The bands that earned the emo moniker addressed politics in relatable ways (Beefeater's Tomas Squip would silence thugs by hugging them and chase away homophobes by sticking flowers in his ass); they preached local and practiced it as well.

Rites of Spring burned brightly and quickly: after only fourteen shows, merely two of which were outside the D.C. area, it was over. And those who felt alienated by the openness of the emo movement quickly mocked its passing. "It immediately became a big joke in the fanzines," says Jenny, "but people absolutely cried at the shows. And to this day I can't go into a gospel music tent without welling up. The idea that music doesn't have the power to change your emotions or to make you think is a slap in the face to everything we know. If you turn on certain kinds of music and want to dance it only makes sense that when confronted with people performing that nakedly, you'd cry. That's the definition of great art." Jenny herself continues to live her life in a manner that is in keeping with her emo experiences. In the early '90s she fronted a seminal indie-rock band, Tsunami, and co-ran a hugely influential label, Simple Machines, based on the Dischordian principals of fairness, quality, and Do it Yourselfism. Today, Jenny Toomey runs the Future of Music Coalition, a nonprofit lobbying and educational organization based on the fundamental belief that "music works better in small groups of cherished listeners than in huge masses of consumers."

What had happened in D.C. in the mid-eighties—the shift from anger to action, from extroverted rage to internal turmoil, from an individualized mass to a mass of individuals—was in many ways a test case for the transformation of the national punk scene over the next two decades. The imagery, the power of the music, the way people responded to it, and the way the bands burned out instead of fading away—all have their origins in those few performances by Rites of Spring. The roots of emo were laid, however unintentionally, by fifty or so people in the nation's capitol. And, in some ways, it was never as good and surely never as pure again. Certainly, the Washington scene was the only time "emocore" had any consensus definition as a genre. Moreover, the relative insularity of the scene allowed the personal connections made through the music to be intimate and lasting. The types of people involved were also limited, so a prevailing liberal/activist attitude towards business and politics—both personal and national—was allowed to flourish. In the following years, as the politics were slowly stripped away from the music, the result was often a direct contradiction of "Remainder"; the "self-indulgence of self-devotion" grew prevalent and became an obvious bull's-eye for a legion of critics.

Better than anyone before or since, Guy Picciotto articulated a sensibility that is both wide-eyed and stiff-upper-lipped, pretentious and self-effacing, artistic and physical. The music his band produced remains utterly fresh and vital; his words tiptoe through minefields of excess, remaining suprisingly clever and occasionally subtle. Those who were moved by Rites of Spring often scoff at their descendants, and their descendants are very often ignorant about their heritage or unconvinced about the existence of a connection. (It is, some would argue, a downward spiral from bohemian to boo-hoo.) But to hear Jenny Toomey talk about Rites of Spring is to hear any teenager from any era talk about the bands that mattered to them, and that, above all else, is the thread from Rites to Dashboard Confessional to the internet and beyond.

"To be honest," she says, "I don't know if it would affect me with the same kind of power now. I was a junior in high school and it was the perfect time to listen to Rites of Spring. They had distilled a certain kind of frustration that is unique to teenagers. The songs were about you and your peer group; the love songs were often about friendships, not sweethearts. It was just an incredible period of time for me."

TWO

KISSING BOTTLES AND TALKING
TO ANGELS

While the emo movement burned out relatively quickly in Washington, D.C., the ideals it espoused, like hardcore before it, spread quickly across the country, infecting and altering the nation's mostly disconnected network of regional scenes. Since the late '70s, punk movements had sprung up and been carefully tended to in unexpected pockets of the country—the more suburban, dull, and culturally isolated the locale, the more likely it was to have a strident local scene. (The country's most enduring hardcore scenes have been Orange County, California, and the Long Island and New Jersey suburbs.) Everywhere that the music went, it changed to better suit the community that formed around it. Punk, then as now, was a life preserver for young people: one size fits all. The conflict between the unity within a scene and the distrust without fueled changes and dialogue in the music and culture. The spread of "emocore"—disseminated through a clandestine network of homemade zines, vinyl, and hearsay—cut a new-style trail of tears across the country, offering sensitive punks an exit strategy from the immolating, furious monotony of hardcore. Barricaded in a solitary room, the door pushed tight to keep the outside world out, hardcore kids suddenly gained a window letting in a ray of sunshine.

In D.C., meanwhile, the trendsetters of the two genres—Ian MacKaye and Guy Picciotto—joined forces in a new band, a quartet called Fugazi. The group's sound was as generous and expansive as its songwriters, drawing in elements of hardcore, metal, funk, and jazz to create music as fiercely confident as it was diverse. Over its decade-plus lifespan, Fugazi has blazed a trail that is utterly uncompromised—unimpeachable in terms of both consistency and politics. Fugazi is one of the best and most influential groups of the last thirty years—and yet, despite some opinion to the contrary, they are not an emo band. Fugazi's fan

17

base is too varied, too diffuse—its themes likewise. Fugazi is a living blueprint for a truly committed, punk/DIY artistic life once both the rage and the tears have faded. Making the group, perhaps, an emo doctoral program, but not emo. People have their preconceived ideas crushed by Fugazi, they don't have crushes on its members.

From New England to Colorado, from Southern California to Milwaukee, frustrated hardcore kids began to see emo as a way to marry the intensity they found so appealing with the surprising and discomforting range of emotions brought on by growing older. All hardcore kids loved the Smiths—the terminally maudlin English pop group fronted by the fey complexities of Morrissey. The Smiths shared a fatalism with hardcore, a sense of theatrics and outsiderness that struck a chord with those usually allergic to quiet music or—gasp—melody. Morrissey's monkish/macho asceticism was a match for hardcore's uncompromising, dramatic worldview; if all resistance is physical, then all emotions should be maudlin. Emo was, in many ways, the perfect marriage between the Smiths and hardcore—a splash of Technicolor in a monochrome world. Across the country bands began to play music in the newly minted emocore style: over-the-top lyrics about feelings wedded to dramatic but decidedly punk music. Though the faces and specifics changed from city to city and state to state, the aesthetic was more or less the same.

"Once punk and hardcore had swelled nationally to hundreds of thousands of people," says Jenny Toomey, "only then did people start grading what was punk and what wasn't. What was once a hugely diverse space quickly codified into the sound of a white boy singing and crying."

Jim Adkins, the singer and guitarist for the latter-day emo band Jimmy Eat World, grew up in the suburbs of Phoenix, Arizona, and remembers hearing the term for the first time. "To me and my friends, emo was always synonymous with hardcore," he says. "I think it's relative to where you grew up, what these words—punk, hardcore, emo—mean. If you grew up in Southern California you're going to have a much different definition of hardcore than if you grew up on Long Island. So, to us, emo and hardcore meant the same thing, really. Bands like Julia, Indian Summer, and Current. They were emo."

While the bands themselves may have varied from scene to scene in the late '80s, the music did little to advance the spirit or sound of Rites

of Spring. (Though one aspect of Rites was clearly lost in translation and transmission: a sense of humor. Many have criticized emo for its self-righteous self-importance, and a dominant vision of Washington, D.C., as an ascetically pure, monkish musical mecca, exists amongst the various regional scenes. Rites of Spring used to have an iron donkey onstage with them.) To some, the sound of hardcore music with impassioned lyrics is the end-all and be-all of emo. This view mistakes musical moment for genre. Emo is the soundtrack to youth, and as times change, so does the music that resonates with young people. The history of emo is one of reinvention and bigger and bigger stages—of shifting musical styles and baggage across generations. The key to tracking its growth, migration, and development lies in following the intimacy that Jenny Toomey felt in D.C.

To that end, two bands stand out as advancing the emo cause into the 1990s. Two groups led the way out of the world of regional punk and a step closer to the mainstream. Two different bands, in a relatively short amount of time, fostered similar cult followings and, in so doing, redefined, reintroduced, and recontextualized the word "emo" for an entirely new generation.

Sunny Day Real Estate was emo's head and Jawbreaker its busted gut—the two overlapped in the heart, then broke up before they made it big. Each had a lasting impact on the world of independent music. The bands shared little else but fans, and yet somehow the combination of the two lays down a fairly effective blueprint for everything that was labeled emo for the next decade. While Jawbreaker found poetry in the stumbling drunks down on the corner, Sunny Day had ecstatic visions of winged deities in the night sky. One looked up and one looked down, but both cemented the place of fearless, emotional indulgence in punk rock.

When Nirvana broke in 1991, the underground was dragged blinking, kicking, and screaming into daylight. Like it or not, subculture was now big business and regional and independent acts gained access to the national stage. There was no such thing as national punk until Nirvana. New distribution networks cropped up; touring routes became codified. A generation of high schoolers suddenly declared themselves fans of independent music; being punk was mainstream. Those who felt their heads spin around upon first listen to *Nevermind* went out in search of new fixes. With the harsh glare of the spotlight thrust upon them, punk bands changed and adapted to suit the circumstances. With the expansion of the emo aesthetic to the mainstream, punk rock no-nos like the cult of personality and artistic abstraction suddenly became de rigueur. If one definition of emo has always been music that felt like a secret, Jawbreaker and Sunny Day Real Estate were cast in the roles of the biggest gossips of all, reigning as the largest influences on every emo band that came after them.

Spanning two coasts, three genres, countless throat polyps, and an entire generation of heartsick boys, Jawbreaker is the Rosetta stone of contemporary emo. Singer/guitarist Blake Schwartzenbach, bassist Christ Bauermeister, and drummer Adam Pfahler formed the band as students at NYU in the late '80s. After moving to San Francisco, the band muscled out its own niche and eventual legacy with a sonic shotgun marriage between the bristly heft of hardcore, the songwriting sensibility of Cali pop-punk, and the tortured artistry of D.C. emo. Schwartzenbach's throat sounded like a rusty corrogated pipe pumping ache and bile from his heart directly to the microphone; his hoarse cries gave voice to scores of similarly disillusioned post-collegiate souls. Too smart for slackerdom, too heartsick to get out of bed, Jawbreaker and their fans were like their namesake: rock-hard on the outside with endless layers of sickeningly sweet complexity buried within.

Jawbreaker's first album, *Unfun,* was released on a tiny indie label in 1990—but while the band's sound was fairly standard pop-punk, Schwartzenbach's lyrical and vocal intensity separated them from the pack of like-minded Northern California bands. *Unfun's* most memorable song is its first track, the bouncy, accessible "Want," which is shocking only in its naked delivery of the chorus; when Schwartzenbach howls, "I want you," the desperation in his voice is palpable. A sentiment that would have seemed sanitized in other throats cuts through the song like a Ginsu through a tin can. The band, along with San Francisco peers Green Day, began to get notice both in the Bay Area and beyond. Brett Matthews, a Berkeley-based music writer, clearly remembers the day he picked up the 12-inch advance single "Chesterfield King," the first song available from Jawbreaker's second album, *Bivouac.* "I had heard of the band," he remembers, "and picked up the record because it had an amazingly cool-looking picture on the cover. But I wonder how things would have been different if I had listened to the record before seeing the band live—because coincidentally I ended up seeing the band that very night. More than anything else, they were a live band that made records. Musically, they weren't too dissimilar from other local bands. But live, they brought the entire crowd into a trance. They could transcend and transfer these emotions to the audience through these instrumental grooves that they would lock into live. I might not always have gotten what they meant, but I always got what it meant to me."

Jawbreaker songs weren't overly sentimental and their shows weren't displays of excess or indulgence. They merely communicated an intangible sense of longing that triggered young people's hearts like defibrillators. "We weren't a political band because we didn't know or care that much about politics," Pfahler says from the video store he now owns in San Francisco. "Our politics manifested in the way we did our business and behaved as human beings."

The band's insistence on focusing on the personal, the lived, the immediate helped improve their songwriting by leaps and bounds; it also centered the spotlight directly on Schwartzenbach. It wasn't that his songs were vague and offered up a malleable palatte for the audience, though they were often obscure and metaphor-heavy. It was that the imagery and word choices were so specific to one man. On Jawbreaker's second album, *Bivouac,* the songs were deeply rooted in the specific concerns of Schwartzenbach. Oftentimes, the lyrics were lifted directly from his journal without editing or comment. The attraction then was to the songwriter; it wasn't the song that the listeners related to, it was the singer.

The charisma of Schwartzenbach was what helped establish Jawbreaker as a national act following the release of *Bivouac.* The music was a rougher, bruised sibling of Green Day's snotty power-pop, but while Billie Joe Armstrong took a perverse, jolly pride in his sad-sack state, Schwartzenbach internalized everything. "Green Day is the mindless, straightforward version of Jawbreaker," Brent Matthews says. "They're very easy on the ears, play what people want to hear. They're a great band, but Jawbreaker is deep and twisted. Blake was writing from his heart—everything, from sweet to bitter to evil, is to the extreme."

Bands like Rites of Spring had attracted listeners because of Picciotto's skill as a representative mouthpiece for the thoughts and fears of the audience. Jawbreaker, with its dominant voice and searingly personal POV, produced emo's first idol. Schwartzenbach was handsome in an unassuming way, but that wasn't the point. His appeal was his publicly private torment. There was a bitterness and frustration in his lyrics that was both universal and magnetic. Schwartzenbach was the poet laureate of scruffy white male angst and, by couching his thoughts in his own inscrutable metaphors, he set a pattern that bands would follow for the next decade. "He has a way of expressing himself about negative and hurtful feelings that most people feel but could never put into words," Matthews says. "He takes fucked-up feelings and gives them fucked-up similes and metaphors to explain them. It creates feelings instead of explaining them which is way more genuine." Much to Schwartzenbach's horror, the Cult of Blake was born.

"In terms of contemporary music, the Cult of Blake is probably matched only by the Cult of Morrissey," says rock critic Chris Ryan. "His music spoke to people in a way I've rarely seen music do. It's probably a lot easier to romanticize having a broken heart than it is to deal with having one. Jawbreaker poeticized being at a dead end very well. There was a stoicism to Blake's lyrics, a remnant of masculinity in the music. It's the same way that Morrissey appealed to weird tough guys. I knew guys who were barely functioning alcoholics or who otherwise listened to garage rock that thought Jawbreaker was the best band in the world. And still there are people who get a weird gleam in their eye when the band's name comes up. It's remarkable."

It's unnecessarily reductive to describe Jawbreaker as solely the mouthpiece for Schwartzenbach's angst—the band did have their fair share of poppy, even cheery moments. But Schwartzenbach's bottomless throat made every sentiment toxic, every simile razor-sharp. His hoarse bellow made it sound as if he were in pain with every breath—and eventually the untrained style took its toll and he actually was. Prior to the recording of Jawbreaker's third album, Schwartzenbach had surgery to remove agonizing and voice-threatening polyps from his vocal chords. But just prior to the operation, the band recorded a B-side that would become one of their seminal and best-loved songs, "Kiss the Bottle."

The song is sludgy and churning, a working-class anthem with a steady, proletarian heart (don't just take my word for it—the song also appeared on a San Francisco compilation called *Songs for the Proletariat*). Schwartzenbach's voice, pre-op, was never as mottled and choked as it was when spitting out the lyrics about two drunks, shaking and twitching, outside a Mission bodega. The song's story is clearly and cleverly communicated—Schwartzenbach's lyrics paint a picture of a lice-ridden liquor store at dawn—but the crushing weight of the delivery and guitars becomes something more than journalism. "I kissed the bottle / I should have been kissing you," Schwartzenbach bellows on the chorus, a wide-screen epic of failure, romance, and failed romance. Though Jawbreaker's strong songwriting attracted a disproportionate number of female fans for a punk band of its era, "Kiss the Bottle," more than any other song, captures the sensitive boy machismo that drew (and continues to draw) male listeners to the altar of Schwartzenbach. With its fictional scrim, "Kiss the Bottle" functions like a country song: the emotional impact is heightened by the specificity, not lessened. "Kiss the Bottle" is Kerouac; it's Bukowski. It's the allure of giving into despair, to doing the wrong thing and at least succeeding at that. Jawbreaker fans may not know lice at dawn, but they most likely know drinking and they certainly know loss—no matter how trivial. While the song could be read as a cautionary tale, it was usually heard as emotional justification. Jim Ward from Sparta, formerly of At the Drive-In, still considers "Kiss the Bottle" among his favorite songs. "Dude, you have no idea," he says. "When we all lived in one big house in El Paso and had no careers or clue we would sit around drinking all day listening to this song and sing along." Ron Richards, twenty-five, editor of the successful zine *Muddle,* finds the song still produces a lump in his throat. "The metaphor is amazing," he says. "How many of us have been in situations like that. The should-haves. I've been straight-edge since I was fifteen—the point isn't the drinks, it's the regrets."

Although Brett Matthews might be loathe to admit it, he is, at thirty, a sterling example of a Blake-o-phile. He's interviewed Schwartzenbach before and still treasures the experience. "Talking to him is everything you'd expect," Matthews says. "He's someone who obviously has the glimmer of genius in his eyes. His answers are backward, really cool, and really smart. Really in touch. You get a sense that a conversation with him—even a stupid one about burritos in the Mission—is like getting an unreleased Jawbreaker album."

In 1994, Ron Richards was seventeen, in high school on Long Island, and desperate to escape the black-and-white suburban backdrop of his life. "Up to then I was mostly listening to classic rock," he says. "If you grow up in the suburbs, it's like you're handed a copy of the Doors, of Led Zeppelin, and you're expected to like it. I was disillusioned and thought there was nothing new, nothing that was representing me." In his junior year of high school, Richards discovered the vibrant hardcore scene all around him and was hooked. "The whole idea of a local scene, of the bands being on the same level as the audience. . . . These were my peers, singing about things that are important to both of us." After gorging himself on local bands, Richards asked his older punk peers where he should turn next. A friend suggested Jawbreaker, and so Richards dutifully ordered the band's newest album, and third overall, *24 Hour Revenge Therapy.*

"When I heard that album," he says, "I fell in love. I listened to it and said, oh my god, this is it. It had the punk edge but the lyrical honesty that touched me. It expanded the scope—Jawbreaker wasn't a local band but there was a common theme. The pieces just fit."

24 Hour Revenge Therapy is arguably Jawbreaker's best album, but it is also far and away its most loved, the best example of Schwartzenbach's innate ability to marry the boozy, bluesy regretfulness of the Replacements with the loose, seat-of-the-pants attitude of Gilman Street punk. The album is sharp and concise; the hooks are as straightforward as the sentiments, which mine Schwartzenbach's seemingly endless vein of insomnia, alcohol, heartbreak, and regret. Aside from its scene-centric digressions, *24 Hour Revenge Therapy* is a breakup album like no other. Rather than relating history or chasing loose ends, Schwartzenbach crafted a soundtrack to the moment after the hang-up or the door slam. It isn't frustration being channeled into art; it's frustration *as* art—and all the songs are eminently hummable, just shy of sloppy, just past precise.

"I was looking for acknowledgement," says Richards, "and that's what that album gave me. That certain things weren't unique to me. Not to be told that I belonged to a scene, but that emotions and feelings are valid. You're looking for acceptance when you go down our path and you don't get a lot of it, especially in suburban Long Island where there were far more 'normal' people than there were of us. So you look for someone else feeling that way. And *24 Hour* said someone else had these emotions, that it's cool."

"We were all about say what you mean and mean what you say," says Pfahler. It was a simple aesthetic but hugely influential. Rich Egan, the founder of contemporary emo powerhouse Vagrant Records, still lists *24 Hour* as his favorite album, and his reasons read like a band-by-band blueprint for his own label's success in the twenty-first century.

"*Unfun* and *Bivouac* are amazing records," Egan says, "but they're way more cloaked in [Schwartzenbach's] English degree. *24 Hour* is just eleven cut and dry little stories about living in the Bay Area—there's not a four-syllable word to be found; it's straight and to the point. And ten years later I still listen to it on the way to work and get the same feelings out of it. I think simplicity is a mark of highly evolved thinking. Whether you're seventeen or fifty, I think it's a sign of greatness because it's not easy to be simple."

Despite its rabid fan base, Jawbreaker always was, in the words of Schwartzenbach, "one album ahead of everybody else." Meaning that by the time the crowds got comfortable with a new album, the band had already moved on, both thematically and stylistically, to the next one. Tired and frustrated, the band decided to break up after the *24 Hour* tours wound down, but Geffen—desperate to build on the phenomenal success Green Day was enjoying with their major-label debut—offered Jawbreaker a contract, so the band entered the studio with friend and Green Day producer Rob Cavallo to give it one last go.

As with so many of its peers in the years to come, Jawbreaker's major-label debut, *Dear You,* released in 1995, was also its swan song. The record's production glistened and gleamed, Schwartzenbach's voice was sanded and smoothed, and the songs were mellow, introspective affairs. The reaction was harsh—those who had entrusted their emotional lives to Schwartzenbach, had viewed him as a tattered, secular priest to lay their burdens on, felt betrayed. Despite touring with labelmates Nirvana and (the by-now famous) Green Day, the album sold poorly and the band broke up.

In the years that followed, Schwartzenbach moved to Brooklyn, DJ'd, and wrote freelance video game reviews for websites before forming a new band called Jets to Brazil in 1998. Schwartzenbach's songwriting had matured even further since *Dear You*—Jets' debut, *Orange Rhyming Dictionary*, crackled with the hook-heavy savvy of Britpop, and its sophomore release, 2000's *Four Cornered Night*, simmered with Billy Joel–style piano ballads and surprisingly stark lyrics (love songs to his parents, shout-outs to his bass player, etc.). But by now *Dear You* was a treasured, out-of-print collector's item, fetching more than twice its retail price on eBay, and bands openly indebted to Jawbreaker's classic sound were making their presence felt on the national pop charts. Schwartzenbach was so adored for what he had done that few were willing to allow him to gracefully move on. Jets to Brazil, though popular, has received unspeakably scathing reviews, boiling with the bitterness usually reserved for a cheating lover. "If Jets were anybody else, I would hate them," says Matthews. "I just don't like that type of music. I think it's very pretentious."

If the fans haven't moved on from Jawbreaker, in many ways neither has Schwartzenbach. His songs have become increasingly self-referential and almost desperate, culminating in 2002's *Perfecting Loneliness* album, where he sings, "when the measure of your worth / is the measure of your work / then you better make it work." Always sensitive, Schwartzenbach has retreated further and further from view. The day Jets to Brazil's tour was to begin in the fall of 2002, Schwartzenbach canceled the entire thing and flew to Canada to be with his parents. Rumors flew that it was stress and the burden of expectation that got to him. No interviews would be given for the forseeable future. "It gets to him," said a confidante of the band. "He refuses to exploit his legacy; he won't tour with any other bands and he won't let the band get any bigger, no matter who might benefit from it."

If his early work with Jawbreaker made Schwartzenbach the J. D. Salinger of emo on wax, he eventually became Salinger in mind as well. When people connect with the thoughts and feelings of your youth, how can you make them grow up with you? With something as deeply felt as emo, it's nearly impossible. Those who grew up singing and crying to "Kiss the Bottle" don't want the same song again; nor do they want something else. The advance nostalgia of great emo records—the visceral thrill of wallowing in failure in anticipation of getting better—all too quickly gives way to real nostalgia.

"If I could go back to every mix tape I made in high school, I think every one had a Jawbreaker song on it," says Richards. "And the majority of them were for girls. Listening to those songs takes me back to specific memories."

The memories have already been made, and they're the ones people have shaped, broken in, chosen to live with. Listening to Schwartzenbach now is like confronting the truth—the way a fondly remembered ex really looked or acted, the often shallow triviality of youth. His music helped countless people grow up, but the sad truth is that these days, they refuse to let him do the same.

When trolling the web for Jawbreaker memories, I encountered the livejournal of a young girl named Leslie.* She couldn't have been ten years old when *Unfun* was released, but Jawbreaker was her favorite band just the same. She wrote:

```
2001-11-25-11:14 p.m.

yesterday i was prettie upset most of the day, but then
would remember i was happie and the reason i was happie
is cuz my very favoryte band of all tyme-jawbreaker
doesnt exist anymore, but the lead singer of jawbreaker,
blake, is in a new band called jets to brazil whych is my
favoryte band that exists. anyhow, i emailed jtb and they
actuallie responded to me and it made me happie, then i
went further and just emailed blake. yesterday he emailed
me back! it made me cry, im in love w/ hym now and hes so
sweet. thys is what he said to me:


    Thank you Leslie
```

*Not her real name. Throughout this book, a fictitious name will be denoted by an asterisk the first time it is used.

I feel like I'm dragging a refrigerator down a dirt road
in hell right
now, but I will take beauty and wonder just the same. I
guess I'm hoping the
low road will deliver some elevated sadness.

Be well.

Blake

The connection is still there for a new generation of adherents, but for those original fans, their need for "elevated sadness" has matured and lessened.

"As miserable as the teen years were, I'd go back in a second," says Richards wistfully. "There was an energy and vigor then that isn't there now. Maybe I'm just old and bitter. But there was a grouping of bands in the early- to mid-nineties—Jawbreaker chief among them—that laid the foundation for everyone that's making music now."

Sunny Day Real Estate formed in the shadow of the grunge boom in Washington state. Originally conceived as a trio by guitarist Dan Hoerner, drummer William Goldsmith, and bassist Nate Mendel, the band expanded to a four-piece after hearing the unsettling and captivating vocal stylings of a teenager named Jeremy Enigk. While the members of the band were fans of punk, they were all accomplished musicians who made no bones about their high-quality gear and musical ambitions. The band's sound was sweeping and epic and Enigk's vocals seemed beamed in from another world. Sunny Day's overwhelming confidence and their intricate songwriting separated them from the Seattle-based pack of post-grunge alt-rock bottom-feeders.

Jonathan Poneman, one half of the brain trust behind Sub Pop Records—the hugely influential indie label that released Nirvana's first record, *Bleach*—remembers being urged to check out an early Sunny Day show in 1993. "The whole thing sounded so cockamamie to me," he says. "An eighteen-year-old kid singing falsetto? But I went and saw the show and—I hate to say this—Jeremy immediately reminded me of Kurt Cobain. Just his presence and the way he lurched over his guitar. And the songs struck me. In Seattle at the time we had all of these really bad, aggressive bands that had a lot of groove but not much going on melodically. Here was a band that was every bit as propulsive, but with a real melodic sophistication."

Poneman signed the band immediately and sent them to Chicago to record their debut album with renowned indie producer Brad Wood. That album, *Diary,* was released in 1994 and quickly became Sub Pop's second best-selling record, trailing only Nirvana. The album's cover was iconic and telling—a traditional family of four, a dad in a suit, a peppy, blonde mom, and two kids, are represented as grinning cartoons. With limbless bodies like children's toys, the four passively beam at the consumer while the toaster quietly ignites, sending chaotic smoke up and out of the frame. There were no song titles listed on the back. In their place was an image of doll-mom and doll-dad, sleeping in the same bed, as far apart from each other as possible. It is from that disconnect that the songs took their cues.

If Jawbreaker concentrated its emotional churning in the stern-browed persona of Blake Schwartzenbach, Jeremy Enigk, Sunny Day's no less charismatic frontman, gathered all of his seething torment and threw it to the winds. Taking as many cues from the grandiose sweep of '70s progressive rock as from '90s punk, Enigk sang desperately about losing himself, about subsuming himself in something greater. The odd and occasionally invented words on *Diary* suggested speaking in tongues— conveying more meaning from their connection to the questing melodies and their dissonance than from the haphazard way they scan. So intense was Enigk's desire to subsume his own problems into something larger, he loses track of language.

Like the most charismatic true believers, Enigk had a way of bringing the listener around to his point of view; cynicism doesn't fly in the presence of such unwavering commitment to doubt. Schwartzenbach's words were lifted from his actual diary; *Diary* seemed beamed in directly from Enigk's convoluted and wonderfully young subconcious. "In the shadows buried in me lies a child's toy," he sang with typical anguish, "tried to figure out memorize their words for hope."

Hearing Sunny Day Real Estate had the same effect on twenty-year-olds as seeing *Star Wars* for the first time had on ten-year-olds: it made them dream *bigger*. In Enigk's dizzying falsetto heights, thousands of punk kids heard the opportunity to reach as far—in sentiment, in instrumentation, in metaphor. One Sunny Day review I found online asserts that the band's music "strikes at the heart of all that makes us human, begging us to profess our deepest sympathies and dearest sensibilities." *Diary* was so over-the-top, yet so out of left field and guileless, that its power was at once undeniable and impossible to repeat.

"I don't think Sunny Day set out to be a new paradigm," says Poneman, "but they were; it was a totally new beginning. Older, so-called emo bands like Rites of Spring and Fugazi I always saw as more intellectual and strident. But Sunny Day was much more romantic. You started to see a totally different crowd at shows—these nerdy college and high school kids that would just stand there and gawk and rock back and forth on their feet. It was a much younger crowd—people who were Jeremy's age, basically. And it was him that it all comes down to. The other guys provided the platform, but it was Jeremy channeling all those emotions, and it was mind-blowing for those kids in the crowd to realize they were in a place safe enough to feel these things. There was a real savant quality to what he did—tapping into something quite effortlessly and without any kind of premeditation. There was nothing macho about it—there was a delicacy, an unrequited love to the whole thing. When you're dealing with a lot of kids who just months before were listening to hardcore or metal or grunge and suddenly there's this peer singing in a falsetto and unabashedly into melody and beauty but there's this colossal rock band behind him. It made it safe for people who are into heavier music, for whatever reason, to explore a whole other range of emotions."

One of those touched by Sunny Day was a seventeen-year-old Philadelphian named John Dispirito. "I was a typical junior in high school," he says. "Going though relationship problems—everything always seems so much bigger when you're that age. Everything is the end of the world. I was listening to mostly grunge, but while Nirvana were filled with angst and anger, my emotions were much more heartfelt. When I saw the video for Sunny Day's "Seven" on MTV I said this is the music that speaks to me more than anything I've ever heard. This is what I'm supposed to be listening to."

Poneman saw the transformation happen—the shift from Nirvana to Sunny Day was a generational transition mostly overlooked by the media. "It was so unrelenting and liberating being able to watch Nirvana do what they did. There was a lot of dancing and pushing around and expression to it. Whereas Sunny Day would refer to these things musically, but there was a seriousness to it—some people would call it pretentious. There was no laughing. It was just this complete intensity and belief in the music. It was unlike anything I had ever experienced before and I don't think I've experienced it since."

In many ways, Nirvana was to Sunny Day what Minor Threat was to Rites of Spring—albeit minus the politics and on a much larger stage. The kids in high school liked moshing to the angsty sounds of grunge, but it didn't make them feel any better when they were home alone in their bedrooms with their magnified problems raining down like hailstones. What Sunny Day fans wanted was to be taken seriously—and in the dizzying swirl of *Diary,* they were.

"Sunny Day is that voice inside your head when you want to cry," says Dispirito. "It's that whining, a sound of frustration. And when Jeremy sings, it's a release; you're letting go a primal scream in your head. Listening to them made me feel that it was OK to feel the way I did. And when I started going to the shows, everyone was like me."

"The last time Nirvana played in town before Kurt's death, they did this Christmas special in an old abandoned warehouse downtown," remembers Poneman. "The Breeders played too; it was filmed for MTV. I managed to get Sunny Day into the taping. So I remember walking to the back of the room and seeing Jeremy there watching the show. He looked bored to death, just not particularly impressed. There was only a few years' separation, but it was really a different generation."

"Sunny Day dared to do things differently first," says Dispirito. "They opened a lot of doors for the bands that came next. Other bands that had their own different things were suddenly like, yeah, let's go for it. We can sound like we want to sound. There is an audience for it."

"Once Sunny Day became popular two things happened," says punk publicist and zine editor Jessica Hopper. "One is that punk bands all over got this gleam in their eye and felt like they could start shredding like that and singing about whatever mattered to them. The other is that the word 'emo' went from being vague and undefined to this specifically emotionally overbearing music. Music that was romantic but denatured of its political, traditionally punk rock content. It was polemic. Everything switched."

Sunny Day's life span as a band was typically tortured for an emo act. After the whirlwind success of *Diary,* the group rushed into the studio to record a follow-up. But the band was splitting at the seams, due, in part, to Enigk's sudden and forceful announcement that he was now a born-again Christian. The naïve questing of *Diary* had taken Enigk to a very concrete and all-encompassing answer; the melancholic dialogue of the album's centerpiece, "Song About an Angel," now read as foreshadowing. "I see patterns occur and reoccur with Jeremy," says Poneman. "He'll get very introspective and down on himself and then he'll reach out and seize onto something. It's a vaguely manic-depressive cycle—to go from so down to grabbing onto something that will inspire and uplift him and make him incredibly productive. After the first record the thing he seized was Christianity. He became kind of an overbearing zealot and made a lot of proclamations that bummed out the other members of the band. Around that time [Nirvana's] Dave Grohl invited the rhythm section to play with him in his new band, which turned out to be Foo Fighters. And it was never really able to be the same again."

Sub Pop released the cobbled-together *LP2* in 1995 to a generally enthusiastic response, but the rest of the '90s would be years of occasional reunion and continued frustration for Sunny Day. Enigk released a hugely acclaimed solo album of orchestral pop in 1996 and, after Sunny Day broke apart for what may have been the final time in 2000 (after the release of the band's worst album, a prog-rock behemoth called *The Rising Tide*), three of the original members reconvened as The Fire Theft, while Dan Hoerner briefly joined Dashboard Confessional and then wrote a children's book. Sunny Day Real Estate seems destined to be remembered only for its first album, more for its brilliant promise than its realization. But in many ways Sunny Day's brilliance *was* its zeitgeist-seizing debut, physically forcing a regime change in the hearts and minds of fans of underground rock. And if the band burned itself out on its own delirious ambitions, well, what's more emo than that?

"Part of what's great about rock music is that there is a fleeting quality to it," says Sub Pop's Poneman. "If something could be made to live forever it would lose its specialness. Music survives on vinyl, but when taken out of its original context it becomes something else. That's what makes it so interesting that *Diary* sells and sells, year after year. New generations are always discovering it. There must be something about that record that resonates with these generations of new listeners. And despite the age difference, I don't doubt it's the same thing that resonated with me: the purity. The vulnerability. And that the songs absolutely *kill*."

Beginning in 1994, the American indie-rock and punk underground that had existed since the early '80s was overrun, strip-mined, and changed forever. Sunny Day Real Estate—part punk, part preacher—pointed the way towards a new underground consensus and aesthetic. With Nirvana broken, big money everywhere, and cynicism dominating the culture, sincerity became currency. Bands were doomed—Jawbreaker by its pessimism, Sunny Day by its optimism—but the roads were paved. Over the next decade emo would retreat again, reform, and be reborn both as a national subculture and, eventually, as something even greater, but in terms of scope, style, passion, and emotion, all of the bands that came next were following Jawbreaker and Sunny Day Real Estate's tearstained map.

THREE

"Maybe," sang Karate's Geoff Farina in 1996 over droning minor chords, "it's harder when you try." For a few shining moments in the mid-nineties, it seemed like every young man between the ages of seventeen and twenty-three was ready to agree but willing to try anyway. It also seemed like every one of those young men was wearing thick glasses and carrying a shoulder-slung messenger bag, but that's not important. Or it's not *that* important.

Sometime after the promised major-label nirvana of the post-Nirvana years and before the end of the millennium tech-bubble glam-pop explosion, the two dominant underground musics of the '80s, hardcore and indie, met in the middle and produced something new. The middle was both a figurative and physical space for this new breed of bands. The songs had the raw anthemic power of punk as well as the DIY, hard-nosed work ethic. But the songs were also smoother, and the chords were chunkier and corralled into sloppy melodies. The voices weren't accusing, they were yearning, and the best and most lasting of these bands emerged from the perceived cultural no-man's-land of Middle America, from the forgotten cities in the flyover states. Braid from Champaign-Urbana. Christie Front Drive from Denver. Mineral from Austin. Jimmy Eat World from Phoenix. The Get Up Kids from Kansas. The Promise Ring from Milwaukee. After years of raging sameness, hardcore desperately needed a brain; after years of studied, ironic detachment, indie desperately needed a heart. What they found was each other. And what it got called was emo.

The emo that came out of the mid-nineties wasn't the better-yourself primer of the '80s D.C. scene; it fell somewhere between the soaringly righteous abstract heights of Sunny Day and the earthbound, cold-water splash of Jawbreaker. This was the period when emo earned many, if not all, of the stereotypes that have lasted to this day: boy-driven, glasses-wearing, overly sensitive, overly brainy, chiming-guitar-driven college music. Despite critical opinion to the contrary, mid-nineties emo wasn't a soundtrack to failure, it was a romantic film score to a million true-life tales about the *potential* of failure. It held back even while it gave everything away.

Jessica Hopper is, at the ripe age of twenty seven, a punk lifer. As a teenager she was featured on the Jane Pratt TV show as an example of a Riot Grrrl. She did time in Seattle as Courtney Love's housesitter. She's a musician, writer, band publicist, and publisher and editor of the influential, intentionally outrageous zine *Hit It or Quit It*. Her most prominent and infamous role, however, is as the Dorothy Parker of underground rock: her temper is the only thing shorter than she, and her bad side seats thousands. But like football coaches say about tenacious special-teams players, she has a knack for being around the ball. From her perch in Chicago, she has observed and played a key role in the development and transformation of emo over the past decade. Sometimes as a cheerleader, sometimes as an employee, but mostly as a scold, Hopper has served as the self-proclaimed and ever-present Statler and Waldorf for a universe of studious, guitar-slinging boys who alternate daily between living in awe and living in terror of her.

"I remember living in the Midwest in the early '90s, the bands were always older than us. It was like no one young had thought to pick up a guitar," she says. "Around 1994 I started hearing the term 'emo' for the first time; people were excited about it. And what it signified were bands that were teenagers, that were our age. It was people from the Midwest, kids that were into Jawbreaker, Drive Like Jehu, Fugazi. And it was all centered around the Promise Ring."

The Promise Ring—easily one of the top five least punk names ever—came together when the various hardcore and postpunk bands of its four members fell apart. Singer Davey Vonbohlen, guitarist Jason Gnewikow, bassist Scott Schoenbeck, and drummer Dan Didier were musically obsessed nineteen- and twenty-year-olds in 1995, bored to tears in their hometown of Milwaukee. As the Promise Ring they took hardcore's thick, blocky repeating riffs and slowed them down, smoothed them out. In the newly created spaces, Vonbohlen—a jolly, athletic, balding fellow with a froggy croon and a pronounced lisp—would sing goofy, though picturesque, words about splitting a soda with two straws and watching the sun come up from the tour van in places like Denver and Delaware.

"We just started playing songs together," says Gnewikow, "and I don't know if it was the right combination or what, but it was all chance, random chance. We practiced twice a week, then wrote some songs, recorded 'em, and people were really excited by it. It was totally naïve and honest. There might have been some dissent from the hardcore kids, but we were in a total bubble. The whole theme of the band was to give something to the scene that we loved so much that it hadn't experienced yet."

And the staid Midwestern hardcore scene—"super cool, super tight-knit, but probably a little bit self-righteous," as Gnewikow describes it—went mad for it. "I had never felt such an urgency as I did around Promise Ring," remembers Hopper. "I had been around a lot of things that have happened from the ground up and watched them progress—different genres getting popular and getting signed—but this was so completely beneath the radar. It was really organic. We were seeing shows at a library; things had been taken underground again. These teeny bands with this Midwestern work ethic and no style making totally poppy cute music that still had an aggressive angularity. For me, at least, it was really pure. The bands were young and no one knew about them. Music was fun again."

"The audience was punk kids, our peers," says Gnewikow. "We booked our tours by calling friends, playing in basements and VFW Halls. It was very unpretentious and cool and the fact that everywhere we went people were into us was amazing, it was shocking. It was so much more honest and low-key, though, than the way things are today. There was no jockeying for status. We just went around and did it, very fast and carefree with everyone jumping around and singing."

By spreading their live show up and down the east coast during all of 1995, the Promise Ring served as the warning shot to the underground communities: something new was happening and it was coming your way. In Delaware, the owners of rising punk record label Jade Tree were looking for their next release. After a few days with the Promise Ring's 7-inch singles, they made an offer, and in 1996, *30° Everywhere* was released. By indie standards, the album was a blockbuster, selling tens of thousands of copies. The album is rough but winning; the only hurdle for prospective listeners is Vonbohlen's often off-key warbling. The songs, particularly "Everywhere In Denver" and "Scenes From France," are forceful and charming at the same time; the effect is like being hit in the head with cotton candy. The band summed up both its appeal and its listeners' mindsets when Vonbohlen sang, "I'm breathing like a boy, full of you."

The record itself was well designed (by Gnewikow, a budding graphic designer and huge fan of the meticulous look of the British tech-pop duo Pet Shop Boys) and mysterious, with double-exposed, sepia-toned images and a single photo of the band that captured the members sitting glumly on a couch, looking particularly young, tiny, and lovelorn. In short, it was like the Cure recording for Dischord, and it made tens of thousands of pining punk hearts go pitter-patter like young schoolgirls.

"I don't think it's a very good record," Gnewikow says matter-of-factly. "But we had been a band for nine months. We had no business making an album like that then. Some songs are only one chord throughout—it seemed like bizarre songwriting for a punk band, but it was still exciting."

Chris Ryan was nineteen years old when he moved from Philadelphia to Boston in 1996 to attend college. Today he's a rock critic in New York, but back then he was just another indie-rocker clutching his Pavement bootlegs to his chest and looking for whatever was next. He was a passionate and literate music fan, but he had never paid very close attention to the lyrics of the bands he loved—which made sense, considering that Pavement's most touching and affecting song to date was called "Zurich Is Stained."

"When I got to Boston," he remembers, "I was entirely by myself. Eventually, I met a couple of guys in classes and we bonded over music. But they had a vocabulary of bands that was entirely unknown to me. I thought there couldn't be anything smaller than indie-rock. But here were these guys in Texas Is the Reason T-shirts. I remember walking down the street one day and they were talking about the Promise Ring, who I had never heard of. They told me that it was an emo band and I was like, 'What's an emo band?' and they didn't know! Even then you couldn't say what it was. But over the course of getting to know them I discovered an entire subculture—and that's what I came to see emo as. It's not a genre. It's a subculture.

"Those guys—who eventually became my roommates—had an emo band themselves called The Shyness Clinic. And what they introduced me to was a dozen or so bands and half a dozen labels that I'd never heard of. Bands like Mineral, Promise Ring, Texas Is the Reason, Karate, Braid. Labels like Jade Tree and Gern Blandsten. It was a much more insular, cooperative community that really had nothing to do with the way I thought music worked before that. I remember seeing Pavement in 1995 play to eight hundred people and thought that was a small show. Well, no. That's a hell of a lot of people. Now I was seeing shows in someone's basement with forty other people and it was considered a hugely important event."

Hearing Ryan talk about his connection to this music is reminiscent of the Frosted Flakes commercials where adults, hidden in the shadows, confess to an illicit and potentially embarassing affection for the sweetened children's cereal. "There was an immediate emotional sugar rush with these records that, sadly enough, spoke to my nineteen-year-old male consciousness," he says. "I had unrequited crushes on girls. I had long-distance relationships. Just a lot of things that seemed very new to me and very heavy and important. And these new bands corroborated all of that."

Emo not only gave Ryan a common language with his new friends, it spoke to him with a musical and thematic urgency that the emotionally cold indie-rock often lacked. "I was always an inquisitive music fan," he says, "and always wanted to find out what my favorite songs were about. And I would read interviews with [Pavement's] Stephen Malkmus or [Archers of Loaf's] Eric Bachmann and they would dismiss the question or say the songs were about Glenn Miller or a Civil War colonel and I'd be like, no! Make it about me! Why can't you just admit to that? Also, a lot of the emo bands were really loud and way more dynamic. It was that shot in the heart, quiet-quiet-loud Nirvana thing, but it wasn't as codified or clichéd then. I remember hearing the Texas Is the Reason single 'If It's Here When We Get Back It's Ours' and thinking, 'This is what I want.' It's not so saccharine that it's pop, but it's an overwhelming, driving rock song. It wound up making sense to me directly in a way that indierock only kind of did."

For many, the New York City–based quartet Texas Is the Reason was the perfect bridge from indie-rock to emo. Born out of the ashes of well-regarded hardcore and Hare Krishna bands, Texas (named after a Misfits lyric) took the yearning, searching melodies and lyrics of Sunny Day Real Estate and stapled them onto a more familiar, churning punk background. Singer Garret Klahn had a jones for the anthemic and took vocal cues from Jawbreaker's Blake Schwartzenbach and Oasis's Liam Gallagher. On "If It's Here . . . ," the standout track from the band's self-titled EP, Klahn breaks free of the didacticism of punk rock, singing directly to the listener: "would you know what to say? / would you know what to feel?" There's a hint of the proactive headshrinking of Rites of Spring, but none of the extremes. Klahn isn't impressed "with anyone or anything," and he's "sick of faking it." He claims he "won't tell anyone" but he's telling you—the listener. You're the only one he can trust, and the pile-driving music raises the level of discourse to DEF-CON 4—he's bottomed out and flailing around for support. To any nineteen-year-old, the desperation is familiar. The fake constraints of society are a punk evergreen, and the questions Klahn asks are the same that anyone, alone in the world for the first time, searching for mystery, meaning, and romance, is already asking. There are no answers, but there's momentum in the doubt and in the guitars.

Though Texas broke up in 1997, the legacy of their EPs and one full-length album (the monumentally emo-titled *Do You Know Who You Are?*) flourishes online. One such anonymous shrine to the band sums up its impact better than a thousand reviews: "I'm not saying Texas is the best band in the history of music, in fact they are not the best band I've ever heard. The point is, their music came to me at a very special time. I was discovering a whole new world of feelings. Their music became a kind of soundtrack to that season of my life. [Everything] was very confusing and so was my spirit. There are no words to explain what TITR means to me."

In his second year in Boston, Chris Ryan moved into a group house with his friends in The Shyness Clinic in the Roxbury neighborhood. With touring bands playing in the basement, sleeping on the floor, and running up long-distance bills on the house phone, Ryan had a front-row seat for the underground emo explosion. Fueled by camaraderie, flyers, and more than a few ever-present zines (including *Punk Planet,*

Change, Commodity, Antimatter, and Hopper's *Hit It Or Quit It*), Ryan felt plugged into a "circuit of information" that seemed wonderfully bigger than his own concerns, while it simultaneously sustained them.

"The thing about emo shows is that there seemed to be a complete lack of pretense," he says. "Not to harp on it, but that Pavement show in '95, it followed a pattern: the houselights went down, the crowd yelled—it could have been REO Speedwagon up there. I was probably pretty naïve, but at the shows in Boston, there were never any encores. Whether it was Karate or Jejune or whoever, the way it happened was, you'd show up at a place—be it the small upstairs space at the Middle East [a venerable Boston rock venue] or at someone's house—and you'd stand around for a while. And there'd always be this funny time when the guy who was standing next to me would get onstage and pick up a guitar. There was no 'You are the audience; prepare for *the show.*' There was no backstage. They were drinking beers and talking about their van with my friends, and then they'd go onstage and sing songs about drinking beer and driving their van. And afterwards we'd all go watch TV or drink more beers. The hardest part was, I would always have an incredible reaction—'Oh my god, this is such a great band'—and then they'd come up to me and ask where the bathroom was."

This low-key, punk approach to performance linked the bands of the era in a way that smoothed over a myriad of stylistic differences. Bands that were lumped together in the emo camp back then varied wildly, much more so than today. The dominant sound was the melodic punk of the Promise Ring and Texas Is the Reason, but peers and tourmates like Karate, The Van Pelt, and especially Chicago's Joan of Arc played with elements of post-rock, including odd instrumentation and ample amounts of droning, wordless minor-key dirges. The Shyness Clinic adored the Scottish noisemakers Mogwai, and emo mix tapes often included the Ivy League folk of New York City's Ida. At the Boston basement shows it wasn't uncommon to see the fresh-faced boys of Braid sharing the bill with the heavy rawk bombast of the Rye Coalition.

The common lyrical thread of the mid-nineties emo bands was applying big questions to small scenarios. The approach was a combination of self-important and painfully shy, regressive and humble—kind of like a deaf-mute in a tuxedo. No band embodied this aesthetic more than Texas's Mineral, a quartet of deathly serious young men. On the group's two albums, 1997's *Power of Failing* and 1998's *Endserenading,* singer Chris Simpson's gloriously ecstatic and defeatist visions of the world are so soaked in religious imagery that it's impossible to tell if he's venerating a high school crush or Jesus Christ. To the band's rabid fans, it hardly mattered—a mostly areligious bunch, there were few things in life more all-encompassing than crushes anyway. On "80-37," Simpson agonizes over familiar childhood images—lemonade stands, the ice cream man—as if they were stigmata, defining his present with a litany of loss: "Those days are gone now and we must carry on / But I will not forget the things I learned on your front lawn."

This sort of indulgent weeping is familiar in teenagers from Holden Caulfield to Dawson Leery (of *Dawson's Creek* fame). As soon as teens are old enough to mark off eras of their life—usually concurrent with leaving home for the first time—the past can become not prologue, but purpose. Nostalgia for childhood becomes heightened, a defense against an uncertain future. This is all well and good, but in other songs Simpson seems paralyzed—emotionally and otherwise—unable to risk potential pain even for immediate pleasure. In other words, he doesn't just miss childhood, he hasn't recovered from it. On "If I Could," Simpson carries on a self-loathing love affair in his mind:

> *I wanted to tell her how beautiful she was*
> *But I just stared*
> *. . .*
> *I sat behind the wheel and watched the raindrops*
> *. . .*
> *And I know I don't deserve this*
> *The capacity to feel*

In many ways, "If I Could" is the ultimate expression of mid-nineties emo. The song's short synopsis—she is beautiful, I am weak, dumb, and shy; I am alone but am surprisingly poetic when left alone—sums up everything that emo's adherents admired and its detractors detested. The music was as somber and yearning as the lyrics—a key part of emo's perpetual appeal is the simple fact that it takes relatively mundane problems quite seriously—and its presentation of the shy narrator as somehow heroic in his defeat was heartening to an audience full of young men who possessed countless unrequited and unexpressed crushes of their own. To scene haters, Mineral might as well have put a bull's-eye on its forehead, so naked and up-front was the song about its own pathos. From this era onwards, there was a defiant pride in emo's loser-ish tendencies—an arrogance derived from superior humility. What was understood by fans as strength came across to others as juvenile, tear-in-your-(root) beer whining.

"If I Could" is about a guileless, innocent romantic, or a creepy, self-defeating stalker prone to indulgent poetry. Either way, it's the same song. To Mineral and its fans, the former interpretation was the only clear choice. In that way, emo was transforming itself into closed circuit—bands of young men sang about themselves and their audience. In effect, they *were* their audience. It wasn't made for everyone, and that was part of its appeal. "Mineral was just embarrassingly honest," says Ryan. "It was like my goth period. There was no line. There was no subtlety. And the songs had no shame. Mineral was the Andrew Lloyd Webber of emo—going straight for the heart every song. Set it up for four minutes and then fucking *pay off*."

Though it came to dominate thousands of young people's lives, the emo of the mid-nineties was far from the national consciousness. The Promise Ring was the most successful of the bands, and sales of its best-selling album, *Nothing Feels Good,* topped out in the mid five figures. The bands made their money and their bones the old-fashioned way: through nonstop, backbreaking touring. Though regionalism still limited the bands' geography (The Shyness Clinic never made it to the West Coast; when the generally obscure California band Tristeza made it to Boston, its members were greeted like conquering heroes), there were pockets of action, cities (usually near a university) that would always guarantee them an audience and a futon to share. For all the accessibility and open emotions, emo was still an underground music and its fans were those already drawn to the counterculture. It was a new way of listening to and being affected by music for the kids involved, a bunch of mostly male, mostly white, college-age music snobs. Even when the music broke barriers, the aesthetic kept things humble. "It seemed like being in the basement was enough, for a while at least," remembers Ryan. "With all of these bands, any hint of mass-market success, they would do their best to ruin it. Like the Promise Ring—even though the songs were really poppy, they had horrendous recordings and the singer had a lisp." In other words, just because it was accessible didn't mean it was commercial.

"That era was the first time I saw people playing music, having shows just for the joy of it," Ryan says. "It wasn't a hippie commune, but it was self-sustaining in a really positive way. We were all around the age where we're thinking, what the hell are we going to do with ourselves? Everybody goes through that phase—where you stake out the things that are important to you and you don't want to have to become an accountant and have a kid. And the social structure this music bred was, if this is what you like to do, it's a good enough way to use your time— even if you're not in a band, if you just like to go to shows and hang out, that's enough."

The desire to use music as a never-never land, a shield against the demands of aging and the real world, is as old as sound, but mid-nineties emo was the first music to so actively celebrate the self-conscious romanticism and high-stakes emotional desperation of the years between high school and whatever comes next. "Peter Pan-tastic," is what Jessica Hopper calls it, and emo did seem to have the same universal appeal as that particular fairy tale. Ryan recalls the crowds at concerts in Boston as "a lot of kids from my school, but I'd also overhear kids talking about how they took the bus in from New Hampshire just for this show and, if they had the money, they'd be back next weekend for another one." There were also thirty-year-olds in the crowd, hoping to use the youthful energy and naïveté as barricades against their own apathy.

The zenith of Chris Ryan's emo-life—and many of his peers' as well— was the release of the Promise Ring's second album, *Nothing Feels Good,* in 1997. "I still remember one of my friends got an advance cassette of that album in the fall," he says. "And to this day that is one of the most distinctive pieces of music in my life. One that has a direct connection to a certain time, a certain place, and a certain group of people. I would walk to and from class with it in my Walkman. I'd listen to it in my car, with friends. It was constantly on that fall. I remember walking around [Boston neighborhood] the Fen, listening to it, trying to figure out what the words meant, just trying to figure it out."

And *Nothing Feels Good* is the perfect album for those moments, a fully realized combination of obvious and inexplicable, specific and vague. The double meaning of the title mirrors the ambiguous nature of young love—there's a mixture of fixation and desolation. "Nothing feels good like you," howls Davey at one point, while another song bears the bleak title "How Nothing Feels." Immature romance has inflated stakes—there's more than a bit of excitement and drama derived from failure, or at least skirting the brink of it. The production was cleaner, thanks to Jawbox's J. Robbins behind the boards. Musically, the band was tighter and ten times as confident: hooks gleamed, choruses went for the throat, the heart, the lungs. The album could get you moving in the morning and tuck you in at night. It was a timetable for a season, an album to live by. Its iconic cover image was of a candy-colored amusement park boarded up for the season. The album is the pinnacle of its generation of emo: a convergence of pop and punk, of resignation and celebration, of the lure of girlfriends and the pull of friends, bandmates, and the road.

Chris Ryan describes the Promise Ring as having "an accelerated life cycle," and the same could be said of that entire emo moment. The music was so urgent, so specific in its lyrics that there was very little room for movement or growth. It was an outburst, a line in the sand against change (or development). Just as Gatsby saw the green light, the emo bands of the era could see the beacon—the road ahead—but could never get there. They were content to muse about romantic possibilities, not potentially unpleasant realities. Their songs were about wanting something terribly, but ultimately wanting the wanting more than the actual object of desire. No matter which way you look at it, that's not a sustainable situation. As Braid sang, "nostalgia is drunk and frustration is gorgeous." Or perhaps Karate's Geoff Farina put it best when he proudly caterwauled, "let me bang my head against the wall if I want to."

For many of the bands—and a majority of their audiences—the essential object of fear and desire was women. "It was almost entirely guys," says Ryan. "There would be a woman in maybe one out of every twenty bands. The audience was men between the ages of eighteen and twenty-three with short hair, glasses, and courier bags, exactly what the critics would say." And, for the most part, exactly like the people onstage.

In Karate's best song, the mournful, elegaic "Every Sister," singer Geoff Farina takes the specific female subject of his song and makes her an object, a stand-in for all women. "Maybe you could be my generation. . . . I can't figure you out." The goal of the moaning is so he himself can "feel better"; she exists merely to give Farina a reason to sing, and then to cheer him up. Women's roles in emo songs were frequently reductive, distancing. Rather than attempting to bridge the gender gap, emo bands set up camp at the very edge of it and then wrote poems agonizing over the distance.

Jessica Hopper—then, as now, one of the most vocal feminists in the underground—became discouraged and then disgusted with the hegemony relatively quickly. "Emo became a total playpen for dudes to be withdrawn and in their own worlds," she fumes. "It was saying, 'We don't have to grow up. We can have these teenage emotions. We don't have to accept responsibility.' It was about being bruised all the livelong day in a very vague way. It was drawing attention and sympathy and, unfortunately, it was very self-perpetuating."

The biggest obstacle to women's voices in emo, however, was the fact that there weren't really any women in emo bands to speak. There was a female bassist in Jejune, a singer in the kinda-sorta emo Wisconsin group Rainer Maria, but the name of another popular emo band of the day summed it up best: Boy's Life. Punk has traditionally—and unfairly— been male dominated, but usually due to aggression; emo was segregated because of expression.

"Sunny Day Real Estate and Jawbreaker inspired people—and the local versions of those bands were what we called emo," Hopper says. "But those local bands—like Promise Ring—immediately spawned a huge legion of imitators. They found the quintessential thing that spoke to boys between seventeen and twenty-three. And their distilled essence from heaven came from [Braid's] Bob Nanna. It was apolitical and cute and the records looked really nice. And everyone was channeling the same waiting-by-the-telephone angst. The first wave of bands actually addressed things; they had political things to say. Braid and the rest of the second wave had songs about friends, girls, the world inside your van. There were Braid songs about being in Braid. It was a nostalgic naïveté, a fourth-grade approach to women. And that became the unifying factor of the music and of the scene."

Beginning in 1993 as a fairly ordinary hardcore combo, Braid expanded its musical horizons when founder (and University of Illinois student)

Bob Nanna hooked up with guitarist/singer Chris Broach. After a shouty first album called *Frankie Welfare Boy Aged Five,* Braid began to evolve in more melodic and expressive directions. By the time its third, final, and best album, *Frame and Canvas,* was released in 1998, the music was reminiscent of the Promise Ring, but with less willfully simple hooks. The rhythms were meandering, the time changes were frequent, and the dual guitars played off of each other in an ostensibly arty manner, often working themselves up into a fine, semi-directionless froth. Much like with the Promise Ring, however, opinions, when they were split, were most often done so over the lead vocals. Bob Nanna's wan croak had its moments of effectiveness, but was more often than not submerged and drowned in the muddy mix.

What Braid did better than any other band of its era was truly live the egalitarian spirit of emo. If emo is, on one level, the ability to move from sympathy for song subjects to outright empathy, then Braid blurred the line even further, engendering empathy for itself. In other words, Braid's charm lay not in the fact that they, the band members, *could* be the audience, but in the fact that, like Mineral, they *were* their audience. Nanna couldn't sing, but he did his best to try, and in that effort lay a definite appeal. When he cries out to a lost lover, his voice is weak, cracking. The sound mimics the sentiment, tapping into the everyguy appeal. We've all been there, and he's going to sing about it. When Chris Broach shouted out emphasis on some of Nanna's words, he expanded the community. The band was a group of pleasant, Midwestern indie guys with a tireless touring schedule that crisscrossed the country with an almost self-destructive frequency. One had the impression that they were a band precisely because they desperately wanted to be a band. Like its college-educated audience, Braid also thought about things too much; the lyrics are often tangled collections of wordplay ("the current erode it / I rode it"), overheated imagery, and confessions. Known as incredibly nice and approachable, Nanna and Broach peppered their sets with covers of songs that everyone in their fan base knew by heart—songs by the Smiths and the Pixies, performed awkwardly but lovingly; the band members were fans above all else, using their concerts to act as listeners in the crowd.

It's hard not to think of Chris Ryan's comments about emo bands' self-destructive streaks when one considers that Braid's best song was never included on one of their albums. "Forever Got Shorter" was first issued as a split single with the Get Up Kids in late 1997, then re-released in Europe in '98, put out on a Tree Records compilation in Chicago in '99, and then once again on vinyl in Japan. Slow-burning and vigilant, "Forever Got Shorter" is a long, stumble-filled jog down a runway towards an eventual takeoff/payoff. Lyrically, Nanna struggles with definitions of distance—the physical space between him and a lover, the theoretical divide of expectations, as well as the metaphorical distance created by writing about an important event in a song; the double frustration of celebrating thwarted desire in a lyric: "Let's go undercover like young lovers should / 'cause I can kiss you better than this letter could."

Over a cascading streak of intertwining guitars, Nanna hangs himself out to dry: "I'll still be lost in poetics or lost in the mail." Later, he sings of "frustration" as all of his attempts to communicate are thwarted—everything from the postal service to the radio lets him down—and he begins repeating the phrase "on the radio," again and again—the aural equivalent of banging your head against the wall. By the end of the song, however, as he and the music build to a propulsive release, the "on the radio" refrain transforms itself into a celebration and it's almost as if Nanna can hear his song being listened to, talked about, burned onto mixtapes, adored. The message may be warped into various disguises—letters, analogies, radio waves, Japanese vinyl—but the song *is* his message and its existence is proved everytime someone listens to it. The letters are received, the broadcast is heard. Braid's wriggling rhythms and melody are desperate to communicate—and communication equals growth, the completion of the circuit.

Despite this glorious moment of success, the mid-nineties incarnation of emo was already short-circuiting itself—Bob Nanna may have been inadvertently speaking for his entire musical generation when, near the end of "Forever Got Shorter," he sang, "maybe I'm a baby / but I think it's time to grow." The appeal of emo to large music companies was obvious—young, self-sufficient bands that had passionately loyal fan bases and songs that cleaned up a little wouldn't be that out of place on the radio. But by the time the music made an impression, it had already burned itself out.

A number of emo bands did jump at the major-label offers that were suddenly dangled in front of them, but all that did finished the same way: broken up. The intensity of the music cost it longevity; so specific were the lyrics and emotions to the fans—and to the bands that made them—that neither could move on with the other. Braid sang in the voice of its audience; Mineral vocalized their fans' innermost thoughts. The music was a welcoming, self-affirming community. All the kids who listened to emo in the '90s were seeking to validate themselves, to join in something shared and secretive. It was the last subculture made of vinyl and paper instead of plastic and megabytes. It was confident enough in its message, but ultimately weak in the messengers. The bands were as innocent as their take on romance—when money, exhaustion, and contracts started to appear, they simply crumbled.

"When business gets involved, it just gets too complicated," says the Promise Ring's Gnewikow. "Your ratio of fun to work starts to plummet. And that strains things." It's a particularly salted comment from Gnewikow—I spoke with him on the phone from his Milwaukee home on a Tuesday in October 2002. It turned out that after seven years, the Promise Ring had broken up.

"For me, personally, it was becoming really difficult to answer for things that we did when we were twenty years old. I love *Nothing Feels Good,* but it colored everything we did after that because we were reacting to it." He sighs. "You have to wonder if there's not a social side to why people are affected by a record. When your peers are into it, you talk about it, obsess about it. It's not necessarily the record itself, but where your life is and what you're doing. At the time we made *Nothing Feels Good* a lot of the people listening to our band were our age. And they moved on and got into different music. And so did we." He pauses. "Once people like you, you can't take it back. And I don't think you can ever really write an honest record again."

And that, ultimately, was what killed the mid-nineties version of emo. Despite the cries of sellouts from the underground and the increased major-label attention, it was the bands themselves that called it a day. Even Peter Pan had to leave never-never land sometime; at a certain point, life beckons in a louder voice than the van. You can choose to have a girlfriend, or to drive as far away from her as possible and then sing about how you made the wrong choice. And the choices for the listeners were, at heart, no different.

FOUR

THE CURIOUS CASE OF WEEZER

In the same year that Kurt Cobain was screaming "rape me" before pointing a shotgun at his own head, a mop-top bespectacled dork named Rivers Cuomo was climbing the charts with a song about his favorite sweater. When Weezer broke big in 1994, Cuomo became geekdom's Jackie Robinson—a breakthrough figure on the national stage who changed the game and the audience of an entire industry. Lazily lumped in with the dregs of the grunge explosion, Weezer's irony was miles apart from his dour peers. Cuomo was a fully formed nerd singing about what he knew best: vintage clothes, random trivia, and trouble with girls. There was no working-class angst and there was no ugliness. Where Cobain used a smirk to defend himself against the world, there was no real distance: he commented on the unfairness of it all, but took it personally. Cuomo may have a bad self-image, but he'd never be the type to pull the trigger—he just wants you to "pull this thread as I walk away."

It made perfect sense that Weezer's second single paid tribute to Buddy Holly. Cuomo may be socially awkward but he's no dummy. Holly was pop music's first cool jerk, a jittery dude in glasses who played the part of suave rocker, subverting the silliness of the dominant tropes by embracing them with a wink in his eye and a swagger in his step. More than any other band of the 1990s, it was Weezer that signified college rock breaking through; its fans were boys and girls who wanted to rock, but maybe after studying for their SATs. The band's aw-shucks appearance and goofy demeanor was the musical equivalent of the school misfit wearing a Def Leppard T-shirt; eventually Cuomo would even co-opt the hoary "rock-horns" hand gesture, reveling in and mocking its power in arenas all across the country. When people refer to the "ironic '90s," they're usually picturing Rivers Cuomo in their head—

a mainstream rock star dressed like the last kid picked for kickball; an outcast who single-handedly made thick black glasses the coolest fashion accessory since a heroin addiction.

Weezer's songs were fast, chipper, and catchier than smallpox—every single track lifted from the band's breakthrough, eponymous debut (aka The Blue Album) could easily have been a one-hit wonder. But the album was a resounding success, selling millions of copies around the world. By the time the band returned with its sophomore album, *Pinkerton*, in 1996, its success, by rights, should have only increased. After Cobain's death, the burgeoning modern rock radio format had become as stale and formulaic as the classic rock dinosaurs it had seemingly usurped. With major labels adhering strictly to the law of diminishing returns, underground bands were snatched up, overpaid, and then dumped after little more than a novelty single. 1996–'98 were the glory years of any future late-night "hits of the '90s" double-disc compilation, with obscure geeky-looking bands from all over the country scoring fleeting success with hook-filled ditties about self-doubt and girlfriends. Apparently, though, someone forgot to send Rivers the memo. Instead of ratcheting it up and cashing in, Weezer submerged. *Pinkerton* was a dark, churning record—the hooks were still there, but this time they were dug deeply into Cuomo's own skin. If the Blue Album was the hipster's night out, *Pinkerton* was the nerd's night in. The mainstream celebrity that the band enjoyed preyed on Cuomo like a rash: he hated himself for achieving it and he hated himself for loving it.

Pinkerton is obsessed with sex—way past the chaste, closed-lip kiss of "Buddy Holly," but far removed from the bawdy, lap-dance soundtrack of bands like Mötley Crüe. *Pinkerton* is about messy, manipulative, confused hook-ups, sympathy screws, and quickies with groupies. It's the sound of a lifelong diabetic given the keys to the candy store, and it has similar results. Songs like "Why Bother," "Tired of Sex," and particularly the seemingly innocuous first single "El Scorcho" present Cuomo as a bumbling Humbert Humbert for the twenty-first century, an apologetic nymphomaniac with an Asian fetish and a guitar. Predictably, the album was a disaster. Reviews were negative and sales were slight to nonexistent. Mortified, Cuomo retreated from the public eye, had painful surgery to correct the length of his legs, and enrolled in Harvard. The pop juggernaut rolled on; Weezer became a footnote while a succession of memorable-to-mediocre singles (by Fountains of Wayne, Nada Surf, Superdrag, Nerf Herder, and others) filled the gap created by their absence and perpetuated the newfound genre of "nerd-rock." Case closed on Weezer.

Except it wasn't. Not by a long shot.

A young generation of teenagers who discovered so-called alternative music through Weezer and its mid-nineties contemporary Green Day had purchased *Pinkerton,* and instead of being put off by its dark themes, they were entranced. *Pinkerton* is an album, on one level, about rejection, and its rejection by the greater marketplace became part of its allure. As the thirteen- and fourteen-year-olds of the Blue Album matured, the negative yearnings of *Pinkerton* became a gateway drug, opening up a new world of painful music to adolescents hungry to understand their newfound pain. Weened on the glory years of alt-culture, these were the kids who, as they descended deeper into the underground, still kept a torch burning for Rivers Cuomo, their original idol. As the years rolled by and Cuomo stayed vanished, *Pinkerton* sold steadily. It was an old friend, an important secret. It was passed down from punk enabler to willing Padawan; it was whispered about on messageboards; it thrived on Napster. Since Cuomo never stuck around to explain himself and the album was generally ignored, thousands if not millions of kids believed that the album was directed at them—it was their life, their story. None of the kids ever forgot about it, and a good number of them went on to form bands. Although no one was paying attention—perhaps precisely *because* no one was paying attention—*Pinkerton* became the most important emo album of the decade.

In late 2000, when Cuomo cast off his self-imposed shadow and decided to rock again, his audience was waiting for him. The Weezer that returned to the road that fall was ostensibly the same poppy band that had rocked the Alternative Nation eight years previously (although founding bassist Matt Sharp had departed, taking a lot of the band's goofiness with him), but something had changed. When Rivers Cuomo took the stage, he was blown away to discover an overflowing audience that looked exactly like him, crying out for the songs they most wanted to hear: the ten tracks from *Pinkerton.* When the album was originally released, Cuomo's defiant geekiness was a solitary attempt to subvert the macho posturing of large-scale rock 'n' roll. Weezer in the twenty-first century represented the triumph of that very subversion. Bizarrely, Weezer's greatest failure proved to be their respirator and their greatest success.

While away, Weezer had become a "classic" band, one referenced with a sad-eyed sigh over what could have been. Two separate tribute records had appeared, both featuring contemporary punk and emo bands (including Dashboard Confessional, Piebald, and The Ataris) meticulously recreating Weezer's most beloved songs. More than punk bands embraced Weezer's legacy—harder acts like the Deftones covered them live, Axl Rose emerged from his own Howard Hughes–like seclusion to proclaim himself a fan. The most critically lauded—and most beloved by their peers—band of the '90s was the English art-rock group Radiohead. But while everybody may *love* Radiohead, no one else would dare try to *be* Radiohead. Weezer was the band that inspires, not intimidates. Something about their unartfully admitted nerdiness struck a chord with everyone who had ever felt unloved or unwanted—which was, despite good looks, fame, or money, apparently everyone. It was clear: Cuomo's deeply personal confessions—often set to hummable, toe-tapping melodies—were the definitive blueprint for twenty-first-century emo. To the bands that had sprung up in its wake, Weezer's return was epochal—the true masters back to reclaim their rightful crown.

The only problem was that Cuomo wasn't having any part of it. Dismissing *Pinkerton* as "ugly" and embarrassing, Cuomo refused to play any of the album's songs on the reunion tour, driving the hordes of fans to a frenzy of orgasmic frustration. The new songs debuted on that tour—and later packaged as the triumphant, platinum-selling comeback record, *Weezer* (also known as the Green Album)—were tight, instantly memorable pop songs in the great Weezer (some would just say "great," as in overly familiar) tradition. But the lyrics were cagey, ranging from the intentionally wacky ("Hash Pipe") to the banal ("Island in the Sun"). Weezer was back, but insisted on being just another pop band. In doing so, Cuomo turned his back on the very thing that kept him relevant.

Pinkerton today is an impressive document and an even more impressive oracle. On "El Scorcho" Cuomo sang, "sneak into your room / and read your diary" years before such an act not only wasn't transgressive, it was expected. *Pinkerton* was, in effect, Cuomo's own diary, and it inspired legions of adherents. But the irony of the album's acclaim is that Cuomo was mortified by it. Drummer Pat Wilson confirms that at one point, Cuomo threatened to buy the *Pinkerton* masters back from Geffen so he could destroy it once and for all. In 2002, Cuomo presented himself to *Spin* thusly: "I see things very clearly and realistically without my emotions coloring things. Of course, I have feelings like anybody else, but rather than let them run my life, I like to exploit them and use them for my purposes." On *Pinkerton*, Cuomo was honest with his listeners before he was honest with himself—and when they loved him all the better for his failings, he couldn't take the heat. In other words, he wasn't ahead of his time, the album was. Six years later, when the time had clearly come, he still wasn't ready.

The Weezer touring machine circa 2002 is a smooth-operating, emotionally dysfunctional operation. The band members are rarely seen speaking to each other, and Cuomo is rarely seen at all. Always notoriously antisocial, the group's renewed success seems to have served as the impetus for a full-on retreat from normal society. "He thinks he's Brian Wilson," said one member of a band who has spent time opening for Weezer, "and so he's trying his best to act crazy." Whether it's an act or not isn't for me to say, but there is an air of craziness around the backstage area. There are rumors of tour contracts forbidding any member of the opening bands from making eye contact with Cuomo; five minutes before the band takes the stage its massive security chief puts the entire backstage area into "lockdown," forbidding anyone from leaving their dressing rooms while Cuomo is transported from his private room to the stage. When performing, Cuomo (who has taken to only wearing suits) plays his stumblebum nerd image to the hilt, holding his body rock-still below the shoulders and addressing the crowd with bizarre parodies of rock-star chatter and hip-hop homilies delivered in a thick voice that could generously be described as autistic. "All right, homies!" he yells. "It's great to see you all singing along my brothers and sisters. Especially when you're *hot chicks.*" The crowds roar every night, while the rest of the band grits their collective teeth and continues playing.

All major tours host "meet-and-greets" for the fans of local radio stations. Intended as an end run around his antisocial demeanor, Cuomo ferries a foozball table with the band's gear from city to city to serve as a buffer between him and his fans. Every evening before the show, a bunch of nervous, excited kids in T-shirts clutching faded copies of *Pinkerton* is led backstage and told that Rivers will spend a few minutes playing foozball with each of them. Awkwardly bent over in his suit and barely raising his voice above a whisper, Cuomo looks more uncomfortable than his starstruck fans, who themselves appear to be caught somewhere between awe and sympathy. I spent one afternoon on a recent tour, and observed Cuomo wandering out into the intense sunshine of the catering area. The members of the other bands sitting around enjoying stir-fry fell immediately silent and stared at him openly. Finally, Cuomo's attractive Asian assistant came running out to rescue him and steered him back to the dressing room. It turned out all he wanted was a yogurt.

For its still growing legion of listeners, the appeal of *Pinkerton* has nothing to do with the sex or weird Japanese digressions. The fact that Cuomo was complaining not about his boring life but rather about living the rock-star life doesn't matter either—all that matters is that he regretted it and felt sick and stupid a lot of the time. But somewhere along the line he stopped sharing with his audience, and his audience felt silly for continuing to hold up their half of the bargain. So, Weezer isn't an emo band anymore. That moment has passed. But *Pinkerton* is an emo touchstone, and the band remains the forerunner and standard-bearer of Vagrant Records' populist punk movement. The greatest of all its legacies is the transformation of pain into something not only listenable, but pleasant. It may have happened covertly and taken close to a decade, but *Pinkerton* proved that pain sold—especially if you could hum along to it.

With Weezer, emo had come a long way from the righteous artistic flailings of Rites of Spring; it had come a long way from the messianic thrashing of Sunny Day Real Estate too. *Pinkerton,* for whatever reason, reduced emo to its contemporary, most popular, and—as we were soon to discover—profitable definition: the toe-tapping sound of sensitive, self-questioning boys complaining.

FIVE

WHO ARE THE EMO KIDS?

They're not traditional punks; they're not frustrated indie kids or disillusioned college English majors. They're not wearing glasses to be cool and they're not wearing vintage T-shirts to impress. So then, who are the emo kids today?

They are the kids from the suburbs, from outside the major cities, and from way, way off the beaten path; kids from the traditional punk breeding grounds like Long Island and New Jersey, places where rampant commercialism and boredom constantly combine to push inhabitants into a desperate search for something "real." Or they are kids from more recent hot spots like Florida and Utah, states where most touring bands don't choose to venture and where rampant fundamentalism leads directly into a more stridently inclusive sort of rebellion; places that lack any sort of blueprint for musical backlashes, transforming the venerable concept of DIY into CIY—Create It Yourself. Emo kids are exactly that—kids, meaning they don't have positions of power in the media; they don't even live in Manhattan or Los Angeles. They haven't really thought the deep thoughts yet—they're too caught up in the majesty of their own private drama and they've found a music that privileges that very same drama—that forces no difficult questions, just bemoans the lack of answers.

No matter the era, punk-rock kids will always be punk-rock kids, the quiet loners or exuberant exhibitionists who sneer at society and reject anything that's been handed to or forced onto them. These kids have their relief from whatever it is that plagues them. There will always be hardcore scenes because there will always be those sorts of kids who need them.

But what about the nonpunk kids who need them too? Kids who are popular—maybe not jocks, but certainly not nerds. Ordinary, non–music obsessives who gamely deal with the day-to-day difficulties of high school, of home, of themselves. Kids who are younger, both male and female, who are not political by nature or by nurture. Lower- to upper-middle-class, often white, these are kids with problems that—to them at least—matter just as much as anyone else's.

Difference is OK—but it's better, more productive, and more pleasant to celebrate similarities.

Punk is inherently oppositional. Screw your mainstream, this is our way. That very opposition is what traditionally limits it. It contradicts itself the moment it becomes popular, or even known. Emo is inherently inclusive. Punks are backed into a circle, away from daily commericial life, until, middle fingers raised, they are all backed up together, defensively a unit for fighting and self-protection. Emo kids run towards the circle, arms up, and huddle together. Better together than alone.

More than ever, kids today who have access to a computer (a number that skyrockets with each passing week) need never be truly alone. Those who claim the highflying techboom nonsense of the late '90s effectively killed the internet age have been looking in the wrong direction. It is today's teenagers who are the first fully online generation—those born in the '70s may have adapted to the reality of a wired world, but those born in the '80s need no such adaptation; they know no other reality. The dominant role the internet now plays in teenagers' lives—most spend at least sixteen hours per week online—is both a profound change and the next step in a larger chain of events that stretches back throughout history. Teenagers have always felt persecuted and have always been so-called early adopters, seeking ways to connect with each other that are unique to their peer group. Think of the telephone, the convertible, the electric guitar. With the internet, teenagers have the ultimate emo tool—a private medium that their parents don't understand, one where they can easily trade, access, and share music, ideas, news, feelings, and support. It took the better part of a decade for an overlooked artifact like *Pinkerton* to become more than a secret—these days it would be unlikely to take longer than the better part of a week.

As the country has moved further and further apart, it's been simultaneously wired closer and closer together. Teenagers were given eyeballs so they could roll them, and they were given towns/schools/lives so they could complain about them. The DSL line snaking out the back of the house is nothing more than a canny update of the tin-cans-and-a-string telephone that linked neighbors together for after-hour chats in more idealized times (i.e., in the movies). Late at night, when kids are supposed to be sleeping, praying, doing homework, they can pick up the digital lifeline and cling to it: for support, for friendship, for music, for answers. Angst and boiling over emotions are carried out; songs that help make sense of the world are carried in. It's an escape hatch for everyone, bringing cultural choices even to those utterly incapable of seeking them out. It's an international emotional plumbing network: reach out and touch someone.

The web is both the ideal medium for communicating music and music fandom and the ideal way of fucking with people's preconceived notions of what music is, should be, and can be. When you take community-centered music—which is what punk has traditionally been—outside of the community, what are you left with? (The age-old pattern of seeing a flyer, sneaking out to a show, writing to a post office box, waiting to get a hand-scribbled note with a 7-inch, and whispering to your friends about it is long gone. One click of the mouse and an entire band's ouvre is available on MP3, anytime, anywhere.) One view is that it transforms it into more of a product. If you divorce punk from the thrill of it, the chase of it, the discovery, and social interactions—what are you left with? A soundtrack to surfing. Another thing that can be consumed as opposed to something that takes a lot from you but gives back in spades. What defines punk? Finding others who are like you or sitting alone in front of your computer? Music that wants you to love it, that fits neatly into a space inside of yourself, or music that pushes you around, challenges you, changes you, makes you come to it?

Online, a messageboard is a rock show—you've got your moderators on stage, setting the tone. You've got the loudmouths in the front, pushing everybody around with their attitude, their righteousness, their need for attention. You've got the lurkers in the back, taking in all the action, not saying a word, holding their opinions close to their chest, giving nothing away but taking what they need and more. But both, at their most basic level, are invented, temporary spaces. A common interest has filled them with people, but all are free to leave whenever they like, and the people who fill them are there as whoever they want to be. They are presenting an idealized version of themselves—tonight, under the anonymous cover of rock, of screen names, the school church mouse can mosh, the junior varsity quarterback can sing, the person who gets ignored during the day can be noticed.

The information superhighway can also be a super–back alley. Indie bands have always relied on word of mouth to attract attention and fans; the rise of the internet as the primary communication tool of teenagers hasn't removed its importance. What it has done, is tweaked it in a subtle fashion. Case in point: When I was bringing my first interview with Dashboard Confessional's Chris Carrabba to an end in November 2001, he mentioned that there was one rising band in particular that I should watch out for. "There's a band from New Jersey called Thursday," he said, while we were paying the check. "They're gonna be huge." I filed away the information and didn't think much of it for a few weeks. By the beginning of December, though, something strange was beginning to happen. On messageboards, on Makeoutclub, on livejournals and blogs, the name Thursday was popping up. Again and again, slowly at first and predominantly from people on the east coast, there were raves about the band's album, *Full Collapse,* breathless testimonials about the intensity of their live show. Soon the word had spread to the California webheads as well. A week later, I caught the end of a Thursday video on MTV2. A few weeks after that, everyone in the *Spin* office was flabbergasted to see some band they'd never heard of called Thursday had crashed into the lower echelons of the *Billboard* charts. In May of 2002, half of the kids I spoke with in Texas had Thursday T-shirts on.

The point isn't that the band wouldn't have achieved national success without the internet—it's that it all happened so much faster. Because of the public/private nature of the computer screen, raving about a band still feels like keeping it a secret. If it goes national, it does so covertly.

Punk rock has changed the internet and the internet has fundamentally changed punk rock. What was once a subculture, dominated by regionality, is now something completely new and unexplored: a national subculture, dominated and defined by those too young to have their voices heard, but savvy enough to make their presence felt.

What a large number of pundits and those in the media forget is that the kids in question are literally kids. While rock critics roll their eyes and point to the superior precedent of the early '90s, post-Nirvana alt-boom (followed by the crushing bust that left the underground be-trayed, decimated, and wracked by a million and one subdivisions) and cringe at the lack of restraint in the music and lyrics, they are forgetting that a typical Dashboard Confessional fan was four years old when Nir-vana's *Nevermind* was released. There is a moment, usually concurrent with puberty and/or high school, when kids come into themselves and begin to pay attention to the world around them on its own merits. A moment when they start questioning their parents, questioning their friendships, their tastes. It's the beginning of a possibly endless process of creating the people that they will become.

Up to now, these coming-of-age kids in America have only had a *Total Request Live* landscape to navigate: a glossy, one-dimensional fiefdom split between the craven rock-star theatrics of prefab boy bands and those of manipulative aggro rap-metal outfits. Hearing emo, then, is pretty close to a revolutionary experience.

"If you expose Saves the Day to someone who only had a Wal-Mart to buy music, all of a sudden they have a situation where they can hear something and make up their own mind," says Dreamworks Records' Luke Wood. "Emo and the internet give kids a vehicle to have a per-sonal and creative life which was never acceptable or accessible before now. When you see them posting on messageboards and singing along with Chris Carrabba's lyrics, it's clear how much they needed this cul-ture in their lives."

When you have such a relatively blank canvas to build on, it's not possible to get too basic about the attraction. Most fifteen- or sixteen-year-olds, when asked what drew them to Dashboard Confessional, answer the same way: "the acoustic guitar." No matter the generation, rock music has never been able to get over the essential argument that acoustics code as "realer" or more legitimate than their noisy, scruffy, plugged-in brethren. So while the twentysomethings of the world were busy going the opposite way—falling all over themselves hyping and praising the "back to basics" value of neo–garage bands like The White Stripes and The Hives (bands that aggressively turn back the clock and hide behind poses copped from artists who have long since peaked; bands that attempt to restore sex, sweat, and mystery to rock)—the teens are gasping for air. They haven't been let down by a decade of irony—they don't know what irony is and quite possibly have never even heard Alanis Morissette's iconic but inaccurate "Ironic." Kids want something real and pure. So do adults. At different stages in life, however, what you're looking for and what you find can diverge wildly.

Dulce is a seventeen-year-old in Arizona, whose music tastes adhered fairly closely to the mainstream until the day she downloaded three Dashboard Confessional songs on a whim. Her description of that day is like that of a blind person learning to see: "I remember the first time I listened to "The Swiss Army Romance" I thought it was so beautiful. I mainly focused my attention on the sound of the song rather than its lyrical content because before listening to Dashboard I never really listened to anything acoustic. It was something new with a different sound for me and I was taking it all in."

Danielle is seventeen and lives in Ontario. "I first heard about Dashboard almost two years ago on a messageboard and decided to download some songs. I fell in love and went out and bought the CD. It made me want to cry and smile at the same time. It was one of the first times that I felt an emotional connection to something. It was like Chris was singing right to me about my life. It was totally different than most music I heard. Not many artists play acoustic guitar and it has such a different sound than an electric. It's really a lot more calming and to me brings out the emotion in music."

Jane is fifteen and lives in Kentucky. She describes how she fell for Dashboard Confessional thusly: "Chris's music appeals to me, I guess, because I really love acoustic guitar and not only are his melodies and rhythms catchy but also his lyrics hit so close to home. Most people can relate to his songs and he sings with such emotion and he has a beautiful voice. Dashboard was unique but I think more artists are going for the 'acoustic guitar' sound now. And most people call that genre of music 'emo' and they all form to make this community of 'depressed emo kids.'"

After a lifetime—which, in these cases isn't very long at all—of hearing voices obscured by crashing hip-hop beats, squealing electric guitars, and meaningless, scripted lyrics written by anonymous Swedes, hearing something as simple as an acoustic guitar and a voice is revolutionary. It is, quite literally, the sound of not hiding, of being yourself, of being real. It makes people, as one girl told me, "sit and think about what the lyrics actually mean. I had actually never done that before."

Leaving those fraught lyrics aside for just a moment, the stripped honesty of the acoustic sound easily parallels the churning reinvention that usually accompanies early high school. Tracy* is a fifteen-year-old living in Virginia. At the beginning of 2002 she was listening to what all of her friends were listening to: Britney Spears, Mandy Moore, 'N Sync. And then something changed.

"I've had a lot of stress and some family issues, especially with my dad," she told me. "And I relieve myself by locking myself in my room and putting music on. Pop music just didn't cheer me up anymore. For some reason, hearing others' problems does cheer me up. Britney sucks. Christina Aguilera sucks. That stuff just gets annoying. Emo isn't all happy-go-lucky music. It's not fake. This is all stuff [the singer] has actually been through and it's amazing to hear him express it like he does. I haven't listened to anything but 'emo and punk' for a good six months. I don't care what people think of me anymore. I'm not gonna be fake. I'm gonna be real."

I asked her in what ways she was fake before.

"I would buy clothes at the mall or wear whatever was in and act however everyone else was acting."

And now?

"I buy clothes wherever I want, whether it's the mall or Goodwill. I made all new friends because I don't want to have fake friends, and all of them are true to themselves too."

I asked her if she could be more specific about the problems that the music was helping her with.

"My problems were really only with my dad. My mom and I are like best friends. My dad hid the fact I have older sisters from me. He never told me [and then] one of them emailed me. He tries to hide things from me, like that he drinks. I'm getting to the point to where I just wanna leave. I told my mom today that I hate him and hope I never see his face again. She had to take a second job because he quit his. We're getting close to leaving. Usually, I lock myself in my room, put a CD on, and just ignore all other things. I guess thinking about others' problems makes me forget my own for that time being. If I didn't have music, I probably would have run away by now. I was very close to it."

If punk was traditionally the long-needed balm to a small but persistent type of outcast who needed it, emo is the same healing agent for the teenage community at large. What most music critics tend to forget as they decry the lack of subtlety, humor, or nuance in contemporary emo is one basic fact: high school is *hard.* It's a miserable, judgmental, cruel war zone of avarice, antagonism, gossip, romance, and self-doubt. It's about feeling things for the first time. The raging emotions of study hall, of P.E. class, of prom and chemistry lab don't have nuance, they have passion, and a particularly self-obsessed passion at that. Some of the issues kids face are as old as time. Others—like, for example, the increased presence of drugs, sex, handguns, and media—are of a more recent vintage. This isn't a caution to adults—some self-congratulating 'do you know where your children are' bit of conservative propaganda. It's just the truth. High school isn't impossible and it isn't a cakewalk; it's not a cartoon and it's not an N.W.A. album. Somewhere between *Saved by the Bell, Dawson's Creek,* and *Kids* is the reality.

The emo kids are young, experienced, wise, cocky, miserable, ecstatic, engaged, detached, clever, charming, dreaming, crying, polite, and trapped. "I'm not depressed all the time," says eighteen-year-old Whitney Borup in Utah. "But I'm certainly human and I don't think my parents want to know that. Music is calming to me. It's a relief to hear other people expressing themselves." They are a generation of a divided, diffuse country looking for any way possible to bring themselves—and others—together. Digitally savvy but emotionally fragile, they look to make meaningful connections via the two most intangible media available to them—music and the internet.

You are disenfranchised, your parents don't understand you. You like girls/boys, they don't like you. You are smart but not smart enough. You are too fat. You are too thin. You have to get into college but you have to finish your eighteen extracurricular activities first. Your best friend betrays you, your girlfriend/boyfriend cheats on you. Your parents get divorced. People offer you drugs/drinks. Maybe you take them, maybe you don't. People are mean to you. Again and again and again. When you come home from school, you sit in the bathroom and cry for an hour. Every day.

With the door closed, you turn on the stereo. Someone is singing about problems just like yours. They're not commenting on them, not judging them, just echoing them, making them real, validating them. You sing along and your tears dry up. You switch on your computer. You're safe in your room. You control everything. You're alone. But you check your buddy list and know, you are anything but alone.

PART TWO

VAGRANT AMERICA

SIX

THROUGH BEING COOL:
VAGRANT RECORDS

The backstage area of Manhattan's famed Madison Square Garden is a lot like Theseus's legendary labyrinth but without the charm (and no sign of the minotaur). Grim winding hallways circle back on themselves; faded concrete lines the pictureless walls. There's little sign of all of the megastar bands that have passed through en route to rock immortality; there are no scars dilineating generations of *Spinal Tap*–worthy excess.

On stage, a diminutive twentysomething with a mop-top of blond hair, a painfully earnest expression, and *My So-Called Life*–worthy acne is pumping his fist like the rock stars of old. His band (median age: twenty-one) has his back, filling in the mammoth arena with precise, pop-laced power punk. "This song will become the anthem of your underground," sings the blond kid. "I'll sing whatever song you want for whatever mood you're in . . . all you want from me is a broken heart and a mouth full of blood!" The twenty-thousand-strong crowd of fifteen-year-old girls in "Punk Princess" T-shirts and sixteen-year-old boys with glasses and angst to spare scream, applaud, and sing along with every single word. It's summer 2002, Saves the Day is playing Madison Square Garden. Emo has broken in America.

Afterward, Saves the Day's singer, Chris Conley, staggers deliriously offstage, sweat pouring down his red and ruddy face. Billie Joe Armstrong of headliner Green Day throws his arm protectively around Conley and asks him how it was.

"Oh man," says Conley, breathless, "it was amazing! It was so amazing. You're gonna love it. Well, I guess you're used to it. But it was— wow. Wow!"

Billie Joe laughs a paternal laugh and pats Conley on the shoulder. "You did it, man," he says. "Good job." And he walks away laughing.

In the dressing rooms, Rich Egan, Saves the Day's manager and founder of their Vagrant Records label, takes congratulatory high-fives and handshakes between cell phone trills. With his black T-shirt, boyish face, and shock of stuck-straight-up blond hair, Egan doesn't much look like the man behind the most successful punk label on the planet—in fact, he doesn't much look like the owner of anything. He's more like the overeager intern. But at six feet tall and the build of a hummingbird, Egan is working the room like a grizzled industry pro. He carries himself with the go-go air of someone who's been incredibly, blissfully, unreasonably lucky; someone who's marginally convinced that there's no reason that his luck should end anytime soon.

In between business huddles with Conley, Egan takes time to talk about his plans for the second go-round of his highly successful Vagrant America tour—a slick, no-expenses-spared package featuring every band on his label. The plan was to have the second Vagrant America tour play arenas, using it as a nationwide victory lap, rubbing everyone's noses in the fact that Vagrant was triumphant, Egan's emo-aesthetic a nationwide brand. Sponsorship deals with Microsoft and Activision are on the table, and last time I saw him, Egan had been busy booking the Garden for an October emo extravaganza. But now, he explains, the whole thing might be delayed for a year.

"Too many variables," he says, smacking his gum. "A bunch of bands wanted to record their new records then and others had other commitments. So instead we're going to do it in the spring and play 3,000-seat venues instead of 10,000. That way we can charge twenty-two dollars instead of twenty-eight. Y'know," he says, with a giant smile, "do it a little more punk rock."

Emo broke in the summer of 2002—it had its tipping point, if you will—not in the mainstream consciousness, just the mainstream media. With Vagrant Records moving big numbers on every release, Jimmy Eat World going platinum, Dashboard Confessional taping an MTV Unplugged, and New Found Glory debuting at number four on the Billboard charts, the word emo—always meaningless at best—became buzzworthy; a cover line to sell magazines; an affectation to make over forty magazine columnists seem down; a semi-current limbo stick against which to judge all music; a catchall, basically, for any music not made by Britney Spears or Limp Bizkit.

At the end of July, I browsed the magazine rack at my local Barnes & Noble. I looked at three magazines and found three curious uses of emo as an adjective. There was *Entertainment Weekly* feeling the need to state that Northern Irish guitar pop band Ash was "not maudlin enough to be emo." There was the British music weekly *NME* describing a song by hip New York quartet Interpol as an "emo slowcore anthem." And then there was *CMJ New Music Monthly*'s eye-catching cover line, "Atmosphere's emo rap" in reference to the backpacker hip-hop group from Minnesota.

Around the same time *Seventeen* magazine ran a two-page pullout spread that doubled as an emo "how-to" guide, detailing how girls should wear vintage clothes and hair barrettes; for guys, v-neck sweaters and visible copies of arty books (Salinger, Vonnegut) were a must. A newspaper in Hawaii ran an extremely silly style piece called "Geek Chic Look Is Clean-Cut," that read like a fieldspotting manual for indie-leaning youngsters. The article marveled over how young people were choosing to wear button-down shirts and shoulder bags instead of baggy jeans and halter tops, and that emo fans actually wrote poetry and valued love. The article could have been published in any of the last four or five decades with the words "punk," "hippie," "grunge," or "young republican" replacing emo.

The media business, so desperate for its self-obsessed, post-9/11 predictions of a return to austerity and the death of irony to come true, had found its next big thing. But it was barely a "thing," because no one had heard of it, and those who had couldn't define it. Despite the fact that the hedonistic, materialistic hip-hop of Nelly was still dominating the charts, magazine readers in the summer of '02 were informed that the nation was deep in an introverted healing process, and the way it was healing was by wearing thick black glasses and vintage striped shirts. Emo, we were told, would heal us all through fashion.

And, at least tangentially, that media-promulgated message began sticking, at least a little bit. "When Dashboard hit the radio, everyone at my high school started wearing Converse high-tops," says fifteen-year-old Emily.* "People started wearing fake glasses and Dickies pants because they were 'emo.' It was something that made you cooler. It was a trend. It was pathetic." And for good or ill, the man most responsible for raising emo to the boiling point was Vagrant's Rich Egan.

Since 1999, Rich Egan's Vagrant Records label has become synonymous with emo, successfully signing disparate bands in the Jawbreaker vein and communicating them to the public at large as a cohesive movement. Through savvy marketing, strident antielitism, and pages ripped wholesale out of the big bad major-label playbook, Vagrant has widely expanded both the audience for—and the definition of—punk. The label's artists have a diversity of sound but are thematically black and white; while the music ranges from acoustic folk to thrashing SoCal skate rock, the lyrics stay zeroed in on uncomplicated, lovelorn confessions. For all intents and purposes, Vagrant bands like Dashboard Confessional, Saves the Day, and the Get Up Kids *are* emo to thousands, if not millions, of music fans. The label's ability to market both itself and its artists on a national scale has resulted in hundreds of thousands of record sales and at least as many raised eyebrows from the ever-vigilant underground. In both the ways and means of its across-the-board success, Vagrant's rise has raised the bar for independent labels and for punk in general. In the hangover of the post-grunge era, most indie bands and labels cried foul and retreated back to their small-stakes spheres. Riding the explosion of internet use among high school students and the universal appeal of his musical formula (cute, bruised boys who fall in love too easily and tour too much), Rich Egan chose a different tack. He hasn't leveled the playing field so much as he's crashed the party.

Jimmy Eat World and Vagrant's first breakthrough act, the Get Up Kids, survived the self-destructive doubt of the mid-nineties emo scene because they had ambition and no time for wishy-washy indie hemming and hawing. Both in their careers and in their choruses, they went for it, all out, no apologies. Vagrant Records is a label built on that same aesthetic. Both its employees and its fans have no problem being behind something that's popular—not to mention populist and more than a little bit pop. In a world where cars are advertised as punk, Green Day members are platinum rock stars, and getting pierced and tatted up is as natural as a sweet-sixteen party, everyone is free to come up with their own definition of punk—and everyone is ready to embrace it. Emo had always connected with young people—it had just never aggressively marketed itself to them. Enter Rich Egan, a man whose idol is Fugazi's Ian MacKaye, but whose entire career, in its aims and its practices, is miles away from MacKaye's Dischord record label. Born and raised in L.A., the entertainment capital of the world—literally miles away from MacKaye's political hotbed of D.C.—Egan is, at the end of the day, just trying to make a buck for his young family. "What we're doing is punk rock because of the ways our bands conduct their business, the way they look at the world," he says. "You can be a punk-rock anything."

When discussing the violent splintering of the mainstream in the late '90s, many writers love to dust off the hoary "there will never be another Beatles" analogy. It's the old 500 television channels routine, except now there are 500 channels competing with 500 Napsters competing with 500 video games, websites, extracurricular clubs, and practices, not to mention over 500 highly trained and Ivy League–educated youth marketers vying for teenagers' every blink. It is just simply no longer possible for one pop group to dominate the culture to the degree that the Beatles did in the '60s, or Michael Jackson did in the '80s, maybe not even like Nirvana did in the '90s—there's far too much culture.

Ian MacKaye and Guy Picciotto's Fugazi is the unimpeachable ideal of American indie: fiercely, savagely independent. Answering to no one, in bed with no one—morally and aesthetically perfect from their music to their politics, lifestyles, and friends. No band was name-checked more during the research of this book by bands setting off on tours sponsored by Microsoft, bands with videos on heavy rotation on MTV2, and bands who discussed Long Island hardcore scenes in the same breath as the past week's Soundscan sales breakdown. Today's punk bands and label moguls talk about Fugazi the way American Catholics talk about the Vatican: worthy of respect and worship, but impossible to reconcile with the realities of modern life. Washington, D.C.—not the actual D.C., mind you, more the idealized construct of the place—is the Holy Scene: fractious, cantankerous, utopian, a relic of a different time, a different century. On Fugazi's classic first album, *Repeater,* the strongest anthem was the song "Merchandise," with its strident cry of "you are not what you own!" On Vagrant.com, Saves the Day has over a dozen different T-shirts, sweatshirts, pins, and stickers for sale.

Ultimately, whether you're with Rich Egan or against him, like many things in the overheated and ephemeral world of punk, it comes down to pragmatism vs. purity. If you're a die-hard, dyed-in-the-wool DIY punk or indie purist, then Rich Egan is the devil, responsible for not only money-changing in the temple, but bulldozing the temple's south wall so as to better install the ATM. You're also probably not reading this book. If you're a punk pragmatist, someone who believes in the messenger, not the message, and in living within the limitations of the system while not toppling it, well then you probably work at Vagrant already. If you're somewhere between the two, like most of us, then you're probably wondering what all the fuss is about.

Vagrant's offices are located on a spartan strip in south L.A., just past an on-ramp for the 10. The office itself is impossible to notice from the road—it's less a building and more like a compound, a gated rust-red structure with an obscured black Vagrant sign just above the door. The label has been growing at light speed over the past three years, and this new space, a former paper-processing plant, has room to grow a bit further. The walls are decorated with giant-sized black-and-white photos of some of the label's best and brightest in action—at that size they're mostly indistinguishable blurs of white men with black sideburns playing electric guitars. There's a receptionist's area and a stack of magazines on a table, all of which contain articles about Vagrant or reviews of Vagrant bands. All of them. It's early summer, 2002, and I'm supposed to sit down with Egan at 8 A.M. but he's not there yet. In fact, he doesn't get there for a full two hours. His apology is a good one: he's living with his mom. It seems that Egan's house fell victim to the same "black mold" spores that infected the abodes of other Cali celebrities like Jerry Van Dyke. Though his wife has picked out a new home—sight unseen while Egan was in New York for one of his band's frequent TV appearances—it's not ready yet. So the Egans and their two kids are shacked up with Mom out by the beach.

A rare worry line creasing his brow, Egan hurries me into his office and settles back into one of the two large leather couches with a satisfied sigh. I turn on the tape recorder, but first he dispatches his assistant to Starbucks. Throughout our talk, Egan smacks chewing gum between his teeth and chases it with an enormous cup of coffee. His phone rings endlessly. The couch looks too large for him—it seems like we're stealing a few hours in the boss's office. He's like a more calculating Tom

Hanks in *Big,* a more rock 'n' roll Michael J. Fox in *Secret of my Success,* getting off on the high-stakes moneyed world that he's infiltrated.

"I'm a dork," he says with a toothy grin, not believing a word of it. It's something Egan says with pride, but it's irrelevant—he fundamentally doesn't agree with the rules of the game that would label him such. "I was never cool growing up. I was always just to the right of cool. And frankly, I probably separated myself from it intentionally."

Rich Egan grew up comfortably in the prosperous Santa Monica and Brentwood neighborhoods of west L.A. His father, Richard Egan Sr., was a well-liked and successful television actor in the 1950s and, by all accounts, young Rich's home life was stable and pleasant. Like many SoCal teens, Rich fell into punk rock by accident. "Growing up here, you were just kind of thrown into it," he says. "By skating and surfing, you're part of punk rock. It's just part of your existence. You're never actively seeking it out." For Rich, punk wasn't a way out; it wasn't a way anywhere. It just was. And so, from the very beginning, he was able to balance out would-be revolutionary music with a decidedly unrevolutionary life. Rich had friends and he had goals. When the music became more about socializing—both for and against things—he began to lose interest. "There was a period when I was younger when all of my favorite bands were playing every weekend. Black Flag, the Descendants, the Minutemen. Social Distortion. But I got completely disillusioned with punk in '85. That was freshman year of high school and all the bands I liked were phasing out and everything that replaced it was meathead, beat-on-people punk-rock lameness."

Again and again throughout his life, Rich Egan rejected anything that was labeled cool. He detested cliques and insider music snobbery. And so at the exact moment when most emo kids thirst for punk, Egan lost interest. He craved simplicity and directness in music, eventually letting his tastes wander halfway across the country to find it. It was the busted-lip and bruised-heart blue-collar romanticism of Minneapolis's the Replacements that made him a music fan again during his first years at L.A.'s Loyola Marymount University. Here was music that took what he liked best from punk—its snarl, its swagger, its unpretentious intelligence—but none of its holier-than-thou smirk. The song that blew his mind and, in many ways, defined his label was the Replacements' classic "Unsatisfied." The song is little more than a fiercely ragged electric guitar and Paul Westerberg's throaty howl rasping out, again and again, "I'm so unsatisfied." There was nothing cool about the song. It was merely undeniable. "It's the most heartbreaking, amazing song," raves Egan, "and it's still punk rock. It doesn't have that beat—y'know, 'too-TA too-TA too-TA.' I was like, 'holy shit.' It was completely revolutionary to me." Uncool kids may not get in fights or dress right or take the right drugs or know the right people, but uncool kids have heart. "I was never hip partly because none of my friends were listening to the same kind of music I was," he says. "All the music I loved was in the Midwest. Even the bands I loved that were here in California, there was always some kind of weird elitist thing, a lot of cliquiness. I either never got accepted into those crowds or never wanted to be. Probably a combination of both." (Egan completed the Midwest/California circle in 2002 when he signed Paul Westerberg to Vagrant as a solo artist.)

Rich Egan's punk rock was a third way in the underground music scene. Too smart for mainstream, too lame for the subculture. Egan was one of the earliest examples of the suburban punk fan to which his label now caters, finding a new definition of punk in the rejection of the rigid orthodoxies of self-proclaimed punk. If punk rock said making money was wrong, then isn't rejecting that and making money the most punk-rock thing of all?

A born pragmatist, Egan still took his inspiration from the purists. "It sounds unbelievably corny, but when I saw *Another State of Mind* [the influential documentary about Minor Threat, Dischord Records, and the D.C. DIY scene] ten years after it was made, I knew immediately that it was what I wanted to do." Egan was eighteen, a college student, and working in the mail room at Hollywood's megapowerful Creative Artists Agency. It was the end of the '80s and the decade's Gordan Gekko money-grab mentality was still in full effect. Even, apparently, down in the mail room. So Egan conspired to get fired (he claims to have hit the "main guy's" golf instructor in the eye with a paper clip which, appropriately, is either the most or least punk thing one could ever do), took a semester off from college, and started a record label.

"We had nine hundred dollars when we started," Egan remembers, "so we bought our business license for three hundred and spent the rest on 'supplies.' I came up with the name randomly. I had a partner from the mail room and we basically dicked around for a few years figuring out how to do it while I was going to school."

Vagrant may have been a last-minute choice for the name of the nascent label, but it couldn't have been more apt. Egan has always taken a perverse pride in his lack of cred. His defensiveness about his uncool personality and his relatively privileged background translates, then and now, into the aggressively self-protective boxing posture seen on the Vagrant logo. We're punk because we're not punk, it seems to say, cool because we're not cool. We're the underdog that you kick around now, but we're scrappy, and we'll bite you back.

The label didn't really come into day-to-day existence until 1994. Egan's mail-room buddy had grown sick of the indecision and ditched California for business school on the east coast. Enter Jon Cohen, a punk fan and fellow waiter who believed in Rich's vision and wanted in (it also helped that Cohen was high school chums with the members of Egan's beloved Jawbreaker). "Rich has always been intense and always been a good salesman," Cohen says in his perpetually measured tones. "He was so focused on his vision of this label, on the big picture, I felt there was no way he was not going to realize it." For a mere $6,000, Cohen was given ownership of half the company.

Flush with the new money and energy, Egan went all out. What had originally been planned as a split 7-inch release from two of his favorite bands, Jawbreaker and L.A.'s Rocket from the Crypt, suddenly became, in typical Egan fashion, a heck of a lot more ambitious.

"I had the idea to make a box set of 7-inches," he says, "but of course my two main bands then dropped out. Thankfully a lot of other cool California bands stepped up. We had Face to Face, Seaweed, J church, the Meices. We did different covers for all five 7-inchers. But I couldn't find a place anywhere that would make a box for five 7-inchers. So I had to get a special custom box made. Then we couldn't print on the box, so we had to have outer sleeves made and then wrapped onto the box. It was ridiculous. It cost me five dollars a unit to make and we sold them for ten dollars, postage paid, because I hadn't stopped to think about saying otherwise in the ad. We printed up a thousand copies, advertised in *Maximumrocknroll* and *Flipside* and we sold out of them as soon as we got 'em in."

The box set was called *West x North-South* (a play on the venerable Texas music festival South by Southwest) and quickly established Vagrant as a reliable name for unpolitical, driving rock that skated the line between indie and punk, as well as a label that, either out of goodwill or ignorance, lavished money on the bands and product, often at their own expense.

"I didn't make dick on the thing, of course," Egan laughs. "But even when we didn't have any money, we always paid the bands. We paid them for recording and we paid them their royalties each month. Because I figured if you take care of the bands, at some point, word's gonna spread that you treat the bands right. And they're the real foundation of all this shit. I saw these other indie labels giving their bands a bunch of free CDs to take out on the road and I thought, that's great and all, but it doesn't put gas in the tank when you're out on tour."

Encouraged by the demand for the box set but discouraged by the lack of profit, Egan and Cohen re-released the entire thing on one CD. Using distribution instead of mail-order, the CD version of *West x North-South* sold an impressive five thousand copies. "And all of a sudden, we had a company," says Egan.

Vagrant's next move was equally successful. The pair commissioned some of their favorite pop-punk underground bands—including a pre-fame Blink-182—and had them record covers of New-Wave hits from the '80s. The compilation, entitled *Before You Were Punk,* was an exercise in fun, the kind of throwaway gimmick that thousands of major labels have used to mixed success. For the cred-conscious underground it was anathema; for the fun-starved music fan, it was nirvana. The comp sold a staggering 70,000 copies, with an equally successful sequel. The label had money, an identity, and a growing reputation for fair play.

"From the beginning," Egan says, "our mission statement was 'treat the bands better than you would treat yourself.' Put the bands ahead of the label, not vice versa. And it worked. Too many indie labels screw over bands not due to malice but due to disorganization. It's this whole 'bro factor' thing. But, really, fuck being bros, bands need to get paid. It hurt us in some ways because we weren't down. We were never cool and that was OK by me. What set us apart was taking care of the bands."

By the late '90s, Vagrant had a burgeoning operation in Santa Monica and contracts with well-regarded punk bands like Boxer and No Motiv.

Perhaps realizing that his bands-first attitude more naturally put him on the other side of the ball (and causing many detractors to claim all of Vagrant can be traced back to Egan wishing he was in a band himself), Egan had also by this time started a management company, called Hard 8, with the sole purpose of looking after the career of L.A. trio Face to Face as they tried to tread water in the major-label ocean. In 1997, a quartet of corn-fed, bespectacled kids from Kansas set the underground on fire with their blisteringly catchy brand of pop punk. Calling themselves the Get Up Kids, the group updated the indie-rock indignation and fast tempos of North Carolina's Superchunk by stripping it of its occasionally ironic braininess. The Get Ups were frustrated lovelorn nerds in the vein of the Promise Ring, but they had the hooks, the chops, the spartan touring ethic, and—most important of all—the lack of a self-destructive streak to make a national name for themselves and sell over 15,000 copies of their debut, *Four Minute Mile,* on micronsized indie Doghouse Records. The group knew they wanted to take a step up, and they needed an insider to help them do it. Based on his experiences negotiating the major-label waters with Face to Face, the Get Ups hired Egan as their new manager.

Egan and the band took meetings with almost every major label before the band decided on quasi-indie Mojo. "I was against it," says Egan, "but the band decided so I spent six months negotiating the shit out of the contract. Finally, the band got sick of it, and said, 'Fuck it, let's sign to Vagrant.' I was like, uh-oh. Because I had always said never the two shall meet. But am I going to tell my clients that it wouldn't be the best thing for them? Because I knew damn well it would be the best thing for them. And they went from selling 15,000 copies to 150,000."

Rich Egan had always said that he wanted Vagrant to become the Motown Records of punk rock, but without the artist unhappiness. But the Hard 8/Vagrant conflict of interest created the potential for a less seemly similarity between Motown and Vagrant: Motown's Berry Gordy was a visionary executive whose role as both manager and label president enabled him to take advantage of his artists to the tune of millions of dollars. None of Vagrant's acts accused Egan of impropriety, but numerous outside eyebrows were raised. The overwhelming triumph of the Get Up Kids and their ability to sell major-label numbers by doing things the old-fashioned way—touring without the support of radio or

MTV—made Vagrant, and caused the industry to take notice. It also made a lot of other labels and punk insiders furious.

"If we trust you enough to be our manager, why wouldn't we trust you to put out our record?" is how Get Up Kid Matt Pryor recounted the group's thought process to *Punk Planet* in 2002. And Egan did his best to live up to the trust, going to outrageous lengths to make the band feel appreciated and, in many ways, feel as if they *had* signed to a major label. Vagrant funded a vanity sub-label for the band to release albums by their friends called Heroes & Villains, handed the group a huge— particularly for an indie label—recording advance (some have claimed it was near six figures), and paid for living expenses. To pay for the Get Up Kids, Jon Cohen's parents mortgaged their house.

The company's total faith in the Kansans was indicative of Egan and Cohen's strategy. "The Get Up Kids were our first example of a band that was underexposed in terms of record sales," Cohen says. "I spent a great deal of time looking at their merchandise sales, their concert returns. It was the first study for us of a band that, bottom line, could and should be selling more records." Armed with Cohen's data, Egan had no doubts about investing the future of the company in the Get Up Kids. On paper, they were proof of what he had always believed: that a band's true connection with a community can be judged on both intangibles (the fans' level of passion and frenzy) and tangibles unrelated to record sales. If bands were in a certain position, Vagrant could use its full-court-press style to take them to the next level. Still, it was far from a slamdunk.

With the stakes so high, it's understandable that the Get Up Kids were Vagrant's number one priority for the next two years. The band toured the country basically nonstop, headlining shows and opening up huge (some would say "corporate") arena rock shows for major-label success stories like Green Day and Weezer. The Get Ups approached touring with the do-it-till-you-drop ethos of an indie band, but traveled with all the amenities of a group on a major label: tour buses, huge merchandise spreads, tour support. Whatever the formula was, it worked. The Get Ups's sales skyrocketed and their name began circulating in all sorts of different social strata—yet the emotions felt towards them were the same that they had encountered back home in Kansas City. They could sell out New York City's Irving Plaza weeks in advance, but were still being dismissed as Superchunk imitators who weren't worth a second mention by the mainstream music press. They weren't cool, but they were huge. By the beginning of 2001, the Get Up Kids were the biggest band no one had heard of.

And there was no good reason why that couldn't change as well. The band's Vagrant debut, *Something to Write Home About,* was a riotously good album, a breathless, headfirst sprint to a consistently hook-filled finish line. Pryor sang with a harmless snarl, the sound of a perpetually picked-on pupil tearing open his flannel shirt to reveal his Superman Underoos underneath.

Something was triumphant with universal appeal—it could easily have been released by a major label, and seemed even more winning for not having done so. With a rumpled, nerdy appeal (like Weezer but without the guilt), the Get Up Kids managed to charm the ears off of nearly everyone in the underground. "Sometimes I'm old enough to keep routines / sometimes I'm child enough to scream for everything," goes one of their best songs. By admitting depth but preaching pop, the Get Up Kids may have been losers, but Vagrant helped them find a way to win.

Flush with the Get Up Kids's success, over the next two years Vagrant made a series of power moves that changed and redefined the company. All of the profits that Egan and Cohen generated from their timeless work were put directly back into Vagrant. Despite the fact that Egan was married with two small children, he claims he didn't even take a paycheck during the growth period. The company expanded to over a dozen employees and moved to its first in a series of successively larger offices. The Heroes & Villains imprint brought the label a number of new acts, including the Get Up Kids' lucrative side projects the New Amsterdams and Reggie & the Full Effect. The new cash flow also served as an enticement to a number of other underground bands ready to make the switch to a bigger label. The highest profile of these was a young five-piece from the New Jersey suburbs called Saves the Day.

In a number of ways, no band better represents Rich Egan, and by extension, Vagrant's sensibilities, than Saves the Day. The group was formed by a physically tiny blond kid named Chris Conley and friends of his from an affluent New Jersey town. Conley was a huge fan of the seminal NJ hardcore/emo band Lifetime; his particular songwriting talent was to channel that band's frustrated pop heart while ripping it free from its scene-specificity. Conley's songs were about, well, being Conley: young, bored, horny, riddled with self-doubt, and wracked by recurring stomach pains. Saves the Day's first album, *Can't Slow Down,* won the teenagers plenty of fans in the New Jersey underground community, but nowhere else. The band's second album title alone must have made Egan sit up and take notice: *Through Being Cool,* The album was equally indebted to Lifetime, but Conley OD'd on Alka-Seltzer for his still churning stomach, boosting the pop, increasing the fizz. The result was a punk album even your mother could love (Conley's no doubt did—the refrain of "You Vandal" includes a strident cry of "I miss my mom!"). The album's booklet read like a how-to manual for the band's fans, depicting a photo-essay about the five smooth-cheeked Saves the Day-ers showing up at a party but feeling—*sigh*—left out. The group dropped out of college to tour the record, building a huge fan base on the east coast and a sizable one throughout the country. When the touring stopped, *Through Being Cool* had sold nearly 50,000 copies, a monumental figure for the band's label, a tiny New York City–based indie called Equal Vision. Major labels were calling and dollar signs were being tossed around, but in the end STD chose Vagrant, and hired Rich Egan as their manager in the process.

"Subtlety is overrated," says Rich Egan, by way of explanation. "Just because I've been on this planet longer doesn't mean that my opinions or my feelings are any deeper or weighty than a fifteen-year-old's. The reason I fell in love with Saves the Day is because their lyrics are so honest, so cut and dry. When [Conley] says 'I miss my mom,' it's so universal, it's awesome. Any kid who is that open with his feelings to write it and then have the guts to get behind a microphone to sing it, put it on a CD and put it out there for the world to see has *way* more props in my book than someone who is gonna write really cloaked lyrics that I have to sit there and try to figure out forever."

Saves The Day's sensibilities not only dovetailed with those of Egan personally, but professionally as well. The band members were scared of the major-label offers, but thirsted for the major-label routine. Vagrant gave them that and more—within weeks of signing, the band was in the studio with high-profile producer Rob Schnapf (Beck, Elliot Smith) and the resulting album, *Stay What You Are,* sold 15,000 copies in its first week, crashing the *Billboard* sales chart and shocking the hell out of the industry once again.

For all their touring and relative world-weariness, the members of Saves the Day are all still under the age of twenty-five. Their appeal to younger listeners isn't forced—the crowds really are their peers. So while Conley's public pronouncements can provoke reactions ranging from mild eye-rolling ("I recommend that everyone on this planet should read Hemingway's *For Whom the Bell Tolls* immediately") to gagging (on what he does in his spare time: "write and play guitar and listen to music and marvel at the trees and be wide eyed that I'm actually here and that things actually exist") in those paid to have opinions about these things, to his fans he's just preaching to the choir. Just a few years the Get Up Kids's juniors, Saves the Day made the Vagrant veterans look like your dad at a high school dance. *Stay What You Are* is as smooth as a sugar pill with hooks like a bait and tackle shop; every one of Conley's twisted, emotional roller-coaster rides is framed as a fist-pumping anthem. Plus, the band is ridiculously cute. By the end of 2002, Saves the Day videos were fixtures on MTV2 and the band had appeared on the Conan O'Brien show, graced the cover of *Alternative Press* magazine, and played Madison Square Garden. The band's fans were also almost entirely under the age of twenty.

With Vagrant topping out at over a dozen acts, Egan decided to take things to the next level. In the summer of 2001, he dreamed up the Vagrant America tour, a barnstorming, coast-to-coast run featuring every band on the label. The tour was a brilliant marriage of old-time carny salesmanship and modern music-biz realities. In order to present a united front, the label shelled out for a fleet of top-of-the-line tour buses and set the bands up in hotel rooms in most of the tour's stops. Sponsorship deals were worked out with Microsoft and Coca-Cola. More than any other event, it was Vagrant America that defined emo to masses—mainly because it had the gumption to hit the road and bring it to *them.*

"There is an aesthetic to our bands—it's not hard to figure it out when you consider my own music tastes equals punk rock plus the Smiths," Egan says. "I sign punk bands that write meaningful lyrics. But the only reason it gelled is because all of our bands toured together. So we became a lightning rod for it. But this would have happened with or without Vagrant because kids are reacting to the crap they've been fed. It happens every ten years or so—they get sick of it and seek out better music. If it wasn't us, it would have been someone else."

Even so, Egan and Cohen put in extra work to make sure their efforts were noticed. To maximize their returns on the Vagrant America tour, Egan invited music journalist Greg Kot to join the tour for a few days in the Midwest, allowing him to jot down the "punk lifers" ' shock at the plushness of their hotel suites, the size of the crowds. The effect of Kot's glowing article in *Rolling Stone* was to equate Vagrant to the dominant, posse-run hip-hop labels of the day. Vagrant was swinging its muscles around, conquering the nation. The point wasn't how much money the label lost on the tour—which, by all outside accounts was considerable—it was how much press and notoriety the investment produced. "Things can always be done, even if you're on an indie," says Cohen. "I always have to become more creative about it. And that's where my strong suit lies."

"Creative" sells the label short. From the get-go, Egan had a vision of who the potential audience for his bands was: people all over the world who were, basically, exactly like him. "Our audience is suburban, very white-bread," he says. "They're not punk kids and it's not a college thing the way indie used to be. It's a junior high and high school thing. Traditionally, those are times when you have to take whatever's spoon-fed to you. Because of the internet, kids are exposed to a much wider variety of choices." It's not unusual to see kids as young as twelve at Vagrant bands' concerts, with traffic stalled for hours afterward due to the high volume of parents in station wagons waiting to pick up their hard-rocking progeny.

Egan was among the first industry people to recognize that the rules had changed in underground rock. When he was in high school himself, desperately searching out music that meant something to him, he—like all punk kids before him—had his punk older brother figure who hazed him gently into a new musical world. "Everyone has that one friend," he says, "and mine's name was Matt Rice. I was clueless in eighth grade and I would go to his house every Friday and he had GBH flyers on the walls and he would play me all kinds of crazy vinyl shit. Kids like him are the ground zeros of their worlds. But now the Internet has taken on that role." What Vagrant realized was that the work had been done on the ground—by bands like Nirvana and Green Day—for punk to transcend regionalism and be a national force. The only way to accomplish that, however, would be to maintain the personal connection of a regional scene—after all, more than 70 percent of teenage punk fandom is about the community, not the music. Suddenly, the internet offered a way to accomplish this. On its first pass through the country, fifteen years earlier, emo had evolved as it traveled osmotically—taking on local flavor and accents as it spread around the country, becoming just another shade of whatever the local scene happened to be. This time there was no need for the older figure, no hazing process to separate the punk from the non-punk, the dedicated from the deadheads. This time, Vagrant could control the message.

"The internet has completely changed and affected every single possible facet of this business and of the subculture in general," Egan says with the zeal of a true believer. "In the old days, it took forever to find out about east coast bands—they would either eventually make it out here or you'd have to wait for the next quarterly issue of *Maximumrocknroll*. Now there's immediate access to everything. There's no ritual to go through, no initiation process. If you sign on, you're in and it's all right there at your fingertips. It's changed punk because now it's possible to connect all of the dots a hell of a lot quicker. Therefore, you can have a kid from Florida playing punk-rock shows with an acoustic guitar and by the time he gets to California, he's already sold out three hundred tickets and it's his first time in the state. The kids out here have heard about him on the messageboards, traded his MP3s, they've ordered the T-shirts and CDs from insound or interpunk.com. It's like instascene. And that's how we've used it at Vagrant. Kids look to us as places to start making their way through the maze. We try not to bury them in shit, because we do want them to seek it out because that's how you weed out your avid listeners. It's like throwing it out there and helping it grow."

Historically and traditionally, punk scenes developed organically and regionally. Now, Vagrant was shaping an organic online community into a national scene based on the potentially uncomfortable duality of bringing music fans together and selling them merchandise. Vagrant placed their URL prominently on their releases, maintained a fresh crop of free MP3s and videos on their site, and advertised on like-minded teen-oriented cyberhangouts. Visitors to the site were recruited to be street-team marketers for their favorite groups—a practice considered questionable to some, but as natural as buying a shirt or passing along a mix CD to others. When it came time for Saves the Day to release a new record, Vagrant had the entire album in streaming audio weeks before its release. Kids responded not only because they liked the music, but because Vagrant was speaking their language. Vagrant.com didn't talk down or pander—it was antielitist, direct. Wandering to the label's site after school was like going over to an older friend's house on a Friday afternoon, listening to new sounds, and taking it all in. For a change of mind, for a new obsession, for a new community, Vagrant on the web is one-stop shopping. "There are kids who quite literally become immersed in this culture in two weeks," Egan says. "Maybe they saw a Dashboard Confessional video and went to the website. Click. And they go, OK, who's Saves the Day? Click. And then all of a sudden we get a mail order for our entire catalog and twelve T-shirts. It's like, OK, you've skipped from kindergarten to twelfth grade but at least you're here with us at graduation."

Coupled with this savvy understanding of its potential market was Vagrant's familiarity with the way the big boys did business. Rich Egan spent time in the early '90s doing menial assistant work at a major label, and his years of managing Face to Face while the band was signed to A&M, coupled with the drawn-out Get Up Kids contract negotiations, gave him a sense of how things were done, how they weren't done, and how they should be done. Together with Jon Cohen's business acumen, Vagrant saw a playing field that was a lot more level than for many other upstart labels. After observing the first major-label indie gold rush, Egan was determined not to let it happen again. When Vagrant became a full-time gig with the signing of the Get Up Kids, the label began manipulating SoundScan numbers in the same crooked-but-legal way that the majors had been doing for years. SoundScan is the controversial record-sales tracking company that, upon its inception in 1990, heralded the blockbuster era of popular music—a trend similar to the film industry, where a big opening week becomes necessary for long-term survival. Because even the people behind SoundScan admit it has faults—many independent stores do not participate in the tracking of sales—Sound-Scan "weights" select mom and pop stores in each of its markets. The idea is to account for the unaccountable copies by registering multiple copies of each single sale at a weighted store. In addition to allowing the bands to sell their own CDs at their shows, Egan and Cohen occasionally targeted weighted stores and invited them to sell records at concerts—with each copy sold on-site registering multiple copies on SoundScan. Vagrant bands also frequently played in-store gigs at weighted stores, signing newly bought copies that would ratchet up the SoundScan. Vagrant understands what most indie labels don't or choose not to stress: good sales figures equals mainstream media coverage and mainstream media coverage usually leads to genuinely increased sales. Egan's anti-elitism goes the other way too—though he claims to relish being the underdog, it seems entirely against his nature to go into a fight unarmed.

"The industry's opinion is less and less relevant to the real world," Egan says. "If I listened to the industry, I would have given up in six months. Instead, I've been in it for ten years and I've never seen the industry be so behind the curve. None of our success—or the other so-called emo bands that we're lumped in with—could have happened back then because there was this whole 'man behind the curtain,' *Wizard of Oz* theory about the music business. Bands are more educated now—they've figured out where the money goes and how you make it from the ones that came before them and also by just doing it. Never has the DIY thing been so readily accessible. Like we said—there's no more hazing process in punk. You get a crash course in it by who you go out on tour with. You can plug into that network so much quicker now, and therefore reach more kids, which means you're going to have some semblance of a career. And I don't see any downside to that."

"I know Rich from when he was working as the day-to-day guy with my band, Sammy, when we were on Geffen," says Luke Wood. "Guys like us have seen it all—the good sides and the bad sides of both indies and majors." Wood is a senior A&R man at Dreamworks Records, respected as one of the few major-label people who "gets it." Wood signed Jimmy Eat World and made them the first emo band to break big on the radio and on the charts. "What we're seeing now with his bands and some others is nice and it's not dissimilar to a lot of the bands between '90 and '93 that had an opportunity to reach a larger audience in the wake of Nirvana. Nothing was calculated then and there's a real purity right now. I hope younger guys who are forming bands realize that's what's important: the songs and the message."

Bands on Vagrant seemed to enjoy all the perks of major labeldom without any of the excess baggage—slots on nationwide tours opening up for bigger bands on the label and on major labels. Egan shelled out advances for records like they were going out of style and hooked up young bands with respected (and costly) veteran producers like Rob Schnapf (Beck) and Scott Litt (R.E.M.). The records sounded great and had shiny covers. The bands traveled in tour buses instead of broken-down vans.

"Because of the rise of computers and Pro Tools, Rich Egan can cheaply make a record that sounds as good as any major-label release," says Luke Wood. "Whereas in the past, a rough, indie sound was a necessity. Bands on [seminal punk label] SST had two weeks in the studio because that's all they could afford. That wasn't a choice, even though sounding like crap eventually morphed into a perverse badge of honor. That's no longer necessary or relevant."

Vagrant's successful emo commercial blueprint left many of the mid-nineties bands shaking their heads. Braid had spent the better part of six years pulling all-nighters on unlit highways, touring mercilessly, with little to show for it other than a devoted, if tiny, fan base. When the band broke up, songwriter Bob Nanna decided he wanted to reap some of what he and his peers had helped to sow. After taking meetings with more indie-centric labels like Jade Tree, Nanna's new group (consisting of three fourths of Braid), Hey Mercedes, signed to Vagrant and soon released an album (*Everynight Fire Works*) that continued the Braid formula, only this time it was wrapped in a shiny, more marketable package. The songs may have remained swathed in layers of distance, but the cover went straight for the gut (and the wallet), depicting two lonely dreamer boys sitting on a hill, staring at the unknowable beauty of the stars. Braid's final album had obliquely presented a *Frame and Canvas*, allowing the music to provide the vision; Hey Mercedes provided an idealized image of the target listener.

It was around this time that simmering resentment of Vagrant in the underground community began to boil over. The label spent the fall of 2001 involved in a legal battle with its distributor, TVT, and rumors soon buzzed on internet gossip sites that Vagrant had spent beyond its means and was desperately taking meetings with major labels to bail it out of its cash woes; that its "creative" business practices were being found out; that Egan unfairly manipulated the artists that he also managed; that as its records sold out of stores, so too had the label.

"My biggest thing with Vagrant has always been that they seemed really vigilantly opportunist," says Jessica Hopper. "They were willing to do whatever was necessary to pick up the emo cache—not to mention the emo cash—and to do it in a really big business way. Egan uses our buzzwords and our aesthetics to tap into this glut of teenage suburban money. They're selling something that a lot of other people felt ownership over and that once had a lot of credibility.

"A lot of these bands were so grassroots, so tiny and struggling. And what happened with Braid is that all of these bands that came up behind them were suddenly getting paid, having videos. And they felt, we worked so hard, we want our due. Egan shows up with the cash in one hand, the vaseline in the other, and the keys to the Pepsi tour bus in his pocket. Look, he's smart as hell to come in and do all of this—use our language, our tools, our signifiers to sell emo cool to kids who buy records at Sam Goody. There's just something about him and his label that just stinks. This proximity to the underground. Like he could be in *Rolling Stone* and say, 'Minor Threat is my favorite band' and it's like *fuck you*. Don't be associated with our stuff!"

If one were to form an opinion about Vagrant solely from the comments to be found on punk messageboards and insider magazines, one would think they were the Enron of rock 'n' roll. "How to Ruin Everything," was the title of *Punk Planet*'s exposé of the label. In fact, the biggest complaint leveled at Egan is that he's a poseur—all of which leads to the age-old questions about who's more punk and who owns it. Unsurprisingly, Egan spends no time concerning himself with what others think. His preferred role as the underdog is profoundly fueled by his considerable ego. Criticism only makes him redouble his efforts, albeit in the direction in which he was already heading.

"I think we're an easy target," he says. "People take the easiest shots they can because it's all so obvious. Like with Dashboard—it's so easy to pick on a kid that's pouring out his heart out with an acoustic guitar. And you'll get a lot of lemmings to follow you bashing on him. Look at my management clients—I identify with all of them because they've taken more shit than any other bands out there. Face to Face were tagged sellouts from day one, the Get Up Kids didn't pay their dues, are too cute; Saves the Day are New Jersey rich kids ripping off Lifetime, blah blah blah. None of them are OK for the intelligentsia to like. But they're successful because they're doing things their own way. Our label is like that. Look—I want to be successful. I want my bands to be filthy rich. I do. And if that makes me a whatever, that's fine. Because, to me, it's such a fuck you to the world. That's the punk-rock side of me, showing it can be done differently and done well."

"I don't want a band to be rich!" says Jade Tree co-owner Darren Walters in response. "I want them to be *supported.* When they're fifty they should still be getting regular royalty checks. I don't think most bands realize all that goes into making them rich. Vagrant is now synonymous with money, with emo, with big biz. They've got it all and then some. But you can think of us as the environmentally conscious stock. You get a decent return on your money and can still feel good about it in the morning."

In 2002, articles on the label appearing in *Time* and *Newsweek,* and emo cresting as an industry buzzword, Vagrant entered into a financial relationship with the biggest of the bigs, Interscope Records. Though the label would still be distributed through indie TVT, Interscope made an immediate cash investment and began to work some of Vagrant's bigger bands to radio. On the one hand, it seemed that the piper had finally come calling, that it simply *wasn't* possible to maintain the kind of business model that Egan and Cohen had set out to make without getting your hands dirty.

"It's a five-year, noncontrolling interest in the label," Egan explains. "But it's the first of its kind because we don't use their distribution or their manufacturing. Basically, they're staying the hell out of our way. But, yeah, I'm naturally distrustful of huge conglomerates. That's not because I think they're inherently evil. I just think they have a responsibility to their stockholders that doesn't extend to my artists. Fortunately, the only thing I have to worry about is my artists, because Interscope doesn't have any rights to our bands."

When he was a young punk fan, Rich Egan envisioned a third way through punk—skating (quite literally) right in between the twin minefields of selling out and keeping it real. Now, with his unique Interscope deal, he's trying to establish a permanent business beachhead for that same philosophy. If the previous generation's bands signed their contracts and were promptly thrown to the wolves, Egan plans to shelter his own acts and allow them to have the best of both worlds, if and when they need it.

The Vagrant offices are spacious and hectic, but also rigorously compartmentalized. In an attempt to demonstrate the separate-but-equal nature of his management company and his record label, Rich Egan keeps a three-room corner of the spread as the headquarters for Hard 8 management. His two assistants are not employees of Vagrant. Next to the Hard 8 area is a small room littered with brightly colored toddlers' toys: cars, blocks, and stuffed animals. This is the room for Egan's children to play in while he's working. The rest of the space has room for the other full-time Vagrant employees, as well as a warehouse space for the merchandise. It's busy and getting busier—not unlike Egan himself. Between his management commitments, his label, his family, and navigating the new relationship with Interscope, there seem to be too many balls in the air; compartmentalize all he wants, but there's no way to juggle it all.

Again and again, Rich Egan bites off more than he can chew and gets rewarded instead of scolded. Because of this, there's a bulletproof aura surrounding him, an impossible confidence. There's a bit of Wile E. Coyote to his professional demeanor. Watching him work the room backstage at arenas on both coasts there's a sense that if someone were only to tell him that he's walking on water, he'd look down for the first time and fall. Hard.

But maybe not. Maybe that's just the natural cynic's point of view. Egan already has the first rule of success down pat: Never care what they say about you. Other than his kids waking him up at all hours for playtime, he sleeps well.

If Egan is guilty of anything, it's hubris. With every triumph of a Vagrant band, Egan ratchets up the stakes, both for the band, his label, and, nowadays, for the entire underground industry. Whether he's smacking his gum around the conference table or flying on private helicopters, he seems to think he's subverting the system from the inside. But it's also possible that he, like Nirvana before him, is damning the underground to a generation of unrealistic dreams. Or perhaps the truth is he just doesn't care. He's out for his bands; he's out for number one. With their constant lyrical woe-is-me-ism, the bands are too.

Egan may err too much on the side of the manager/fan as opposed to the savvy, running-with-the-big-dogs exec, because just as his label has ridden to prominence on the back of the word "emo," his bands have run away from it—scared (perhaps rightly so) of being tarred with its unsavory connotations; of going down with the empty buzzword ship while the media moves on to its next big score. To that end, all Vagrant artists are free to make exactly the record they most want to make, regardless of the result. Saves the Day's members grew their hair out, soaked their image in some resin-stained '70s bong water, and have taken to declaring themselves "just" a rock band. The Get Up Kids were so burned out by the rigors of the road and the tempestuous demands of an emotional, teenage fan base that their third album, 2002's *On a Wire,* aggressively trashed their successful formula. Gone were the breathtaking, breakneck hooks; in their place were solemn, country-tinged laments. Their fans were aghast and sales reflected it. In any number of ways, being a die-hard supporter of artists' rights comes into direct conflict with being a savvy businessman. If emo means anything anymore, it stands to reason that it does so because it has become a sellable product. Stray from that formula, and offend an already sensitive group of consumers.

But its tough to bet against Rich Egan. Ultimately, he understands his audience because he *is* his audience. Vagrant is, above all, a triumph of the self. Egan knows that the average Vagrant fan is the kid caught in the middle—neither an outcast nor a straight conformist. A kid with a little bit of money and a small collection of problems. A kid, in other-words, just like him.

In 1984, the entire hardcore and emo movement came out of one man (Ian MacKaye) and one scene (Washington, D.C.). In the years that followed, the terms and ideology that MacKaye (along with Guy Picciotto and others) espoused diffused across the country and across genres of music, creating an atmosphere of self-contradiction, confusion, and accusations. But for a brief moment in 1984, emo meant something—both in sound and in the minds of those who listened to it. Now again, thanks to Rich Egan, the term has solidified once more around the rules, taste, and ideology of another individual. But, unlike MacKaye, Egan isn't expressing himself—he's marketing the expression of others. As with most underground phenomena, the politics have decreased in direct proportion to the increased fan base. Love him or hate him, Rich Egan has located and stayed true to the core of what makes emo so appealing in the first place: a universal desire to be both unique and part of something larger.

And Egan absolutely believes that the emotional connection with the artist will triumph, even if his own careerist goals expand past the intimate confines of a club. "I think these kids are looking for what every kid in high school is looking for—a social connection with other people in the peer group," he says. "And getting it through this music is where the entire peer group seems to be heading. Once we get up to the three or four thousand kids a night that Dashboard is now attracting, the experience is like showing up to a high school dance. It becomes more about the kids showing up and interacting than it is about the music. But if the bands weren't connecting with these core kids, then none of it would be possible.

"The musicans on stage are essentially peers themselves; they're writing about things that make sense. Not about some highfalutin', unreachable ideals. They're writing about getting their hearts broken and stomped on by someone in homeroom. And the music intelligentsia tends to scoff at that and laugh at it. But fuck 'em. That's really important to that kid. To a kid at fifteen—it's as important as an adult getting a divorce. It's his whole world crashing down on him. So when those kids go to a Dashboard show and scream at the top of their lungs, that's a cathartic experience for them. And it's really gratifying to be a part of that. Especially having kids now and seeing that their feelings are so honest and immediate. Everything is life or death to them. It is awesome to be a part of it."

SEVEN

THE MIDDLE: ON TOUR WITH JIMMY EAT WORLD

In the fall of of 2001, the Paul Fedor–directed video for "The Middle"—a brief, charismatic song from Jimmy Eat World's third album—began appearing regularly on MTV. On first glance, the video seems as banal as any other. The band appears in the center of a living room, performing—workmanlike, sweaty—surrounded by a throng of outrageously attractive teenagers clad in nothing but their underwear. Underneath the catchy chords and sweet-voiced choruses, the song is a vague self-empowerment anthem—"it just takes some time / little girl, you're in the middle of the ride / everything, everything will be all right." At first the T&A seems a bit gauche. But watch a little longer and the trappings of a significant plot begin to emerge.

The protagonist of the video is a thin, blond everykid who arrives at the party alone, wide eyed, and more than a little freaked out by all the skin. Rather than stripping in the doorway—as others around him do—he moves, zombielike and isolated, through the house, past taut-bodied, lace-bra-wearing hotties and thick-necked pectoral studs. It's the inverted, adolescent nightmare of anyone who was ever picked last for kickball—instead of showing up for school in your tidy-whities, you end up at an all-naked party in your Levi's. When the kid opens the fridge he interrupts a frantic make-out session (though the deep-frozen male is kind enough to hand our hero a beer without taking his mouth off his lady); later, he stands awkwardly in the shallow end of the pool, fully dressed, clutching his bottle like a life preserver while ostensibly liquored-up cheerleaders cannonball off the diving board. And through it all, Jimmy Eat World plays, manfully, to the frantically waving and chanting goons: "Don't you worry what their bitter hearts are going to say!" But the truth is, they're not singing to their easily excitable audience; the individualist credo is flying over their intoxicated, rah-rah heads. We, the audience, realize what we're supposed to: that Jimmy Eat World is actually singing to our hero. "Just try your best / try anything you can / it doesn't matter what they tell themselves / when you're away."

But the kid in the video doesn't quite get the message and, finally, in a fit of misguided confidence or conformation, he pushes his way into a closet and begins stripping off his clothes, banging into the wall, banging into himself in a desperate search to fit in. No! we think. Listen to the band! Just be yourself! And in the nick of time, the camera pulls back. He's not alone in the closet. A shy-looking skinny girl is in there too. She's just removed her top and is struggling out of her jeans. A pause. They look at each other. (Yeah, they've got great bodies, but that's not the point.) Slowly, they begin to recover and re-cover. As Jimmy Eat World crescendos through the last chorus and the clueless nude jocks cheer, our hero, fully dressed, walks back outside into the cool, Arizona night with his fellow outcast, hands in each others' back pockets. Everyone else got naked; he got the girl. Message received. Independence preserved. Mission accomplished.

The clip was a roaring success for any number of reasons—not the least of which was Fedor's brilliant strategy of having his cheesecake and eating it too. In just 2:45 it introduced a band, coded in this case as a Real Band: nice guys who play their own instruments, genuinely mean something (see: the sweat, their lack of makeup, their willingness to play suburban house parties), and who, despite their popularity and position on MTV, are *actually singing to you.* It also—in some ways unintentionally, in other ways not—helped to codify an aesthetic. The jocks may be dancing to Jimmy Eat World, but they're not really listening. The outcast hero may not get naked, but he's the only one who actually scores. Intimacy isn't showing off your Victoria's Secret—it's putting your arm around someone's shoulders. The video was an oasis amidst MTV's usual jacuzzi of tank tops, speedboats, and belly-button rings. There's something else out there, it promised, beyond the flash, hype, and sex. Not some faraway boho aesthetic—when you're seventeen, just sitting in Starbucks with a copy of *The Fountainhead* and a cappuccino can seem like the Left Bank—or even a whitewashed, sitcom version of reality. Rather, there are intelligent, emotional choices to be made within high school's realtime, realpolitik millieu of keggers, sexual confusion, pointless cruelty, and random hook-ups. Bands like Jimmy Eat World are your gateway to them.

It's an odd position for a band to be in—just a few short years removed from the major-label dustbin, an amiable failure relegated to the remainder stack, Yet, largely on the strength of "The Middle" video, the group broke through in a big way in 2002, going platinum with their third album *Bleed American* (retitled *Jimmy Eat World* after 9/11). It's rare enough for bands to get a second chance in our hyper-accelerated, quick-return culture. To get not only a second shot, but to get it at the exact right moment to best take advantage of it, seems downright fantastical. In a business based on flashy, millionaire hares, Jimmy Eat World has become the standard-bearer for all tortoises. Slow and steady might not win the race, but it certainly won't lose it. Nice guys may not finish first, but they can go platinum if they work at it long enough.

In the spring of 2002 I met up with Jimmy Eat World in the parking lot of a nondescript Sheraton off the highway in Dallas, Texas. The band tour bus is outrageous, extravagant—shiny wood paneling, two big-screen satellite TVs, videogame system, DVD, stereo, kitchenette—but par for the course when the course in question is the Pop Disaster Tour, a gargantuan, multicity behemoth that's uniting the two biggest bands in pop-punk from the last decade, Green Day and Blink-182. Jimmy Eat World is the handpicked opening act for the western half of the tour, playing half-hour sets in daylight to mostly apathetic or absent crowds. In comparison to the fleet of semis that transports Green Day's pyrotechnics and the fact that Blink has three such buses—one for each of the band's members—Jimmy Eat World's bus, shared among the band and five crew members, seems downright quaint. It's a muggy Thursday-morning bus call for the band, and one by one they stagger out of the Sheraton to head for the venue.

It seems half of the Jimmy Eat World touring operation went to a Slayer concert last night, the other half went to a strip club run by the local speedmetal kings Pantera.

"I met my future wife last night, dude," announces Mike, the amiable drum tech.

"Was she a stripper?" asks drummer Zach Lind.

"Yeah."

"Well, did you make an emotional connection?"

The rock 'n' roll stereotypes are all inverted on this bus (which is cleaner than the hotel room I just left), the photo-negative opposite of *Almost Famous*. It's the crew that sit with me, lasciviously detailing the previous night's exploits with assorted strippers, groupies, and chemicals, comparing notes, begging me not to use their real names, while it's the band that's expressing disappointment in the fact that their plans to attend a baseball game the night before had been washed out by rain, making cell phone calls home to wives and fiancees, and speaking reverently not so much of the intensity of Slayer's performance the night before, but of the true dedication of their fans.

"Man, I went into the bathroom last night and saw this guy in there actually cutting his face," says Lind, a wistful note creeping into his no-nonsense voice. "He was smearing the blood all over and then just started grinning, staring at himself in the mirror. I bet his friends were psyched. Now that's dedication."

"Has anyone ever cut themselves for you?" I ask.

Lind takes the question seriously. "No, I don't think we get many fans like that," he says. "Our fans just bake us cookies."

The Tupperware container that Lind gestures towards sits on the edge of the bus's kitchenette. Bassist Rick Burch emerges from his bunk and blinks at the light, then at the Tupperware. "Are these stalker cookies?" he asks, helping himself to one. "They're pretty good!"

The venue in Dallas is yet another in a proud line of utterly faceless, outdoor performance "sheds" and pavilions that have replicated like fruit flies across the blasted suburban nothingspace that surrounds the country's biggest cities. The cities I'm scheduled to visit with the Pop Disaster Tour are Dallas, San Antonio, and Houston, but I end up seeing none of the cities themselves, just the long, flat fields lying fifteen miles outside of the city centers that play home to America's myriad gypsy big-ticket tours. Each has a clearly labeled green room area. Each has a catering room serving variations on a theme of tacos, lasagna, and cold-cut sandwiches. Each has endless beer concessions, $7 hot dogs, $20 parking, and strategically placed concession rotundas selling $15 hot pink Blink-182 thongs. It's no wonder the band rarely leaves the climate-controlled splendor of the bus.

Today, though, the need for laundry far outweighs the need to avoid the anxious teenagers waiting outside in the parking lot, so most of the band members set out early in search of a working washing machine. While waiting to do a load, Zach Lind agrees to eat lunch with me backstage.

Sitting in the air-conditioned, octagonal catering room, Zach forks soggy tacos into his mouth and attempts to self-analyze. The drummer is a compact, burly man with small, no-nonsense eyes, and he speaks in clipped, monochromatic bursts. At twenty-five, he's the youngest of the band, but he comes across as the oldest. He's sturdy, dependable, unemotional. His father was a major league ballplayer, and he fields each question—be it softball, curveball, or knuckler—with the same workmanlike rigor. Lind is also the only member of Jimmy Eat World to spend any time interacting with fans on the band's quietly mushrooming website.

"I look at the messageboard all the time," he says. "I like to see the feedback. I'm always looking for ideas to make these fans happier. And what I've realized is that there's a shitload of kids out there that don't need the radio and they don't MTV to find out about music. These kids know what they like and they know how to get it. And all they need is a CD-R and a web community."

While Lind has a very clear perspective of the band's career from a right-brain sensibility, when it comes to the ineffable *je ne sais quois* that attracts kids to the music, he's utterly clueless. In terms of Jimmy Eat World's appeal—whatever it is that has allowed them to carry die-hard fans across generation and genre gaps—he's like a tree that can't see itself for the forest.

"Lyrics aren't really that important in Jimmy Eat World," he says, shoveling up some stray bits of taco. "We have them because we need them. Within the band we never talk about them. I don't know what the songs mean." He pauses and takes a sip of soda.

"In what way don't you know?" I ask.

Lind looks at me like I'm speaking German. "Literally: I don't know what our songs mean. And we don't talk about it. It's not an issue. I'm just not a lyric guy."

Later in the afternoon, about a half hour before their set, the band agrees to do an on-air interview with the local modern-rock radio station. The station has set up a broadcast booth just to the right of one of the venue's multitude of merchandise stands and has a stereotypical-looking jock manning the mic—the sort of ageless, dyed hair/thick neck sort of fellow who is either called "Boomer" or "Mike G." and blesses the nation's disenfranchised youth with buzzwords, promotions, and up-to-the-minute slang in every one of America's major radio markets. All around me, the incredibly young audience is milling about. Scrawny fourteen-year-olds with greasy, spiky hair and fake tattoos brandish newly purchased Blink T-shirts; chain-smoking Southern girls in midriff-bearing tops gossip in groups; stern-faced fathers with moustaches and jumbo beers stand watch, checking the time every ten seconds. It's a mall audience, people likely to be called "punks" by school principals and security guards, but not actually *be* punks. Spread out behind the radio station's table, Jimmy Eat World members are anonymous and genial, and they all take turns speaking to the female DJ back at the station's HQ. The banter is surprisingly unforced and the four seem to lean on each other when one's enthusiasm wanes. Finally, Boomer (or Mike G., depending) mentions that the station has presents for all three of the bands on the Pop Disaster tour. It seems that the members of Green Day have already picked up theirs, but he points out a listener-crafted macaroni painting of Blink-182's faces. And what does Jimmy Eat World get? Four copies of Ben Marcus's bizarre and elliptical postmodern novel, *Notable American Women.* The irony of an emo band receiving copies of a nearly impenetrable novel about a childhood spent in an Ohio cult dedicated to the idea of an "emotion-free" society is apparently lost on the folks back at the station.

At precisely 7:30 P.M. with the sun still shining brightly in the westward corner of the sky, Jimmy Eat World takes the stage in Dallas. The band's set is spartan, save for a curtain featuring a detail of Arizona. The seats around me are maybe half full; those present when the band kicks into the intoxicating tom-tom beat of "A Praise Chorus" either stand up and cheer or sneer to their friends and wait to be impressed. The performance is remarkably tight and focused for such a diffuse context. There are a few kids in the front row who jump up and down when the band plays two songs from their cult-favorite second album, *Clarity,* and popcorn-laden people stream in from the concessions area to see what all the noise is about. It doesn't feel like a concert so much as an auction—Jimmy Eat World as the latest item to bid on or ignore, a group offered up to be your next big thing. Song after song, the concert has all the warmth of a business lunch, but the band is game; singer/guitarist Jim Adkins sweats up a storm and sings out each lyric for the thousandth time as if it were the first. The effect is like watching the world's best jukebox, but all around me in the crowd are fans, most of them standing solitary in their rows, shaking their arms to the beat and mouthing the words like gospel. There's a sad-faced giant with a shaved head and a varsity wrestling T-shirt solemnly singing the ultra-emo sentiment "once I almost touched your hand"; there is an overweight African-American girl in a green shirt just down my row. The fans stand up like receptors, telephone poles, homing beacons—fearlessly alone and shameproof, yet too far away for me to reach any of them afterward. Jimmy Eat World ends, of course, with "The Middle," and suddenly everyone in the amphitheater is standing, rocking out, doing like they do in the video. Most seem shocked that this relatively boring-looking combo is responsible for their favorite song on the radio to do their homework to, but no matter. Jimmy Eat World, as always, is just there to play. Its music is the soundtrack to these kids' lives—some more personally than others. Both band and audience take what they can from each other and, for now, it seems like that's enough.

Jimmy Eat World was formed in 1993 in Mesa, Arizona, by four fast friends: Tom Linton, Jim Adkins, Zach Lind, and Mitch Porter. The quartet celebrated the end of high school by playing sloppy, energetic punk shows to friends and local scenesters—the group's odd moniker was derived from a picture drawn by one of Linton's younger brothers depicting another brother—Jimmy—devouring the planet; for obvious reasons, the name is usually assumed to reference Adkins, much to his chagrin. After winning over the regional crowd, the group began touring farther and farther outside of the Phoenix metro area. Porter left soon after and was replaced by Rick Burch.

The way the band ended up on Capitol Records is typically accidental—the band often seems like the Forrest Gump of indie, constantly stumbling into success through an odd combination of luck and good attitudes. In 1995, the young band put out a split 7-inch with Denver's Christie Front Drive. A junior talent scout at Capitol named Loren Israel was trying to sign Christie; when its members rebuffed him, he flipped the 7-inch over and the rest is history.

Despite its presence on a major label, Jimmy Eat World was actively embraced by the emo community of the day. The reason being the guys didn't act any different, both because they couldn't afford to and because it wasn't their style. Though it might have been odd to some at first, a band on the same label as the Beatles opening for Mineral or Braid, loading in its own equipment, and getting drunk at the bar eventually became a common sight to concertgoers all over the country. Jimmy Eat World was the ghost in the machine, an under-the-radar ambassador to a world completely antithetical to the one to which it most belonged.

The band is blasé when asked about why and how they, as a major-label act, were embraced so completely by an underground scene.

"I have no idea how it happened," says Burch. "It just happened. But no one gave us any grief about it because we weren't trying to be slick about it or anything. We were just like, hey, this is us, this is our situation, this is our music, and whatever."

"We were working hard," says Linton. "We had a little van and we weren't trying to fool anyone. I think everyone knew we were on a major, but that scene was where we were most comfortable."

"It's not like Capitol was helping us out," says Adkins. "We had to do a lot of it on our own. So we just fell in with a group of people that were also helping themselves out. And that just happened to be bands like Christie, the Promise Ring, Boy's Life. Our label situation was quite different than those other bands, but we were all starting out at the same time. I never felt like an outsider; I mean I listened to the same music and liked everything that crowd liked. It wasn't like we were sneaking in. It's just the way it happened. We got lucky. And we ended up playing shows for the right people, for people who would like our music."

Lind is more blunt. "I don't know how it happened," he says.

The truth is, no matter what label had its logo on the spine, Jimmy Eat World's first album, *Static Prevails,* sounds no different than any other independently released emo album of the period. The sound is muddy, the lyrics are searching and grandiose, but when good moments burst out of the morass they have a lusty, naïve gleam about them: the soaring antisuburban ennui anthem "Call It In the Air" and the modestly lovely "Episode IV" (which was Blink-182 guitarist Tom Delonge's wedding song) stand out. Though Linton serves as the primary singer, it is Adkins who, though shy about the spotlight, scores the album's most memorable moment on "Call It in the Air" when he, with almost jarring emotional recklessness, sings, "Become your dad!" It's an unimpeachable earnestness—the band was fed up with the apathetic culture that surrounded them, but was also pretty unclear as to how combat it other than by hopping in the van and playing another show. The truth is, Jimmy Eat World was a bit green to be making an album, and the band spent the next two years crisscrossing the country, learning to become a better band the hard way. And despite the major label behind them, they were pretty much left to their own devices.

"As soon as we signed to Capitol, we were like, 'Rad! We're on a major label. We're going to put out records!" gushes Rick Burch in mock childlike wonder. I'm sitting having lunch with the two least talkative Jimmies, Burch and guitarist Tom Linton, in a hotel restaurant. Burch is tall, floppy-haired, and has a pouty mouth—his general demeanor is stereotypical for bassists: relaxed and removed.

Linton, short-haired and almost painfully earnest, shovels up some macaroni salad and concurs in his trademark half-stoned, half-wistful sounding voice, "Yeah. All these promises they made to us that never happened.

"Because *Static Prevails* happened. And while we were touring we realized, wow, this doesn't mean anything. You get money to record and they'll actually make the CD, but everything else was up to us. And they had some ideas but they were just so bad."

"Like what?" I ask.

"Oh my god," says Tom, through his iced tea.

"The 7-Eleven tour," says Rick.

Tom puts the tea down. "Yeah, so we went into this meeting at Capitol, and they're like, hey! We've got this great idea! You guys travel around the country and right after high schools get out, or junior highs, you guys set up by the local 7-Eleven and just start playing!" He collapses in laughter.

Burch picks up the slack. "They were like, you guys have a PA—you can fit that in the van, right? Just pull up, set up at about 2:30, so when people show up at 3:05 for their thirstbuster or whatever you're ready to go and just start playing!"

I say, "It seems like they knew you'd be playing to kids. But they were clueless about how to reach them."

Both Burch and Linton nod. "Yeah, exactly."

"The basic idea of touring, and building slowly—that just didn't register with them?"

"No, not at all," says Rick. "Because that actually takes time. They're very impatient. They want it now. And they don't really want to work that hard. But we always had problems in the beginning."

"Talk about trying to fit in," says Linton. "In the early days, '95, '96, there was that big ska thing. And for some reason we'd always be on those shows. And no one would respond. It was like, we might as well not be playing shows!"

Jimmy Eat World's second album, *Clarity,* is one of the most fiercely beloved rock 'n' roll records of the last decade. It is name-checked by every single contemporary emo band as their favorite album, as a mind-bending milemarker that proved that punk rock could be tuneful, emotional, wide-ranging, and ambitious. A 180-degree left turn from *Static Prevails, Clarity* made punk beautiful. Underpublicized and perhaps a few years ahead of its time, the people who found *Clarity,* found it them-selves—they searched for it, they discovered it. It was given to them by a precious ex, a close friend. If two people knew about it, it was a shared secret, a common emotion. If punk rock has always been about commu-nity building, sneaking *Clarity* onto your stereo after lights-out was inti-mately crafting a community of one.

"*Clarity* makes you feel a certain way," enthuses Matt Watts of the young emo quartet The Starting Line. "You can put it on and no matter what you're feeling, nothing goes through your head. Everything stops. It's just unreal. Every single emotion that a person can go through is captured on that CD."

For such an emotional album—or perhaps precisely because it is such an emotional album—no one in the band has very much to say about it (Lind: "It's a very endearing, comfortable sort of record, I guess." Linton: "It's more experimental." Burch: "It's kind of scat-tered."). *Clarity* is an album in search of its title and from the first song, "Table for Glasses," it is apparent that for Adkins, clarity is something to be found in community. He needs "somebody" to tell him how to feel, he needs a guide to his own emotions. His way of address-ing this is through the songs on the record—the same record that would soon provide the same service to thousands of equally confused young listeners.

"I bought *Clarity* on a whim in 1998 when I was feeling really depressed about life in general," says seventeen-year-old Debbie via email. " 'Table for Glasses' was the perfect opening track because I was so confused and also naïve to think that I was the only one that felt that way. And then I heard Jim sing, 'lead my skeptic sight / to the table and the light,' and I was hooked. I never thought poetry like that was visible in music."

"I promised I'd see this again / I promised I'd see this with you," Adkins sings on "Just Watch the Fireworks." The initial vision of beauty—of what we can only assume is the fireworks of the title—is incomplete on its own. It takes one to have an experience, Adkins says, but two to make a memory. Adkins perpetually craves this double-tracked harmony, both in life and on record. He sees things and wants desperately to share it with someone—whether that someone ends up being his wife, another individual, or an anonymous teenager in the crowd is irrelevant. His boldest act is making the request—putting himself out there. This is nothing if not a working definition of emo.

If *Clarity* is more concerned with the emotional struggles of its songwriter, it wages the defining battles in the music as well as the lyrics. The dominant audio trope is the multitracked vocal. Again and again, Adkins uses his newfound studio expertise to create beautiful moments of singing with himself. When his voice or lyrics are at their most fragile or vulnerable, a second Adkins appears, swooping up out of the studio crackle to lend strength and harmony. So desperate is Adkins for community, he's willing to fabricate it on record. Much in the same way that *Clarity*'s early listeners found solace in Adkins's voice on their stereo, Adkins seeks comfort in himself. Two sets of eyes transform an ordinary moment into an extraordinary one; two voices can lift the mundane into the sublime. "I am but one small instrument," he sings on the final track, "Goodbye Sky Harbor." But the song doesn't end on such a negative (and solitary) note; rather it stretches on almost absurdly past the sixteen-minute mark, building into a crescendo of multitracked, nonsensical sung melody. Layering "ba ba ba"s with "da da"s like a child would assemble Lego blocks, Adkins builds a defiant community of sound. Out of one small instrument, many. There is comfort in the gibberish, a pattern in the chaotic unravelling. *Clarity* as an album and as a title is about stripping back to the essential, to the most vital elements. The first twelve songs struggle with the limits of self, "Goodbye Sky Harbor" explodes them. Music saved Jim Adkins when he was younger, now, when he needs it most again in his life, he's saved himself.

"*Clarity* was the first record from that generation that could have been palatable to millions of people," says Chris Ryan. "It's really pretty and the songs are compact and you can understand the lyrics the first time through, but they don't beat you over the head. You can take whatever you want from the images. I thought that record was going to make them really big. Surprisingly, it didn't."

Despite the placement of the shimmering single "Lucky Denver Mint" on the soundtrack to the Drew Barrymore comedy *Never Been Kissed* and a warm critical reception, *Clarity* bombed commercially when it was released in 1999. The charts were filled with teen pop and the newspapers were filled with Nasdaq porn. There seemed to be very little place for an intricate, introspective jewel box of an album. But the record made its mark where it counted—with the fans (many of whom still go slack jawed at the mere mention of it), and with their peers.

"*Clarity* is one of the best records ever," says Dashboard Confessional's Chris Carrabba. "When VH1 or whomever does another one of those top one hundred albums lists a decade from now, it should be on there. When it came out—and I really can't remember this happening with another record—for two months it was all I listened to. From my car to my Walkman to my room to my car to my office. To anywhere. It was huge to me. And you make a moot point by calling it an emo record. It's just a staggering work of musicianship."

"Jimmy Eat World proved with that album that this music could be very, very big if you just trimmed the fat and dotted all the *i*s," adds Ryan. "It had the familiar, pop-punk sugar rush but with more introspective lyrics."

But it wasn't to be just yet. After another year of relentless touring, Jimmy Eat World and Capitol Records parted ways. To many, it signified that the band was just another major-label casualty, an almost-famous Icarus that flew too close to the sun, got burned, and ended up with nothing to show for it.

The reaction within the band, though, couldn't have been more different.

"People ask me all the time if we felt like quitting then," says Jim Adkins. "Are you kidding? I threw a party when we got out of our deal with Capitol!"

Instead of packing it in, Jimmy Eat World redoubled its efforts. Bursting with optimism and some cracking new songs that swelled with a less specific, populist vibe ("When we were touring on *Clarity,* Jim was a pretty avid journal keeper," says Burch, "just observing kids and their interactions and I think he drew on those observations a lot for his new lyrics."). The band set out on a three-week tour hoping to raise enough money to record some basic tracks for a new album on their own dime. After posting the tour dates on the website, the band left a message urging fans to come out and buy T-shirts, that every dollar spent was an investment in the future of the band. The guys then posted the earliest demos of *Jimmy Eat World* songs on Napster, encouraging their fans to listen to them and learn them in advance of the concerts. Every single show sold out and, flush with success, the band headed straight into a Los Angeles studio with friend and producer Mark Trombino. They had never looked back before; why should they start now?

"For us it's always seemed like this constant—we've always seen progress for the work that we're doing," says Adkins. "Always. It seemed like the normal thing to do. We just had confidence in the record, in the songs. We just felt sure that it would all work out, even if no label wanted the record. We would just take out a loan and put it out ourselves."

But a strange thing had happened in the year the band was label-less. *Clarity* had sold over 70,000 copies, but, more important, it had sold them to the right people. Though the group had never lacked for friends in the music business, its best friends were now in positions of power. John Silva—Nirvana's old manager—took the group under his well-connected wing. And, as bottom lines shrank, the thought of a band that had recorded an entire album themselves—thereby negating a huge cost to the label—and that had a preinstalled fan base that had funded the recording of it, seemed like a tremendous investment. Jimmy Eat World had transformed itself from the scapegoat of everything that was wrong with major-label excess in the '90s to a Web-savvy poster child for the possibilities of large-scale DIYism in the twenty-first century, all without ever stopping to think about it.

Luke Wood became a fan of the band when his own group, Sammy, opened for Jimmy Eat World in the mid-nineties. Wood was now a senior A&R rep at Dreamworks, the privately held label founded by David Geffen, Jeffrey Katzenberg, and Steven Spielberg. After months of wooing—and proving that he was, in his words, "a 100 percent true fan"—Wood signed the band to a multialbum, multimillion dollar deal. Though some industry wags shook their heads, Wood was convinced. "I felt like *Clarity* should have sold two to three million copies," he says over the phone, while what sounds like a machine spitting out Jimmy Eat World airplay information like an old-time stock tickers chatters in the background. "And this is a band that is productive and one that comes armed with a very strong, devoted fan base. I knew that this is a group that can make a partnership with a major label—and that's what it truly should be—work in the way it's supposed to. Together, we can get Jimmy Eat World's amazing music to as many people as possible."

With *Clarity,* Jimmy Eat World crafted the perfect album for those who were predisposed to search it out and listen to it. On *Jimmy Eat World* they went hunting for new ears.

Even without the brilliant positioning of the video, "The Middle" is a radio dirty bomb: a totally unexpected blast of something fresh, vital, and directed. Many people have said that discovering punk is like receiving the answers to life-changing questions you didn't even know you were asking. If so, then for hundreds of thousands of young people, hearing "The Middle" on the radio was like being handed a cheat sheet two-thirds of the way through the final exam.

Jesse, a high school senior from Texas, describes the first time she heard the song:

> Last summer was a horrible time for me. I go to a small private school and everyone was spreading vicious rumors about me. All of my friends turned against me and I was so lonely and upset. I couldn't understand it. Then one day I was sitting in my room and "The Middle" came on. I hadn't paid attention to the lyrics that much, but all of a sudden I heard Jim say 'everything is gonna be just fine.' I broke out in tears. It was like Jim was speaking right to me because every word he said related to what I was going through so perfectly. Now, whenever I'm upset, that song helps me through it.

While many of the old fans turned their noses up at the song (but not the band) as it became more and more popular, Jimmy Eat World finally lived up to one of *Clarity's* most memorable lyrics and took back the radio. "The Middle" was one of the most played songs of the year and reached an entirely new and willing audience. Ten years after Nirvana made nerds cool, Jimmy Eat World made it OK for jocks to cry. The band—and emo itself—had its breakthrough hit. The first breakthrough album followed closely after.

Where *Clarity* goes inward in search of salvation, *Jimmy Eat World* is outgoing, boisterous, confident. It is searingly well produced—guitars crunch, drums pound, keyboards glisten. There were no, as Adkins would put it, "deep album tracks," no more ten-minute meanderings about fireworks—the band quite literally couldn't afford them.

After the snarly rage of "Bleed American," the album begins in earnest with the second song, "A Praise Chorus." Over thudding drums and an insistent guitar buzz saw, Adkins addresses his youthful listeners boldly, directly: "Are you gonna live your life wondering / standing in the back, looking around? / are you gonna waste your time thinking / how you've grown up / how you've missed out?" For a moment, it's the same "carpe diem, dude" sentiment as "The Middle." But then the tone changes: "even at twenty-five you gotta start sometime . . . / I'm on my feet / I'm on the floor / I'm good to go." Adkins is once again singing to himself, but without any of the poetic fringe of *Clarity*. There's no hiding this time, and in order to get himself back on track, Adkins asks for music: "come on Davey / sing me something that I know / I want to always feel like part of this was mine / want to fall in love tonight." Right on cue, Promise Ring's Davey Vonbohlen appears out of the rhythm, singing fragments of older songs; "Crimson and Clover," "Our House," "Kickstart My Heart." With his fellow musician/muse providing fellowship, Jim's voice crescendos. It's a beautiful, electrifying song that functions on two levels. It's an emo song about the power of an emo song that equals and surpasses the highs it's describing.

"Honestly, it was after hearing 'A Praise Chorus' that I knew I had to sign the band," says Luke Wood. "That song typified the way I feel when I go to shows. You feel disenfranchised, but when you get to the concert you realize there's other people like you. When Jimmy Eat World play they're just as much a part of that community as the audience."

The album is about self-medication—more specifically the Jim Adkins Diet—where music, any music, equals salvation. It's not maudlin or specifically emotional; nearly all of the songs are in the second person. That's why the other band members don't even care about lyrics—they're not a specific sort of band. They're positive energy, forward movement. Let's all help each other help ourselves. As a band, as a construct, they are nothing when left alone.

"Jim's songs are a dialogue with his inner self," says Luke Wood. "But it resonates because everyone is having that same dialogue. I actually feel that when Jim goes to see a band he loves, the feeling he has is no different from the feeling he has when he's onstage, singing his own

songs. Now, half the time you see a band the singers are up there thinking about getting laid or being drunk. I think Jim goes into a zone that is
not all that different from where I am, absorbing myself in a Jimmy Eat
World show, singing along to every word."

Jimmy Eat World was released in the summer of 2001 and Soundscanned 30,000 copies in one week. With the industry shocked upright,
a cavalcade of glowing, "survivor"-type magazine profiles appeared (all
of which called the band emo). On the back of typically relentless touring, the album went gold almost immediately. In July 2002, it went platinum. With its poppiest, most universal album to date, Jimmy Eat World
broke out of the indie/emo ghetto, but by doing so, the band also
defined its sound *as* emo for hundreds of thousands of new listeners.

Jim Adkins is a pleasant-looking fellow. Slightly taller than average, he
has a wide-open, trustworthy face and a certain heft about him that
makes him seem more like a close friend's older brother or that guy in
the back of your English class who kept to himself but had suprisingly
insightful things to say about Dostoevsky. More than a little self-
effacing, Adkins is as unlikely a lead singer as you're likely to find, and
it makes sense that he gradually absorbed the role rather choosing it
outright. When the band started, he was the spastic guitar player and
Tom Linton was the main songwriter, but, over time, the shy Adkins
simply wrote more songs than Linton—a trend that has continued
through to their present success. His speaking voice is slightly husky,
and he is prone to saying things like "dude," laughing nervously, and
using the words "rock 'n' roll" as an adjective. Onstage he favors short-
sleeved, black button-down shirts, he sweats a lot as he sings, and his
mop of brown hair forms little curls to either side of his forehead that
swing back and forth like curtains being operated by a nervous, teenage
stagehand. He's an odd combination of wide open and incredibly
guarded. To visitors and fans he's almost painfully polite and solicitous—inquiring about their thoughts, opinions, and safety like a cherished, trusted friend. But a great deal of the kindness, while genuine,
seems reflective. If he keeps the focus of the conversation on you, there's
less of a chance the spotlight will swing back to him, which is where he
least wants it to be.

On the bus, Adkins seems like he's always emerging from the bunks in the back (I find out later that he's addicted to the Xbox that's hidden away in the second "chill-out" room located in the rear). Everyone, crew and band alike, seems particularly solicitous around him, deflecting conversations his way, keenly aware of his presence in the room, and Adkins plays his role perfectly, usually walking into company with a well-timed anecdote or interruption. In a production of this scale, individual relationships are hard to crack, but there is a definite sense that Jim is the breadwinner in the family and that it's a role that is not to be disturbed. Obviously there are some heartfelt and goofy friendships powering the quartet, but the business, public, on the road for two years, functioning side of things seems to operate on a quietly different blueprint.

En route to San Antonio, he finally sits down to talk.

"There's always a faction of people that want to have their favorite band in a little box in the basement where it's theirs and no one else's," he says. "I don't know. I think about it sometimes. It's just hard enough to make sure you're doing the right thing for yourself. That's the only thing you can can really do—make what you're presenting something you would feel comfortable on the other end of, as a listener or fan."

"Do you ever check out what the fans think on the web?"

"Sometimes, but I put more stock in personal interaction, talking to somebody rather than reading their post. At this scale it's difficult . . . these shows, they're not really ours. There aren't really as many fans that want questions answered or want to have a conversation. There's a whole lot of autograph signing to get through."

"When they do catch you, what do kids like to talk to you about?"

He laughs. "Mostly the stuff I don't want to talk about! Specifics. I just think that if someone found something that affected them in a lyric—like they found something that helped them deal with a problem or maybe it reminds them of that summer when they met their girlfriend—to me, it just seems like that should be enough. You've succeeded. You've taken the work and found something in it and made it yours. I think it's up to the listener to have a reaction to it."

"So they've succeeded when that happens, not you."

"No, I think I've succeeded. Maybe not for the same reason. There's no correct way to like something. You have your own reasons for it. I succeed when I'm in the studio and I've just put on the last tambourine part and it's done. It's there. That's the song. Then I win."

"Does the song then become everyone else's when you're done in the studio?"

"That's kind of the way I hope people take the music. It's theirs."

"But it seems like, with the kids waiting outside the bus to talk to you yesterday, the people lining up by the backstage gate yelling out for you, that it's not enough for some kids. They want to connect it back to you."

"Sometimes. I like it better when people tell me they like something and tell me why, rather than say 'in this part, what do you really mean?' It doesn't matter what I mean. All the songs, they mean something to me. Very specific things to me. But it's not about me."

"But do you ever think about why it is that things that mean so much to you seem to translate so intensely to other people?"

Jim clears his throat three or four times and looks away. "I don't know. . . . Because I don't think I'm the most gifted lyricist. I wouldn't for a second think that what I have to say is important. But . . . I don't know." He laughs nervously and looks up. "Maybe the delivery is catchy."

"I was wondering if that ever weirds you out."

"Not until now!" More nervous laughter. A truck honks at us from the passing lane. "I don't spend a whole lot of time thinking about it. You can either drive yourself mad or become a total asshole figuring out why so many people accept the work that you're doing."

"You seem like a very private person."

"Yeah, I think so," he says. "I don't have any desire to start my acting career, I'll put it that way. I've started to notice the press wants to get some dirt on us. Some English journalists asked us what the most secretive thing about us is. I told them: we're boring. They said to tell them anything but that. But it's the truth. We're not doing this to stir shit up. We're not doing it to get our dicks sucked. We're doing it because we find fulfillment in writing, recording, and performing music. That's as simple as it is. Anything beyond that . . . it doesn't really have anything to do with us."

"With you being the songwriter, it must be hard to avoid everyone trying to plumb you for secret depths."

"I shy away from really getting into 'me' with people. Just because I play in a band—that's not the way friendships and trust are built. It doesn't work like that. You have to hang out with somebody and know 'em for a little bit before you really get into their shit."

Jim stares out the window at the passing Texas brush. He's such an unassuming, nice guy that I can tell he'd sit here all day with me if I asked him to; he wouldn't resent me for it, but he certainly wouldn't enjoy it. Talking to Jim Adkins is loads of fun; interviewing him makes you question your need to do it. After an hour, I feel like I have the songs; what more do I need?

Jimmy Eat World is successful precisely because its members have no idea why they are successful. Deep thoughts may occur to them—for a time Adkins's recommended reading on the band website was Eric Schlosser's *Fast Food Nation* and Noam Chomsky's *9-11*—but searing self-reflection just isn't in the cards. Asking the occasional serious question of any member of the band is like turning on the lights at a bar: intrusive, disorienting, unexpected, and unplanned-for.

They are the calm in the middle of the tornado. Outside, the gales of punk politics, big business, and the fickle taste of teenagers blow fiercely and unabated. Inside, in Jimmy Eat World, it's the same as it's always been. Maybe a little bigger, maybe a little more money in the bank. The band's ploddingly workmanlike—some would say infuriatingly dense—take on their career has seen them through.

"We just do what we do," says Burch, with the sagacity of a Zen monk, "and we are who we are."

To the peers that Jimmy Eat World has outgrown, the band's huge success is both logical and maddening. "It's totally bizarre to be around Jimmy Eat World now," says Promise Ring guitarist Jason Gnewikow. "Three or four years ago they were opening for us. Now kids are racking their copies of *Jimmy Eat World* next to their Creed CDs. Their story is amazing because it's just so *them*. Everything was so simple and easy. They just seem so unbelievably unaffected by anything. I'm like, 'why can't I be you?' Because I'm a total control freak. They've always been the band where if they were a total failure, they'd probably just think it was a bummer. I'm not complaining because they're totally justified now. It's just that their participation in their life is so casual it's bizarre."

When it comes to their career, the members of Jimmy Eat World are about as un-emo as possible. "I think we have it pretty together," says Adkins. "We love what we do and it's important to us. But you can't take it too seriously. It's a fucking rock band. There are so many things out there that you can't control—you just have to let it go or you'll go insane."

Hanging out with all four members of the band together—particularly post-performance—is lazy like a late-November football game with friends. After another successful, anodyne-daylight performance in San Antonio, we're driving straight through to Houston. Some of the crew disembarked at a gas station off the highway, choosing to make the ride with some leggy, midriff-baring fans who seem to appear backstage at every venue in Texas. Jimmy Eat World members sprawl across the bus's couches, crack Pepsis, and crack jokes, obviously comfortable with each others' silences. While everyone lazily watches a racy episode of MTV's Darwinian dating show *Dismissed,* Lind is the only one to stick to business, asking me what other band's messageboards I've been following. Lind's demeanor is gruff and he doesn't beat around the bush. He's genuinely curious about what younger bands are doing online, how kids respond to them, and if there are elements that they can integrate into their own websites. His face is implacable, but it's possible to see the heavy gears rumbling and turning behind his eyes. "Have you seen the telephone feature?" he asks.

One of the cooler interactive elements of jimmyeatworld.com is the ringing phone—visitors to the site can click on it and listen to a phone message left by a member of the band. It's a clever way for the group to stay in close touch with the fans without having to wade through crowds of them or even visit the site themselves—Lind merely dials a number on his cell phone and directs the other guys to leave a message on the webmaster's machine. It's possible for a message to be uploaded as quickly as the next day, though the band has been lax of late.

"Jim," Zach barks, "it's been awhile since you left a message. Want to do one now?"

Jim tears his eyes away from the screen—two young women in bikinis are flanking a lucky fellow in a hot tub, desperately doing anything to avoid being "dismissed." "Sure," he says, and takes the phone from Zach.

Tom taps me on the shoulder. "Did you hear the message I left? It was sooo funny."

Zach breaks in. "Tom didn't know it was recording. So he kept starting to talk, screwing up, saying 'shit!' and hanging up and trying again."

Tom is displaying his oddly proud/happy/blush face. "And they put all of the calls up on the site! It sounded sooo stupid."

From the back of the bus, Jim's voice rings out. "Hey everyone, it's Jim here. We're driving through Texas right now. Thanks a lot for coming out to these Pop Disaster shows. It's great to see you all. . . ."

Zach asks what other bands I've been talking to and I mention that I'd been having trouble setting up interview time with Chris Carrabba of Dashboard Confessional.

"Why?" says Lind bluntly, looking perplexed.

"I don't know," I say, "I think he's deciding whether he wants to be a part of the book. He's worried about getting lumped in with a scene."

Lind snorts. "Huh. If there's one guy who should learn to deal with being called emo, it's Chris Carrabba."

Onscreen, one of the bikini-clad girls gets dismissed right out of the hot tub. Burch chuckles and changes the channel. Lind pops open another Pepsi. The bus rumbles on.

If Jimmy Eat World is happily untroubled by its ascent from Boston basements to arena rock, the band members also seem quite ignorant of what they may have given up along the way.

"It's way less personal than it was," says Burch with a shrug.

"Yeah," says Linton. "It kind of sucks."

"There are more autograph hounds now than people that just want to chat," says Adkins, "but it's cool."

"I don't blame kids for being frustrated about the size of this tour," says Lind. "We want to gain new fans but without alienating the older ones. I think most of our fans understand that, but some are dogmatic—'I wish Jimmy Eat World would be like they were before this album came out.' When they say that, I have a hard time not replying and saying, hey, I can afford paying health insurance now for my daughter and wife. Whereas before I couldn't. And that's a good thing. I understand it's not the fans' problem—but these kids who are fifteen, sixteen, seventeen, they don't live in the real world of adult responsibility and they don't see the bigger picture as an adult would."

Lind's thoughts are anathema to punk rock, but a pretty healthy attitude for a long-term music career. The truth is, Jimmy Eat World works
best on a mass-market level anyway. Unlike its mid-nineties emo peers,
Jimmy Eat World's songs sound magnificent on the radio and on film
soundtracks; the songs on the platinum breakthrough record are generational calling cards, not digressive mopes plagued by and written about
self-sabotage. "They have an unusual band DNA that allowed them to
come back stronger than ever," says Dreamworks' Luke Wood. "They've
got the business guy, the creative guy . . . it's just a wonderful chemistry
among the four of them. They're not concerned with the drama of a
scene, not interested in marketing themselves. And by not being
obsessed with that stuff they're incredibly like their fans. There's a real
sense that the most important thing is the music." As Jimmy Eat World
works "The Middle," they also work the middle: the line between art
and commerce, between punk and pop, between cynicism and caring,
between one generation's private music and another's public pain. The
band in 2002 is a headache-free machine, traveling the world, simultaneously rebuking and defining an emo movement of which they have no
clear understanding. Quiet, retiring Jim Adkins is the machine's furnace,
glowing white-hot and roaring hotter still with every successful concert,
every CD purchased, every life changed around.

The backstage of the Houston venue is a bit more cramped and cavelike
than the previous two, which is all right since the humidity keeps most
everyone in the air-conditioning anyway. In the long afternoon before
the show, the band sits around and watches more MTV on the dressing
room television. In between videos, the trailer for the forgotten-before-
it-opened teen comedy *The New Guy* comes on. The film concerns a
nerdy outcast who repositions himself as the coolest kid in his new high
school. The soundtrack to the commercial is, of course, "The Middle."
As soon as the opening chords start playing, I sneak a peak at Jim, who
is watching the screen with a befuddled look of pleasure on his face.
When the commercial ends he turns around with a grin. "Hey," he says,
"that ad paid for my new kitchen."

The band's set is concise and enthusiastic, same as ever. Jimmy Eat
World is not a band that seems to have off nights—they've been at it for

too long. Near the end of Green Day's performance, I wander backstage and cautiously push open the door to the dressing room to see how everyone is doing. There's an eerie silence emanating from behind the door, and when I step into the room it's one of those moments when the record skips to a stop at a party and everyone in attendance stares— except this time they're desperately grateful for the interruption.

Rick is seated on the couch, surrounded by two friendly looking young women; Jim is sitting cross-legged on the floor, flanked by two slight-looking men. There are modestly diminished bottles of Budweiser on the table and more than a few cans of soda. Jim turns to me at the door with a beseeching look.

"Andy!" he practically yells, "come in and talk to us!"

A random collection of young people and friends with Phoenix con- nections have come to the show and Jim is determined to give them a good time. Of course, he seems just as uncomfortable in the situation as they do. It feels weird taking the reins of a conversation away from rock stars, but Jim and Rick still aren't very good at being rock stars. Grouped awkwardly around a tacky wooden coffee table in a dressing room with bad art and worse, bright lighting, we could be at any fresh- man mixer—a bunch of overly polite, overly sober young people trying to maintain a cheery atmosphere. Talk turns to New York City (one of the girls is planning a move) and eventually things relax. Despite his social worries, Jim is in a good mood tonight—there's a long drive and an off day ahead of them, so he's relaxed, having a few drinks, and smil- ing. Eventually, Tom shows up with some young ladies in tow, seeking refuge from the fireworks of Blink-182's stage show. The spreading good mood is genial, infectious. Green Day drummer Tre Cool walks in, sits down, and, for awhile, makes himself the center of attention, his perpetually stoned-sounding voice rising high above the sound of the TV. Rick is joking around on the couch with some random fans. There's a total disconnect from the rock 'n' roll theatrics going on just a few hundred feet from the dressing room. If a stranger were to walk in, he'd be hard pressed to identify the members of the chart-topping band.

At one point, Jim and I are standing together underneath the TV and I ask him about the house that I'd read he'd recently bought in Mesa. The biggest smile I've ever seen from him spreads across his face. "It's great," he says. "It's the oldest part of town—houses from the '40s and '50s. It's an amazing neighborhood and there's ivy up the outside walls. But there's nothing in it yet because I haven't had time to set it up yet! It's mine but I haven't lived in it."

"When do you think you'll have time to really settle in?"

He laughs. "We've planned to keep this going until February. Then we'll probably let ourselves take a break, unless things are going so well it would be stupid." He pauses. "I love this, but I'm really looking forward to some time off."

What I didn't know then was that not only was Jim due to be married a month or two later, but Amy, his fiancee and longtime girlfriend, was expecting their first child. Both his career and personal life were maturing at the same time, a tough scenario no matter what the circumstances. Here he is, smilingly talking about domestic matters, while the dressing room—the eternal hearth of rock-star excesses and clichés—fills up with random Texas coeds with artificial breasts and sharpies for the band to sign them with.

While one of the guitar-techs has laughingly put the catering table oranges in one well-endowed backstage visitor's cleavage, Jim has been quietly talking to some pretty, preppie-looking girls who have somehow found their way back. While the lighting guys drain the rest of the whiskey, I overhear Jim thanking the girls for what they've said to him just as vociferously as they're thanking him for what his music has done for their lives. The girls ask me to take a picture of them with Jim, and I do; Jim puts his arms around them protectively and smiles big.

Later that night, with the crew doing their best to pull the groupies for themselves (the band is either too married or too amused to partake of the action), I get Jim to pose for another picture. The crew razz him good-naturedly and he agrees to pose the way a rock star should. The picture itself is an amazing document—Adkins, wild-haired, is in the center, his head thrown back, pouring a bottle of vodka all over his face; he's flanked by one girl hoisting a Budweiser can and another wearing a bikini top. But the picture is essential Jimmy Eat World: the bottle was emptied already by the tech guys and Jim refilled it with water. Not long after the flash went off, he retired to the bus to call his fiancee and turn in at a reasonable hour for the long drive to New Orleans.

I'm reminded of what Chris Carrabba of Dashboard Confessional told me once about Jimmy Eat World. "Together, I think we might save the spirit of rock 'n' roll but ruin the aesthetic for a little while. What I mean is, it's not a fashion thing. Bands like us are never gonna be rock stars. I'm not unapproachable by nature so how could I become that? Just because I've been in magazines? When I met Jim, he started laughing and said 'Hey, I've seen you on TV.' And I said, 'Me too!' It was silly. So if we're idols, we're the most accessible idols there could ever be. And maybe that diminishes the cool factor, but who cares. At least it's real."

When I leave the arena in Houston that night the bus is already gone, driving through the dripping Texas midnight en route to New Orleans, and Atlanta, and Florida, and Europe, and the east coast, and Europe again, and the west coast, and so on. For the next few nights at around 8:20 P.M. I think of Jim and the rest of the band onstage at some faceless shed, playing the same songs to another ten thousand faceless fans. Still sweating. Still wanting to fall in love tonight. Still hoping someone else does too.

EIGHT

DEEP ELM

For Jessica Hopper, the end of emo happened quickly and mercilessly. "There was a definite time when emo was okay—both as music and as a term," she says, "but it became more of a caricature. I remember John [Szuch, the founder of Deep Elm Records] asking me 'Do you like emo?' And I was like, I don't call emo a genre. I like emo bands. All it was was an aesthetic allegiance—the records look nice, you're seeing shows in basements, and the music falls somewhere between Jawbox and Sunny Day. But when John asked me that it started to foster distrust. This dude is trying to hone in on our shit. All of a sudden there were these people that popped up who were trying to market themselves as emo; trying to sell it to people that were outside of our community. And you could spot them a mile away. Very quickly there was suddenly an emo product sold to meet this new demand for it—it was basically Sunny Day fans who wanted more Sunny Day."

Szuch worked in finances in New York City for much of the '90s before giving it up, moving to North Carolina, and founding an indie label misnamed after a Dallas suburb (Deep Ellum) out of his own pocket. As with many indie labels, the music Deep Elm releases closely mirrors Szuch's own tastes: punk rock, mixed with the melodramatic pomp and circumstance of Roger Waters–era Pink Floyd. The label's best-known product has been a multipart series of (mostly) unsigned band compilations titled "The Emo Diaries." Szuch claims the name was settled on after "The Indie Rock Diaries" was ruled out by the bands included on the first release (Jimmy Eat World and Samiam were both on major labels at the time) and "Emotional Diaries" wouldn't fit on the cover. The various volumes have an open submissions policy and stake a claim for emo as more of a shared aesthetic than a genre; the bands included hail from all over the world, and the musical styles range from racing punk to droopy, noodley electro. Still, the prevalance of the series—coupled with its maudlin subtitles *(The Silence of My Heart, I Guess This Is Goodbye)* and manic-depressive tattoo cover art—did much to codify the word "emo" and spread it to all corners of the underground. Despite this, Szuch vigorously denies Hopper's claims of exploitation: "How come there is nothing in the Deep Elm press kit about emo?" he wonders. "Is it just very poor marketing? Look, if I was trying to market music, I would have chosen rap. Music belongs to no one except those that made it."

Hopper's view is that of the punk traditionalist—the music belongs only to those who pay their dues to a scene, and mainstream, big-business marketing tactics are anathema to it. Some might point out the apparent contradiction in this argument—Hopper, after all, was hired by Jade Tree Records to be the Promise Ring's publicist. The irrefutable point remains, however, that as the '90s wore to a close, the music that was being labeled emo was making a connection with a larger and larger group of people. The aspects of it that were the most contagious—the sensitivity, hooks, and average-guy appeal—were also the easiest to latch onto, replicate, and mass market. As with any phenomenon— exactly like what happened with Sunny Day—when business enters into a high-stakes, highly personal sphere, things tend to go awry very quickly.

First to go were the hipsterati. Hopper, who had come close to producing a special "emo guide" issue of her zine, excised it from her vocabulary and from the official press bios of the bands with whom she worked. The more national magazines took notice ("Emotional Rescue" blared *Spin*'s late '90s genre trendpiece, which outed the Promise Ring as Sarah Maclachlan fans) and the more kids began identifying the music that they loved as emo, the more the bands ran for cover. "It was all a big joke to us," remembers Jason Gnewikow of the Promise Ring. "All of the bands would laugh about it—even as *Sassy* or whatever was naming us cute band of the month."

As fans threatened to storm the emo bandwagon, the groups couldn't jump off of it fast enough. The popularity and bankability of the word— if not the music—transformed an affiliation with the mid-nineties version of emo into an albatross. While Deep Elm continued to provide its small but dedicated fan base with ample servings of its take on emo without any hiccups, no label felt the burden of its recent history more keenly or, well, emotionally than Jade Tree Records.

JADE TREE

"I wish someone would explain it all to me," says Darren Walters, co-owner of Jade Tree, on the phone from his label's Delaware office. It's late in the afternoon on a Friday in September 2002 and he sounds tired. Very tired. "I mean, who are we? We're constantly searching for an answer. We've put out more records and worked harder this past year than in any other in the thirteen-year history of the label. But we still don't know what's going on." He sighs. "I guess we'll just keep doing what we're doing and see what happens. The music world is so crazy, you know?"

Thirty-two-year-old Walters and thirty-one-year-old Tim Owen have been friends for two decades and have run Jade Tree together since 1989. The label began as a part-time venture between the two of them after their individual labels (Walters High Impact and Owen's Action Packed) went nowhere—Owen had the vision thing, but no organization, Walters paid the bands, but couldn't find enough of them to pay. In 1994, the pair discovered and released music by two hugely influential bands, Lifetime and the Promise Ring, transforming Jade Tree into one of the most hyped, admired, and successful indie labels in the country. It also created the image of Jade Tree as the emo capital of the world, a tag Walters and Owen would spend the next half decade distancing themselves from.

In 2002, Walters suddenly found himself thrust into the industry's role as Rich Egan's public scold, the honorable ying to Egan's glitzy yang, and the first person on speed-dial when a major publication needs a foil to let a little bit of air out of its otherwise hugely inflated Vagrant stroke-piece. Walters has tut-tutted Egan's way of doing business in *Punk Planet* and in *Newsweek*, yet he's never met the man. Talking to Walters as the sun sets on the east coast he doesn't sound anything like a raging, DIY firebrand. He mostly sounds confused.

"We're at the cusp of figuring out if we're a boutique label or a big label," he says. "It's just getting so weird. All of our friends, our rivals, everyone we know is famous now except us. It's never been our goal, but Jimmy Eat World? How the hell did that happen? When it happened to Green Day it didn't affect us. But my old friend [and former Promise Ring bassist] Scott Schoenbeck is onstage at the MTV Awards with Dashboard Confessional. The Promise Ring is on Conan O'Brien. And I'm like—they were on my label! I cannot process that. It's beyond belief."

Walters grew up in Wilmington, Delaware, spending much of his youth traveling to see punk shows in nearby Philadelphia and Washington, D.C. "Hardcore, especially straight-edge hardcore, which is what I was into, was dying in the late '80s," he says. "It was getting harder and harder to find new bands. So after two 7-inches I decided to bag my label and concentrate on going to school and becoming a teacher. But in 1989, Tim asked me if I wanted to be his partner in a new label. It was going to be called Jade Tree and our parameters would be—there would be no parameters. Whatever we like, we will release records by. And we went from there."

At the time, Walters was touring with his own band ("it sounds trite but we were an emo band in 1992") and encountering a New Jersey hardcore lifer named Ari who had a band called Lifetime that no one particularly liked. "I had heard that the band was changing," Walters remembers, "but I blew it off. But in '94 they sent us some new demos and kept calling us, so we said what the hell. Lifetime had become amazing. It was the demos for what became *Hello Bastards*. And the world was not prepared for that record."

On *Hello Bastards* the trio took all that was great about the east coast hardcore scene and fused it with the tunefulness and undeniably honest barrage style of Jawbreaker. But while Jawbreaker was a national group, to kids on the east coast, members of Lifetime were their peers. Songs like "Rodeo Clown" rode exhilaratingly catchy riffs, relating fragments of a story specific enough for anyone to relate to and vague enough for anyone to fill in the blanks with their own lives. "Last time I saw you I tried to move through the crowd," Ari Katz screamed. "I was calling your name but the band played too loud." Lifetime turned its back on the irony and cynicism dominating the headlines and the world of indierock (one song was titled "Irony Is for Suckers") and sang love songs as pure as blues standards ("I'm Not Calling You" moaned the chorus again and again as Katz confessed, "I'm feeling quite pathetic"). While Jawbreaker sang about boats and drunks on the corner, Katz sang about the gym being neutral territory and misinterpreted looks at basement shows. It was a milieu immediately familiar to the hardcore audience, and setting it to music raised it beyond art towards something approaching catharsis. Lonely in high school in North Carolina, Adam Lazzara of Taking Back Sunday heard *Hello Bastards* and promptly had some of Katz's lyrics tattooed around his elbow. "I feel like that band saved my life," he says. "I picked up *Hello Bastards* and was just like, 'That's it!' I might as well have written it or they might as well have written it about me." The album was a lightning bolt to the national punk scene, selling tens of thousands of copies and putting Jade Tree on the radar, if not the map.

Around this time, Owen and Walters were still separated, running the nascent company from two different states. "Tim was living at the headquarters of Equal Vision Records in New York," Walters remembers. "They were primarily doing hardcore stuff at the time, but they had started as a Hare Krishna label. So the only two non-Krishnas living there were Tim and his roommate, Norm, the guitarist from Texas Is the Reason. When Texas came back from tour, he brought back a demo of this band called the Promise Ring. I heard it, and I heard some guy who can't sing. I thought they were kidding. But I kept playing the tape and there was something that grabbed me: For some reason, there was something about it that reminded me of U2. So I thought, what the hell. They were doing a huge amount of touring at the time, so when they came through Philly I took them out, bought them tons of Coca-Cola and candy bars and sealed the deal."

"That time period was extremely exciting," Walters says. "They came through Philly five or six times in 1996, and each time you could tell that new people were showing up. We could tell we were in the middle of something big with them because their fan base was growing so quickly. The band sold four thousand copies of [their Jade Tree debut] *30° Everywhere* on one tour before it was even out. I was amazed the entire time. I couldn't believe we finally had a band that people adored."

Just like that, a hobby was transformed into a business. "All of a sudden it's apparent that we can't operate the same way anymore. I was working as a product manager at a software company and Tim was still in New York. But I quit and he moved down here with me at the start of 1997, around the same time we released [a compilation of early Promise Ring singles] *The Horse Latitudes*. And wham. Home run, right out of the park. It was then we knew we'd reached a different plateau. We needed to give the next record everything it deserved." Among the things it deserved were biz conventions like publicity and radio promotions— all of the things that Walters and Owen had always, in true punk fashion, railed against. But all of a sudden it seemed natural: they had a band that people liked, that got raves in mainstream press, that sold thousands of copies all over the country. Major labels were calling them, the spotlight was bright. In response, the two tried to step back from the frenzy and rely on their original credo of personal satisfaction above all else.

"We wanted to avoid being pigeonholed," Walters says. "We didn't want to be genre specific. If you have bands getting bigger it identifies you. Which can be good, especially since no one latched onto our original idea, that we put out anything we like. Lifetime and the Promise Ring appealed to similar fans, but we knew we wanted to continue to push our boundaries. So we signed Joan of Arc. And Euphone. So now we have emo and instrumental jazz and avant-indie. And we thought wow, this is great. This is how we want it. Everything was taking off. But businesswise we knew we wanted to grow organically. We wanted to avoid giving out advances. We wanted to maintain our fifty-fifty split on profits. We wanted to be fair and treat bands fair. But all of a sudden you have questions you never thought about before. Like: what's fair? Because, at a certain level, bands need publicity. But who's gonna pay for publicity? And what are people gonna think about us? Publicity seems like the antithesis of what punk is about. We were thinking, Ian [MacKaye] wouldn't do this, would he? What are we gonna do?" He pauses for a moment. "I fucking hate what Egan said in *Newsweek*, about offering the bands the 'best of major labels,' because that's what we were trying to do! That's not what they do. We want to make our bands live by their own means, help support them in any way we can, but without compromising our ethics or theirs. So we decided we could live with publicity and radio. And then there's video. I always thought punk was against video. But one of my favorite bands is Duran Duran, and they did beautiful things with video. So I couldn't think of a reason to be against them anymore. What the hell—the Promise Ring wanted to do one and it's not harming anybody. We just tried to ride the line with how we got bigger."

Punk rock, like most attractive ideologies, works best in theory. In practice there are a million and one variables to consider, reject, assume, and dodge. Walters lived those choices—the tough, money-related ones—in real time, and his voice takes on a mix of wistfulness and stubborn pride when reflecting back on it all.

"Dischord and [venerable Chicago indie label] Touch and Go were our models all along because they're constantly lauded for their business practices. You can't find anything bad about them. But we met with Ian MacKaye a few years ago and it was funny—he just didn't see the point of having a publicist. And the truth is, if you tie yourself to any genre or locale or idea, you're sunk. You'll get noticed, but not in the long run. We realized then that we wanted to create our own business model. More than what our idols had done but still less than the majors. We decided to do all this stuff—radio, press—but in a cool ethical way so we can attract bands that want to get bigger, but without all the cheesy major-label games. All that shit is too complicated."

I mention to him that what he's saying sounds awfully close to what Rich Egan had told me a few months ago, but Walters is quick to highlight the differences between the two labels, particularly when it comes to money—that Egan does everything for the bands, that he's unapologetic about wanting his bands to be filthy rich.

"A label that gives $100,000 advances gives bands an inflated sense of themselves. We do things on the cheap here. I don't want to make one band a great experiment, throw money at it to see if it works. My goal is longevity. If I were to throw $100,000 at something, this label would be sunk. My responsibility is to the artists that I have now, and its for the length of their careers. One of those advances is the recording budget for five other bands. I can't do that. That's money out of everyone else's pocket. I try to make people aware of how their money is spent and what the return on it is so they can make a comfortable living."

There's a lot of integrity in Jade Tree Records and a lot of quality. But there's also a whiff of the bridesmaid. "We had the emo crown when it wasn't something to be stolen," Walters says. "I wasn't so afraid of it then. But now everyone says it's gonna be like grunge, it's gonna kill us all. Did Vagrant steal it from us? I don't know. Do I want to even say we had it in the first place? Our biggest band was Promise Ring, and they defined us. We grew together, so much so that we always say it was like a chicken and the egg thing—who created who? And in the end that's why we parted ways. Things got testy, they wanted more from us because they feel that they created us. We want to do certain things because their success was partly due to us. No one wanted to budge on it. So they signed to Anti [Records, a boutique label with ties to punk monolith Epitaph Records]."

In mid-2002, the Promise Ring released its long-awaited fourth album, and first away from Jade Tree, *Wood/Water*. The album was recorded over a long period in England with famed Britpop producer Stephen Street and it shocked many on its arrival. Gone were the chunky, pop hooks—in fact, gone were the hooks altogether. In their place were pastoral, meandering melodies, whiffs of texture, and downcast rhythms. On the album's best track, "Stop Playing Guitar," singer Davey Von-bohlen openly questions why he's making music in the first place and if the world in general wouldn't be a better place if he just read more books instead. Immaculately and admirally constructed, the album is pro-foundly joyless; so intent was the band on restraining its more familiar, exuberant impulses that *Wood/Water* sounds like pranksters trying des-perately not to crack a smile in chapel. To date, the record has sold 50,000 fewer copies than the Ring's previous Jade Tree release, *Very Emergency*. In late summer 2002, the Promise Ring went on tour, open-ing for their former support act Jimmy Eat World. When Davey strummed his acoustic guitar to thousands of eager teenagers at a sold-out Roseland Ballroom in New York City, he was greeted with implacable silence, the sight of an entire generation of music fans regarding him like they had just caught their dad moshing. The members of the Promise Ring are musicans and they can make whatever sort of album and music they want; it's not for us to judge where their muse takes them. It did seem sad, though, and more than a little unnecessary.

"The period that surrounded the release of *Nothing Feels Good* defined my life," says Walters. "It's so definitive in terms of emo, in terms of everything. It was a classic and I don't really want to hear what they do after that. I want my same old Promise Ring. So they went their way and our relationship has survived. We saw Davey backstage at the Jimmy Eat World show in Philly and he told me, 'If we were doing the same thing now that we did then, we'd be rich. But we don't want to be doing it.'"

Walters yearns for the glory days of Promise Ring, when the phenomenon was part and parcel with the music, when the songs were fresh but the community they engendered was thrilling. When the band decided to turn its back on the past, to grow and evolve, Walters, on some level, wasn't ready to go with them. And yet, despite his protestations, the same could be said of Jade Tree. In 2002, the label released Cub Country, an acoustic Jets to Brazil sideproject, the first post-major-label album by NYC glamcore veterans Girls Against Boys, and the debut record by Denali, a dirge-filled marriage of goth, punk, and trip-hop. Sometimes the label seems willfully obtuse in its selection of releases; Walters's confusion is evident in Jade Tree's scattershot schedule.

The label and partnership will survive. Walters and Owen have never compromised themselves or their bands. Their musicians will remain comfortable for as long as they make music, and possibly long after that. But stability only gets you so far in such a high-stakes, highly emotional business.

Near the end of our conversation, Walters again sounds melancholy. "Sometimes," he says, "I feel like we created the boat and then missed it altogether."

DRIVE-THRU RECORDS

If Rich Egan and Vagrant Records divined a formula that would bring the underworld to the world, and Jimmy Eat World built the bridge from the old world to the new world (and Jade Tree drove off in search of a way around the divide), then it was Richard and Stefanie Reines of Drive-Thru Records who figured out how to sell the bridge. A brother and sister duo from New Jersey, the Reines transitioned smoothly from being the biggest pop-punk fans in Southern California, to becoming lord and lady of an empire of the stuff. From cheerleaders of once ignored bands like Blink-182 and Jimmy Eat World on their contentious and addictive mid-nineties public access TV broadcast, *Sideshow*, the Reines poured their enthusiasm, confidence, and quick tempers into Drive-Thru, a major-label-aligned hit factory for bands that fit the Reines's mold to a T: young, polite boys who write shameless hooks.

Drive-Thru today is the McDonalds of emo—no matter what you buy, you're guaranteed a high-quality, nearly identical product. Drive-Thru T-shirts and CDs dominate Hot Topic stores, the much maligned yet hugely influential (and ageless) mall chain that traffics exclusively in teenage culture. They are the public face of the pin- and patch-scarred backpacks that line public fountains and food courts the world over.

On the phone from their office in Sherman Oaks, California, the Reineses sound like teenagers themselves. Though both over thirty, they jump over each other's words, finish each other's sentences, and swear like sailors. "Me and Richard have always loved things that are in some way, shape, or form catchy," says Stefanie. "When we were doing our TV show in 1996, we were the ones that took Blink-182 into major labels and told them that they had to sign them. When they were like 'We don't get it,' we were like fuck this! We'll start our own label."

Firmly established on the principal of only releasing music that, in Stefanie's words, achieves the level of "If I don't fucking listen to this CD in the shower, in the car, while I'm brushing my teeth tonight, I will fucking lose my mind," the Reineses ran Drive-Thru out of their garage until one of their first bands, a motley trio of post-Blink-182 goofballs called FenixTX, attracted major-label interest. When the band decided to go with MCA, the label did as well, entering into a partnership that provided the Reineses with cash and capital in return for a clause in Drive-Thru bands' contracts that dictated MCA's right to call any one of them up to the big leagues at any moment, without any discussion what-soever.

Drive-Thru's biggest band is New Found Glory, a likeable quintet of young guys from the same South Florida scene that begat Dashboard Confessional. The group has amiable members with un-rock-star names like Cyrus Palooki, and a bassist who goes to great lengths to display his everyguy potbelly, New Found Glory's songs have tightly wound cho-ruses and subject matter more appropriate to cafeteria gossip than the *Billboard* charts. While the music is all about crowd-surfing and losing yourself in the infectious swirl of community, the lyrics proudly display broken hearts and hidden depth. "I'm sick of smiling / and so is my jaw / can't you see my front is crumbling down?" asked the first song on *Sticks and Stones,* the New Found Glory album that stunned the world when it debuted at number four in the summer of 2002. It's an interesting contradiction—the celebration of misery, the simultaneous privileging and subsuming of the self—but one that's pure emo, no matter what the band or its label says. The band has spent the majority of its existence on the road, playing night after night to thousands of screaming fans who know every word to every one of its songs. Their videos use this base of strength to their advantage, mocking the clichés of traditional, self-serious, T&A-ridden clips. Indeed, as much of New Found Glory's popularity is due to their untroubled relationship to fame and the mass market as it is their uncomplicated music.

"We don't want to put ourselves high up on a pedestal," says New Found Glory singer Jordan Pundik. "There'll be girls at our shows acting all crazy and we're like calm down. I'm just a kid too. And that's why we sign autographs until everyone's gone, why we hang out with our fans. Because that's the way I wanted it to be when I was going to shows."

Pundik's cell phone fades in and out as the band's tour bus crosses the Rocky Mountains. The previous night was a riotous show in front of eight thousand fans in Salt Lake City and Pundik's voice is scratchy and hoarse. Tonight is Denver. "If it wasn't for all of our fans telling all of their friends about us, we wouldn't be where we are now. I don't take anything for granted. Like, everything we sing about is real. Real things that happen to us and people in general. And they can easily relate to that. We're not up there with leather pants and a crazy light show. We're real kids too. And I think that's what's great about punk in general. It's accessible. That's why I got into punk: it seemed real to me. A real feeling."

At Vagrant, Rich Egan has built a punk brand founded on antielitism and simplicity. The bands at Drive-Thru are of an even younger generation—one for which punk isn't intimidating and secretive. Rather, it's the opposite—a world where it's downright *normal* for people to be upfront with their emotions, to be kind to each other, and to do what they most love to do. A world where a bunch of ordinary kids from the ratty side of Florida can top the charts and a tempestuous brother and sister can become record moguls based solely on their love of a killer hook. With the doors blown off and the bar, if not lowered, then at least seriously changed, anyone is now free to crash the punk party.

"A lot of our fans are not punk," says Pundik. "They're normal kids. Last night there were a lot of nicely dressed girls right up at the front.

And I don't care. I'm not limiting the band to just one type of person. As long as they're enjoying the music and feeling something, I think that's great."

"Any scene that becomes elitist sucks," says Richard Reines vehemently. "I hate it, I despise it. I love it when it's not 'I'm cooler than you,' because we were always on the other side of things. We had our own zine when we were fourteen and we'd hang out at hotels to meet the bands. But back then, every band thought they were rock stars. They had asshole managers that would push them right past us. I was like, 'Are they blind? There are kids out there!' I never forgot that. Now I'll go to shows and if I see kids wearing Drive-Thru T-shirts, I'll grab them and have New Found Glory meet them. We do that for all the kids because that's what I always wished happened to us. We're all about getting music to kids. We want the bands to be heard. If people have a problem with that, fuck you."

Drive-Thru wears its populist mantra like a badge of honor. "Look," says Richard, with indignant anger rising in his voice, "unless you're a hippie living solely off the land, then you're not punk rock. Everything is owned by a corporation. Even the food you eat. The Sex Pistols were on a major label. So were the Ramones. So either you really claim it and go for it, or you're gonna shut the fuck up. I'm not fucking punk rock because I don't want to be like those other assholes. Our bands know what's like to be a fan, they know where they came from. They don't hide backstage, they're not cokeheads. Everything—fan and band—is completely on the same level."

Drive-Thru backs up this idea through its signings—a seemingly interchangeable crop of young, vaguely punky boy bands that produce eminently hummable guitar pop in the vein of Blink-182 and New Found Glory. Themes are limited to girl trouble and hangin' with the dudes. The bands hail from all over the country, but come out on Drive-Thru as missing pieces in one large, uber-regional scene. One of the better examples of these bands is Pennsylvania's The Starting Line. Within two years of forming, the group saw its first album, *Say It Like You Mean It,* debut on the *Billboard* charts.

"We owe our entire career to the internet," says guitarist Matt Watts. Bored and isolated in the overwhelmingly suburban wasteland of Bucks

County, Pennsylvania, Watts and two friends went searching for a singer on America Online's user profiles. The only potential frontman who emailed back was then-fourteen-year-old Kenny Vasoli. After posting some demos on mp3.com, the young band was offered its first-ever gig opening for Saves the Day. A few months later, a California indie label with loose ties to Drive-Thru contacted the band about putting out a record. When the record eventually did come out on Drive-Thru in 2002, it was produced by Mark Trombino, the man responsible for producing all of the band members' all-time favorite album, Jimmy Eat World's *Clarity*. The band's songs were earnest and likable, their live show rough but energetic, but thanks to the nascent national punk network, the band managed to, in Rich Egan's words, skip directly from kindergarten to graduation. Their songs are perfectly polished, yet emotionally raw and immature. With titles like "Saddest Girl Story" and "The Drama Summer," they seem more suited to yearbook signatures than a punk record. The Starting Line, quite literally, *are* their fans.

"After we play we're always out there trying to meet as many kids as possible," says Watts. "There's not always time but we make time. The kids are our age, after all, so it's cool just to relate to 'em, see what's going on in their lives."

"They're not weird, they're just like us," agrees guitarist Mike Golla.

"That's what's great about Drive-Thru," says Pundik. "They find young bands that suck when they start and get them sorted out, put them on tour, tell them to write good songs, and be cool to their fans. They are so supportive."

The Reineses like to say that they run their label like a family—a line that nearly all of their bands happily parrot. ("If Drive-Thru signs a band, we know we can automatically be friends with them," says Watts cheerily.) To back up their claims, the label released a sampler in late 2001 with a mafia theme entitled *Welcome to the Family*. The CD was distributed exclusively at Hot Topic stores and came packaged in a CD-sized pizza box. While aspects of the project—the *Godfather*-like cover image, the pictures of bands acting out classic scenes from various mob movies—are cute, the overall impression is one of music as product, not just an all-around good time. Not only are the disc's eighteen tracks by eleven bands mostly indistinguishable from one another, the most prominent aspect of the packaging is a full-color foldout catalog featuring members of New Found Glory modeling official label merchandise and mugging for the camera. There are over thirty-three T-shirts displayed, along with countless stickers, pins, posters, patches, hoodies, hats, keychains, and even playing cards. It's one-stop shopping for the dedicated fan, but it's also superficial self-definition—tellingly, none of the prices are listed on the sheet—as immediate, reproducible, and disposable as a pizza.

Unsurprisingly, Richard Reines sees it differently. "There is no emphasis of merchandise over music," he says emphatically.

"Up until recently all I did was wear band T-shirts," says Stefanie. "When you're heavily into music you want people to know what you're into."

"It's how you make friends," says Richard. "You see someone wearing a shirt and guys can meet girls, girls can meet guys."

"It's just an extension of the kids' taste and us being involved with it," says Stefanie. "Plus we really do try to make high-quality merch."

"I mean, why not a Starting Line shirt over some skate company's shirt?" asks Richard. "This way you're supporting people, not a company."

Everyone associated with Drive-Thru seems to have a similar approach to punk rock. It's a for-profit venture, and they refuse to be bullied into feeling bad about that just because of opinions or aesthetics.

"We've worked our asses off for years, struggling, trying to scrounge together money," says Stefanie. "Our bands are putting their lives on the line and I want to be able to help them and help ourselves. I want to make a living doing this—and isn't that the goal in life? You always hear that having a career in music isn't OK, but it's OK to be an actuary or whatever. All these other indies play the game of 'hide-the-major'—like [polemic punk outpost] Fat Wreck Chords, who are distributed by RED, which is owned by Sony. We want to be the label that proves that being associated with a major isn't selling out and isn't lame."

"People always call bands sellouts," says The Starting Line's Watts. "But the example I always use is: if your dad got a promotion at work, you'd be so excited for him. He goes to work every day, he wakes up at 5 A.M., works his ass off. And if he accepts more money for what he does, no one would ever call him a sellout. And this is the same thing. We give up everything for this."

Allowing that, it is also worth noting that Drive-Thru is selling a 100-percent cotton pair of The Starting Line thong underwear to the band's majority female audience.

"Thongs are cool," says Golla sheepishly. "We like girls."

NINE

SAD GIRL STORIES:
WOMEN AND EMO

Though they may disagree on almost everything else, one characteristic shared by Vagrant, Drive-Thru, *and* Deep Elm is that none of the labels has a single female artist signed to its roster (as of this writing, two Jade Tree bands had female members). Though emo—and, to a certain degree, punk—has always been a typically male province, the monotony of the labels' gender perspective can be overwhelming. If the stereotypical emo boy was tear stained and sensitive—the truly romantic and special one left alone on Friday nights because he's too shy to ask out the most popular girl in the class who's secretly pining for him—then the triumph of that lonely boy's aesthetic has resulted in yet another groupthink mentality. If the sensitive boys had once quietly cursed their fate and the girls who ignored or dumped them in the privacy of their bedrooms, now that they had microphones, amplifiers, and an established nationwide network of fans, they were more than happy to scream their litany of complaints as loud as they could.

Though Vagrant and Drive-Thru's emo acts are a long way from the naked misogyny of hair-metal or some hip-hop, there is something equally disturbing in their one-sided fury at all of the females who did them wrong. The way typical emo bands sing about women is a volatile mixture of Ian MacKaye's strident puritanism—as in sex equals fear, failure, weakness—and self-obsessed sexist solipsism. If mid-nineties emo was mostly about not meeting girls or running away from them, emo's national generation dumbed it down and amped it up. Now emo songwriters were one-sided victims of heartbreak, utterly wronged and ready to sing about it, with the women having no chance to respond.

"I actually think emo today is more misogynist and macho than rap-metal or hip-hop," says Jessica Hopper. "Ever since it was stripped of its politics, it keeps women on a pedestal or on our backs. It relegates us to the role of muse or heartbreaker, an object of either misery or desire. Emo just builds a cathedral of man pain and then celebrates its validation."

Vagrant's most successful artist, Chris Carrabba of Dashboard Confessional, wrote an entire album about his broken heart. His hit single is addressed to a nameless woman who has left him alone "cuddling close to blankets and sheets," staring at strands of her hair which are "everywhere / screaming infidelities." The woman on the record is never named, even as she transforms from salvation ("Living in Your Letters") to ruin (pretty much everything else). Carrabba validates our trust more than some of his labelmates because, in the end, he is just as brutal with himself as he is with the heartbreaker. But for the most part, emo is a monologue, an entire genre built on the principal of *j'accuse;* a kiss-off with no one returning the kiss.

"I wish that I could hate you so bad / but I can't," goes one memorable lyric by Taking Back Sunday, and it best sums up the contemporary emo approach to relationships. Songs are, all at once, an admission of sadness and a celebration of that sadness. Singers revel in their misery and suffering to an almost ecstatic degree, but with a limited use of subtlety or language. It tends to come off like Rimbaud relocated to the food court. Drive-Thru band Allister titled its album *Dead Ends and Girlfriends,* while The Starting Line dedicates a particularly bouncy number to "a girl who turned this boy to stone." New Found Glory's biggest hit was a song called "My Friends Over You," an incredibly bold anthem celebrating the hoary cliché of bros before hoes:

> . . .
> *Though you swear that you are true*
> *I'd still pick my friends over you . . .*

The song is a party and the video a wacky pep rally, but the message places all the blame on the woman in question—even though the protagonist led the woman on, it's still her fault for sleeping with him. He chooses a life of hijinks with his band over a meaningful relationship—or even sexual encounter—with the woman.

On "3,720 to 1," The Benjamins, another young Drive-Thru band, sing about a fantastical mission to outer space that's really a thinly veiled Dear Jean letter. The singer has chosen to abandon his girlfriend in order to save the universe. By couching their fear of commitment in the context of a juvenile space fantasy the band is not just celebrating nostalgia, it's living it like a code. Safe in their band world from the female Scyllas and Charybdises that lurk just outside of it, The Benjamins choose to watch *Star Wars* again instead of doing something really risky, like, say, going to the school dance. This sort of emo with its female phobia celebrates a perpetual adolescence. (The cover of New Found Glory's *Sticks and Stones* depicts a boy and a girl wrestling on the cover, and then making out on the inside.) The singers may pretend to be hanging themselves out to dry by copping to crying and being sad at night, but in the heightened emo environment, where broken hearts are badges of honor, it's a hollow boast. Their scars are a sign of pride— you're the one onstage bragging about how upset you are—but there's no attempt at actual conversation or relationship building.

Some emo bands take cues from the darker end of hardcore and make songs that can be heard as virulently antiwomen, couching disturbing physically violent sentiments in sensitive, poppy clothing. Saves the Day's Chris Conley, for one, sometimes rides his obsession with bodily pain to dangerously misogynistic conclusions. "Rocks Tonic Juice Magic" is one of the most musically engaging and addictive songs on *Through Being Cool,* but its lyrics counterpoint a tale of dark obsession with glimpses of juvenile romance. It begins, "Let me take this awkward saw / and run it against your thighs / cut some flesh away / I'll carry this piece of you with me" and later continues the violent theme with, "I'll take my rusty spoons / and dig out your blue eyes." The song is fueled by bitterness, a common punk theme, but the protagonist seems fixated on removing all agency from the girl who mistreated him—he wants to sever her legs, taking away her movement, and her eyes, eliminating the messy reality of her own point of view. He wants to buy her lemonade solely to throw it in her face and make her cry. And yet at the end of all of this bloodshed, he's still swooning, wishing he "could somehow" win her back, missing their long-gone "nights under ocean skies." He's neither grown up nor moved on. While it's impossible to know what Conley's intentions truly were with the song, it is more than a little disconcerting to realize that the lyrics that cause thousands of fresh-faced teens to sing along in unison are as brutal as any of Eminem's well-publicized and pilloried revenge fantasies.

Brand New, a young emo band from Long Island, got some national exposure for their infectious single "Jude Law and a Semester Abroad." But even the song's why-hadn't-anyone-thought-of-this-first subject matter is marred by spiteful fantasies:

> *Even if her plane crashes tonight she'll find some way*
> *to disappoint me*
> *By not burning in the wreckage*
> *Or drowning at the bottom of the sea*

Brand New cop a familiar emo pose in their disappointment. Even when the evil girlfriend dies, it's still all about the singer; she's letting him down even in death. But even "Jude Law . . ." seems like petulant, harmless venting when compared to fellow Long Islanders Glassjaw, a band that was signed to Warner Brothers Records on the strength of the emo boom, despite lyrics that would make even the Hillside Strangler blush:

> *you filthy whore*
> *shut up and swallow my pride for me*
> . . .
> *I don't give a fuck about your dignity*
> *that's the bastard in me*

Thankfully, violent fantasies such as these are prevalent but not dominant. The most common treatment of women is a more insidious type of sexism, an immature vision of women that's all-too-appealing to young people years away from having their first serious relationship. As with many of its other themes, emo's standard treatment of women has been reduced to a Möbius strip—never stretching into anything new, only parroting opinions, hopes, fears, and anger that already existed in the all-too-eager crowd. From imagery to lyrics, women are powerless victims—even when they've been proactive and ended a relationship, they're perpetually denied the last word.

Vagrant's Hot Rod Circuit released an album called *Sorry About Tomorrow* that featured a cover image of an emotionally ravaged young girl hugging herself to stop from crying. The band has already apologized for hurting her—even if they haven't done anything yet. The girl is voiceless and faceless, and yet it is still possible to catch a tantalizing glimpse of cleavage. She is sexy in her bottomed-out desolation—the band's and the consumers' only role is as voyeur.

Something Corporate—a name either obnoxious or charming depending on your placement within the punk divide—is a young band on Drive-Thru/MCA that released its debut album in late 2002. The album, *Leaving Through the Window*, is actually a helpful primer of all of the above points. The record cover depicts a gorgeous, statuesque model hanging out of a window—she's clearly distressed, but not so distressed as to forget her makeup. Our glimpse is godlike and omniscient—we're both looking down on her and looking down her shirt. The overall effect, perhaps unintentional, is that we are on the other side of the window from which she's leaving, that she's running away from us.

The songs on the record take the opposite tack, presenting the band's nineteen-year-old songwriter Andrew McMahon as the emotionally stable wise man ready and willing to aid any confused young women in his path. *Leaving*'s first song is an overwrought piano ballad called "I Want to Save You" and appears to be the emo boy's wet dream writ large. There's a sad yet beautiful girl who wakes up after another anonymous one-night stand: The girl is "messed up" (i.e., she has sex and parties), but all she really needs is to be told that she's beautiful—and, since she is, that's a selfless act McMahon is only more than too happy to perform. The chorus builds to a crescendo of simplicity: "I want to save you!" McMahon sings over and over again. The swollen romantic nostalgia of emo seemingly reaches its nadir in this one song—McMahon wants to be her Romeo but he'd never, ever, like, sacrifice himself for her. He is the sun and the son; she's just some confused chick who could use a good shoulder to cry on and then, maybe, a hickey. Dude.

"This sort of stuff is an emotional outlet with no sense of balance or responsibility," says Jessica Hopper. "It's incredibly self-indulgent. There's no culpability and no personality. Women are just things that do things. Emo in 2002 is just a passive-aggressive rewrite of the Rolling Stones' 'Under My Thumb.'"

Despite this, the curious thing about emo is that its fans are democratically split evenly along gender lines, with some bands—Dashboard Confessional and The Starting Line chief among them—*more* popular with women than men. "Part of the reason for that is the same reason with everything," says Hopper, "because the dude is cute. It's also expressive—in its way—which automatically appeals to teenage girls. There's also a fetishization of the emotional aspect of desire. But when I was a teenager and was into Sonic Youth it was partly because [guitarist] Thurston [Moore] was cute, but I also wanted to play guitar like him. There are no role models for young women to feel like they have the power to take an active role in this scene."

The only female-fronted band that gets lumped in with the general crowd of emo groups is Florida's The Rocking Horse Winner—it like all emo bands, disputes the claim. In this case, however, it's true. The band plays sunny, chiming, uncomplicated guitar pop in the style of The Sundays or The Cranberries. The only reason the Rocking Horse Winner is considered emo is because lead singer Jolie Lindholm has dueted on record with her friend Chris Carrabba from Dashboard Confessional. "Personally, I don't think there are enough women playing in bands," says Lindholm. "I have a hard time finding bands with female singers that I'll listen to. Maybe it's just 'cause girls aren't that interested."

"It does bother me," says eighteen-year-old Whitney Borup from Utah. "I get sick of hearing guys complaining about their girl problems sometimes because I'm from the other point of view. I do want a girl to sing about boy problems so it would be easier to relate. I think a girl emo band is far overdue. But I think that itself is part of the appeal of emo. It's boys saying stereotypically 'girl' things and being accepted for it. There's this feeling that guys just don't care, that they break up with girls because of 'getting action' and nothing else. And emo boys don't seem to be like that. Plus boys can do raw emotion better with their voices than girls can—mostly because of anatomy. I know that when I started a band, I just didn't like the sound of it. I couldn't scream right."

"No girl has ever come up to us and said, 'Hey you guys, we want to say what we have to say with our own songs,'" says New Found Glory's Pundik. "Our songs are about relationships, but anyone can relate to it. Even though we might say 'girl' in the song, girls come up to us and say that they've had the same problems with their boyfriends and put it into their own perspective."

Despite emo's purported sensitivity, many of the old gender fault lines remain. Perhaps when this generation of emo fans begins to form their own bands, a new female-voiced wave of heartbreak songs will emerge—perhaps they'll be more articulate and nuanced, perhaps not. In the meantime, the place where the real male/female dialogue is occurring and the rules are being rewritten is not on record, but online, where the huge number of women fans have their say and assert themselves in varied and surprising ways.

It's also possible that fearing for the ears of young female fans is presumptuous—that the unifying appeal of emo may just be that, at heart, emotional devastation knows no gender.

"It doesn't really bother me," says eighteen-year-old Iris Chi. "Whenever they sing out about how they hate this girl or that girl, I just change it in my head so that the 'she' becomes a 'he.' Eventually a girl or a guy will break someone's heart, so it doesn't matter if they target a certain sex. I think all love problems are the same."

TEN

With the glut of media at our fingertips in the beginning of the twenty-first century, attention spans are shorter, nostalgia is now instant, and every semester—every day—can bring new love and new obsessions. A label like Drive-Thru—with its uniformity of product and high turnover rate—guarantees a fresh, personalized emo product for each of these micro-generations. From New Found Glory's songs about the glory days of high school, to Something Corporate and The Starting Line's songs about being in high school while you're writing the songs, every potential rift in fandom is addressed. On an early EP, New Found Glory covered ironic, iconic pop songs in a cheeky manner. Their choices ranged from Cyndi Lauper, to Limahl from '80s-trivia-answer Kajagoogoo. Only two years later, label mates Allister covered an ironic, iconic single by the Backstreet Boys in a similarly cheeky manner. It took years to get from Rites of Spring to the *Emo Diaries;* it took months to go from a New Jersey high school to Madison Square Garden. Everything is sped up, and should a Drive-Thru band decide to grow up or mature their sound, there will be a hungry quartet of boys waiting in the wings to take their momentum and their fan base.

Indeed, popular culture has become so accelerated that the current crop of emo bands are already primed to build on the success of their "ancestors" from only two or three years previous. When Jimmy Eat World went platinum and New Found Glory debuted on the *Billboard* charts, major labels began binging on emo-affiliated bands like it was last call on the buffet line. Emo groups with only a dozen shows under their belts became the objects of million-dollar bidding wars; indie debuts were underwritten by forward-thinking big-league A&R guys with deep pockets. With teen pop fading, integrity became a selling point, a blast fax from on high that would help bridge the credibility gap between the Napster-abused record industry and the Napster-starved public. Backstreet Boy Nick Carter released a solo album featuring real guitars. Christina Aguilera's guttertrash R&B makeover tanked, replaced on MTV by neofolk teenagers like Michelle Branch and Vanessa Carlton singing about beauty and hand-holding. Avril Lavigne replaced Britney Spears not because she's any less produced or pretty, but because her image (skateboarding, hiding behind bangs, men's ties) reads as more "real."

Punk is historically nihilistic, based on subverting the system and striving against it, whatever the system may be. The punk descendants who populated the alt-rock boom of the early '90s at least acted like they hated being on MTV, sneering on the red carpet at award shows. The kids in bands today came of age in a time of optimistic skepticism about the system—when they buy into it, they at least feel like they know what they're becoming a part of. And they're willing to buy into it in order to guarantee a big audience, because not only did Nirvana prove that that's possible, it's kinda the point, right?

The middle-class suburban kids buying these records are children of a very different late-nineties mentality: greed might not be good, but wealth certainly is. For many of these kids, their first taste of punk came via the middlebrow jokers in Blink-182, who played the role of punks without actually being them. Perhaps in the *Total Request Live,* glitz-swollen world they made their mark in, they were punk*er*—but like Eminem, they never took on any target more difficult than a sitting duck. Their breakthrough video showed the tastefully pierced and tattooed threesome aping Backstreet Boys dance moves; of course, only the MTV watchers knew the difference. To adult eyes, there was little to distinguish the "dangerous" looking Blinks from AJ, the inked-up and leather-clad "dangerous" Backstreet Boy.

In the go-go dot-com bubble, everyone had money: what made you punk was what you did with it. Somewhere in the midst of this, "punk" came to equate *Jackass*—the DIY comedy show on MTV where the laughs derived from dwarves crashing skateboards and dudes stapling their ass cheeks together. Thanks to a dominant mainstream culture and the prevalence of MTV, everyone was in on the same joke. Every court needs a jester or two: Blink might parody Backstreet, and Eminem might mock Britney, but they were all buddy-buddy at the award shows. There was no discord; everyone's goals were the same: cash.

"It's a little bit disturbing," says Dreamworks' Luke Wood. "When the music business consolidated in the '90s, the creative people were pushed out, leaving only the conservative, mercenary types. This creates a problem when you have diverse scenes and styles, and eliminates the hoary idea of signing a band for a career. It has a lot to do with desperation and a need for instantaneous returns. Balance this against the pace of youth marketing becoming totally out of control, and what in the grunge years might have been a four- to six-year cultural cycle is today *maybe* four to seven months. It's crazy out there.

"The industry really does look at emo as the new raprock, or the new grunge. I don't think anyone is listening to the music that's being made—they're thinking of how they're going to take advantage of the sound's popularity at retail. In the shadow of raprock and teenpop, everyone looked away from the underground for a moment and the seeds started to sprout again. But all the bands that used that time to develop national fan bases—Jimmy Eat World, Saves the Day, Thursday—those bands are signed and spoken for. If I could convince the whole industry to look away, to put emo back in the basement and let it grow for three years, I certainly would.

"The bands that have the stamina, leverage, and fan base to exist in the major label system are already signed. If you sign a band solely because they sound like Saves the Day meets Jimmy Eat World, you're basically waiting for a novelty radio hit. Look, you don't need a major label to find that band now—indie distribution is fine and besides, the kids all get it online anyway. But instead the industry goes through the motions, through the feeding frenzy, and it's gonna be a disaster. It's a movie we've all seen many times and, unfortunately, the ending is never any different."

But maybe it just will be. Integrity may now be bought, packaged, aggressively marketed, and sold, but the truth is that records—at least as we used to know them—no longer exist. Today's emo fans make up the first generation that thinks of downloading first, shopping second.

There is no real need for a tangible product. The attraction is all about emotion anyway—and there is little more intangible as that. With indie bands brokering lucrative contracts and major labels scouring basement shows, the traditions have been muddied, the script flipped. The heart of emo returns to the heart of punk rock: the live show and, above all, the community. But in today's world, community means something very different. Emo has always been a listener-determined and listener-driven subculture. With the advent of the internet, subculture is now open to everyone, anywhere, anytime. An intimate underground can now stretch from ocean to ocean, from rec halls to arenas, from MP3s to MTV. What does selling out mean when no one is buying?

In their video for "The Taste of Ink," a scruffy punk band called The Used plays a show in a cramped, sweaty basement. The kids in attendance are everykids, working dead-end jobs, having hopeless romances. They live in a suburban wasteland. Their eyes are dead. Yet when they get to the basement, they feel alive. They sing along, they dance and jump, they point their fingers back at the band on stage who are singing the words the kids feel in their hearts: "and I'll savor every moment of this / so here I am / alive at last." The kids and the band raise their middle fingers to the roof and celebrate their youth, their moment.

The Used's debut album is on Warner Brothers Records. The band is from a tiny town in Utah.

BETWEEN RESISTANCE AND COMMUNITY

Down in the basement, The Insurgent is playing. Loudly. "I saw the signs advertising decay!" its members scream to the thirty people standing in the front, cramped against the wood-paneled walls, against each other. The music is blisteringly loud, archly political, and aggressively sloppy, the kids in the crowd are so amped up that they keep getting in the way—stealing the mic, pushing the guitarist, tripping over the wires.

Upstairs someone's mom is making vegetarian tacos for everyone. Outside, it's the suburbs. A quiet, sunny weekend afternoon on Long Island. From the street you can almost hear the thrashing. But it's hard to pick it out over the anodyne buzz saw of lawn mowers and the Jets game broadcast.

"Saw the graveyards on your strip-mall street," screams The Insurgent. "Saw the standards I refuse to meet!"

At the ripe age of twenty-one, Ben Holtzman and Joe Carroll are veterans of their local DIY punk scene. From early infatuation with the MTV-ready sugar rush of Green Day through to the proactive euphoria of mosh pits in storm cellars, the two have taken what they love best about punk and channeled it into a design for life, a call to action. In 2001, the two made a visceral, engaging documentary entitled *Between Resistance and Community: The Long Island DIY Punk Scene* that captures a bare-bones, political strain of punk standing in direct contrast to the pop hooks and comforting hugs of Rich Egan's emo empire.

"Growing up on Long Island, you get the impression that all you're supposed to do is consume," says Holtzman over coffee. "That's your place in the world. If anything, you're supposed to grow up, go to college, get a good job, settle down, get a wife, and be part of that system. Continue consuming. And that's your life. A lot of kids in the Long Island DIY scene look at their parents as examples and say, we don't really want that life. Your parents are miserable, the only happiness they get is from buying things. Punk, for a lot of these kids, is about rejecting that script and trying to create something else, something not based on consumption but on community values."

"On the one hand I'm very angry about how we're told to live our lives and what I see as my potential future on Long Island," continues Carroll. "On the other hand, the way I want to fix that is by caring a lot and working with people and building communities. It's that anger that leads to wanting to build something else."

"Punk is the combination of not caring at all and caring a whole lot," says Holtzman. "It's like, all right, fuck the system, yeah. But let's try and create something in opposition to that, more than just singing about it."

In their ripped T-shirts and cutoff shorts, Holtzman and Carroll fit some hoary punk stereotypes but obliterate others. The two are idealistic realists, able to balance the big-dream rhetoric of true believers by focusing on things they can control: their own lives and their community. Holtzman has large, probing eyes and a politely argumentative hitch in his voice—he's an openly gay Vassar College senior with a particular passion for gender issues within his chosen subculture. Carroll is a bit scruffier and more earnest—he dropped out of film school when he realized he could get better experience actually making films instead of talking about them all day. After months tossing around ideas for a first documentary, the two settled on "What we know, what we're a part of, and what we're proud of"; *Resistance* has since screened at various film festivals up and down the east coast.

The DIY scene chronicled in the film is Ian MacKaye's righteous idealism brought to life—an intensely close community of fifty to sixty kids who have made not only their own scene, but their own world; middle-class kids who play fiery, political music to their peers in basements, tour in their parents' Toyotas, and eschew any and all trappings of fame and success. Labels of any kind—not only major—are scorned. Crowd participation is 100 percent—the performance *is* the connection between band and audience. DIY kids eat, sleep, breathe, and dream together, cobbling together a network of like-minded young people all across the country. Values aren't myopic, either—the documentary shows DIY kids organizing food drives for the homeless, addressing their scene's tradition of sexism, and playing a giant game of parking-lot kickball.

"As cliché as it sounds," says Carroll, "walking into my first show really felt like home. Seeing that there are kids who think similarly to me, have similar interests, and here they are in their own space, where it was possible to meet other people and exchange ideas. In a lot of ways I was very scared the first time I went to a show, but it was just so exciting for me to discover punk on a DIY level in my own hometown."

Punk has always thrived on Long Island, particularly hardcore. But in the last two to three years, as emo has boomed on the national stage, the priorities of many of the bands have changed. The DIY scene has always been a separate entity, but the differences have rarely been so stark.

"These days there seems to be a huge focus on getting bands to a larger level, becoming national and selling tons of records," says Carroll, "as opposed to building with what you have on Long Island."

"Some of the hardcore kids that have seen our movie just found it laughable that kids would be spending their time in basements trying to build a community rather than rocking out," Holtzman adds. "Punk and hardcore have always had an anti-sellout mentality—that you don't want to be a rock star, that that's a bad thing. But with the rise of emo recently, that attitude has sort of washed away. With bands like New Found Glory and Saves the Day, there's no backlash to what they do because it's become expected with the style they're playing that they're gonna be about singing about girls and signing to the biggest label they can."

The rise of these bands, to Holtzman and Carroll, is all about simplicity. Not only is the central emo tenet of taking relatively minor problems seriously easy to swallow, the music is easier to get. To Holtzman and Carroll, ease of use equals ease of thought.

"When I got into punk, it was really difficult to find out about DIY bands, but at the same time I was impassioned by it," says Holtzman. "I was impassioned by the chase; I thought it was awesome. It was something you really had to put effort into in order to find out about. And that doesn't exist to the same degree now."

"The dominance of the internet leads to the loss of a whole personal feel that is integral to punk," says Carroll. "It's completely different to get someone's hand-stapled zine in your hand as opposed to reading it on the Internet."

"The greater accessibility is probably a good thing, but you're losing that hands-on, community feel that is so essential," says Holtzman. "If music becomes something you can just 'get' then it becomes easier to sell, more of a product."

"But look," Carroll interjects, "the DIY scene is a lot more closed off than the emo scene. It's very, very hard for kids to walk into our scene—we're talking about a set group of kids. This is a real shame. And I think that's why you're going to see more people heading to a Saves the Day show—musically and thematically it has a much broader appeal."

"Absolutely," says Holtzman. "It's the depoliticization. I don't think there's anything that's not safe about a band like [rising Long Island emo act] The Movielife. No one's talking about anticapitalist politics at a Movielife show. That's not part of the equation at all. That's just not what the band is about. But in the DIY scene, the political side is integrated, it's tied, it's inseparable. It's part and parcel to what's going on."

Holtzman and Carroll have made the choice to live their lives as punk. Isn't it worthwhile that emo has brought some of the values that they hold so highly—community, honesty, music—to those who would never feel either motivated or comfortable to seek out a DIY show?

"Look, I'm sure the kids who listen to New Found Glory think that what they're listening to is a lot more underground than the Backstreet Boys—and they're right," says Holtzman. "I think that everyone wants their music to be *theirs*—it's not surprising that Movielife fans want their band to have an antirock-star mentality."

"And that's somewhat valuable, as far as breaking down certain walls," says Carroll. "But I suppose I wish it was other values that were trickling down as well."

"There are bands coming out of Long Island like Taking Back Sunday who seem to have some elements of the DIY bands that we love," says Holtzman. "And at the most basic level those are some of the most appealing aspects of a basement show—that closeness, that ability to be one with the band. But to take elements of that—the very surfaceness of it all makes me a little sad. You can grab the singer and sing along with him. But you know what? At a basement show you can talk to him afterwards. You can go to a diner. Seeing emo bands trade on bits and pieces of our culture creates a fake connection. The band is still going off to their dressing room afterwards. They're still making crappy videos and continuing a rock-star persona."

"That antirock-star attitude—even in small doses—can be very empowering," Carroll says. "That, 'Hey, I'm a regular guy, I go off and make music and you can do that too.' But when that style is just being used to sell a product, when it's watered down, the message is lost. It's just another marketing tool."

"It just seems like a misappropriation to us," says Holtzman. "They're taking these things that we find very important and skewing them. But at its best it's taking kids who would otherwise be listening to Britney Spears and giving them a different mentality. Maybe they'll learn to appreciate that they have the power to do things themselves and they don't need a corporate music industry to sell them things. Look, I would never say a band couldn't make a living off of their music. They can do whatever they want—it's more about what I choose to support. If the goal is to become huge, to become rock stars, there's little that I find inspiring about that."

There is something more than a little ironic about two kids from the suburbs who got hooked on Green Day videos lecturing high schoolers about their misplaced values. But Holtzman and Carroll have taken their emo moment—that intense feeling of connection—and instead of wallowing in it or allowing it to pass like just another phase, have transformed it into a blueprint. DIY is empowering, but it is, at heart, a cul-de-sac. It exists in opposition to getting bigger, it exists because it won't get bigger. In their documentary, in their lives, Holtzman and Carroll seem to suggest that one has to move beyond all limitations, even the rigid, self-imposed kind.

"A lot of the kids in the DIY scene are finally starting to realize that they can't live in their parents' house forever," says Holtzman. "There's been more effort towards communal houses, which aren't life solutions but a step towards sustainability. We're going to need to move out of the basement and towards community spaces." He mentions the duo's next documentary subject, a proposed community center on Long Island called Freespace that's being opened by a handful of activists. The building is designed to be a free school, independent media center, and lending library.

"You have to take it out beyond how you put together your record and sell it at a show," says Carroll. "You have to take those values and apply it to your life."

"If I talk to old friends from the hardcore scene who aren't involved in it anymore, they look at it like a phase," says Holtzman. "But the DIY kids view it more as a lifelong set of ethics. If emo or punk or whatever you want to call it is nothing more than a genre, it's gonna fade away. Just like any other product or trend. Emo will die and then that'll be it."

Holtzman and Carroll agree that if the emo moment is opening up a whole new generation of kids to the importance of community, it can only be a good thing. But the question is what comes next.

"If anything, punk should be expanded as far as it can," says Carroll passionately. "The building of communities and crossing borders is absolutely essential. A lot of bands will say the only way to do that is by signing to a larger label and giving up some of your values. I don't think that's necessarily true. As it stands, there's a very strong DIY network that supports bands coming all across the country. If bands put more of an emphasis on thinking that way and trying to expand that network then it could become even more viable. I definitely don't think that punk should stay on some small level. I think it should always be accessible to anyone at all that's interested, anytime, anywhere.

"The way I view punk rock, my life, the scene, everything is as a work in progress. I'm building them towards something else. All of these new emo bands are singing about high school, and crushes, and summers, things that happened in the past that their audience can easily relate to . . . I have no tolerance for nostalgia. I think it's bullshit. Punk needs to grow and expand and do new things. It needs new voices; it needs new ideas. Otherwise it just becomes stagnant."

THURSDAY

The bus ride from Manhattan to Tenafly, New Jersey, is dramatic; as soon as the skyscrapers recede, the backyards, the baseball-card shops, the trees begin in earnest. The streets are lined with personalized strip malls with natty, tiled roofs. A closer look reveals the shadow of the city even here—nestled in amongst the Irish pubs and Italian bakeries are Pakistani groceries and Judaica boutiques. Near the end of the line is the central stop for Tenafly, an intersection abutted by a quiet, manicured park and an abandoned white bank building draped with a banner celebrating fifteen years of championship Little League.

The sky is a brilliant blue in the late afternoon of midsummer 2002. I sit on a stone stoop eying the passing SUVs and station wagons. There's a honk from the street—a tiny, lived-in red Toyota has pulled to a halt. Behind the wheel, grinning and waving, is Geoff Rickly, lead singer of Thursday, one of the most creative, beloved, and compelling emo bands of the day.

"Oh, I used to love Superchunk," he says, catching sight of my T-shirt. The car is littered with Dunkin' Donuts bags and CD cases. Music blasts out of the car's tinny speakers; the radio is rigged with a beat-up Discman and the wires spill out everywhere.

Rickly steers the car down some side streets, up some more, and finally pulls to a halt next to a modest house on a pleasantly shady lane. Thursday released their second album, *Full Collapse,* a year ago on indie Victory Records to absolutely no reaction. They are currently in the process of negotiating a multi-million-dollar, multialbum contract with Island Def Jam, arguably the largest label in the world. The house belongs to Rickly's parents. He's twenty-three years old, dog-sitting for an ex-girlfriend, and preoccupied with the three videos from Blockbuster that are going to be late if he doesn't return them tonight. Rickly is handsome in a doofy sort of way, with floppy hair and wide, almost feminine eyes—the cumulative effect is that he appears happy but constantly bracing himself for bad news.

The house is warm and pleasantly cluttered. There's a rich, fruity smell permeating the kitchen—something's on the stove. Rickly lifts the lid of the steaming pot. "I'm cooking my jeans," he says, poking at the hot, damp pants with a wooden spoon. "Someone told me it would shrink them faster if I boiled them in cider vinegar. We're going back on tour next week and I hate breaking them in onstage."

Missy, the wild-eyed puppy that Rickly is caring for, is already half the size of him and barking loudly for attention, so he rolls around on the carpet with her for a few moments, making sure to have me duck down into the basement to see where the band practices. Tucked in amongst the old ping-pong table and wicker chairs that seem to populate every suburban cellar is enough music equipment to stage an entire festival. "Do your parents mind the noise?"

"No, not at all!" Rickly says as he extricates his arm from Missy's teething clutches. "They love what we do."

It was Chris Carrabba of Dashboard Confessional who casually mentioned Thursday—a band no one had ever heard of—as his peers most likely to become the biggest band in the world. This was in the fall of 2001 and it would be close to a full year until they would get any sort of mainstream attention. But the key wasn't that "no one" had heard them. It's that the right people *had* and were telling everyone they knew. When the band crashed into the lower registers of the *Billboard* charts nearly a year after the release of their debut album it was shocking to everyone except the group's fans.

Seeing Thursday in concert is the closest one can get to watching an emo how-to filmstrip. As soon as the band takes the stage there is a palpable energy transfer in the room—every sullen-eyed teen in the place surges forward like magnets to a refrigerator. They throw their bodies towards the stage maniacally, jumping and lifting themselves on top of each other to get closer to Rickly, to testify his words back to him with waving arms and soaring voices. And Rickly gives it all back, leaping onto the PAs, saluting the crowd, swinging and tossing his microphone like a cheerleader and swaying and swooning like a punk-rock Morrissey. Crew-cutted preppie boys climb each other's backs like stepladders; boney girls clutching notebook diaries dance silently to themselves, alone in a crowded room.

The band's music combines the spiraling, epic, pop songcraft of The Smiths with the militant uppercut of hardcore, and then runs it all under a black light. Songs are willfully arty, with Rickly's clean, reedy voice teaching a graduate-level course in heartbreak. Familiar emo tropes are complicated, subverted, and raised to heretofore unheard-of heights of excess and indulgence. "Understanding In a Car Crash" finds Rickly waxing poetic in the "splintered pieces of glass," daydreaming over mixed metaphors of "the youth we lost," while the rest of his band mucks around in the blood and bone, screaming and shaking him out of his coma. Elsewhere, Rickly dreams robot dreams: of killers stalking, of a world without language, books, or paper. "Autobiography of a Nation" imagines digital cable TV as a Leni Riefenstahl film, while "Standing On the Edge of Summer" conjures up a love that's "pulled like a punch / burnt like a cigarette." Thursday's records are filled with moody impressionistic photographs and immaculately precious doodles (such as an internal time line of the album, helpfully pointing out the "requiem for a permanent midnight" that occurs thirty-four minutes in). Thursday combines the dark screams of Linkin Park with the ethereal melodies of Coldplay, so, on one hand, there's little reason why the band shouldn't become a national sensation. Yet, more than the music, it is the band members die-hard dedication to their fans, to making themselves accessible, that has accelerated their ascent.

Rickly spent his childhood moving up and down the east coast, changing schools frequently. He was a self-described "miserable fat kid," who felt isolated and alienated from his peers. It wasn't until high school in New Jersey when an older acquaintance passed him a Bad Brains tape and invited him to a punk show that Rickly found community.

"Three towns over, in Westwood, there was a garage where they did these super DIY shows," he says. "That was my indoctrination to punk—illegal shows in a garage. And it was really great—kids would come out no matter who was playing. The garage was tiny—one-hundred people would pack it—but the energy was awesome, overpowering. Everyone treated each other equally and sang along to everything. But it's funny—I still don't think I equated punk with a lifestyle at that point. I guess I was sort of a punk, but I really wanted to be a teacher. I had tons of friends. It was just something I used to do."

Rickly spent his weekends at the garage but his weeks listening to the Smiths and the Cure, as well as gobs of decidedly unpunk goth and industrial. He was a vociferous reader, and after graduation he headed to Rutgers University in New Brunswick to pursue a degree in education.

"I had tried being a singer in tons of bands, but I would always get kicked out because I couldn't sing," he says. "Literally. They called me 'Tone Geoff.'"

His own musical ambition thus limited, Rickly started organizing shows in the basement of his house in New Brunswick, playing host to an entire generation of emo and hardcore groups that sprang up in the wake of local heroes Lifetime. "There was so much going on," he says, "so I invited half local bands and half touring bands and made my first show donation only. The performances were amazing but no one donated! So I ended up paying all of the touring bands the money that I had for school. I had to use my friends' books all year, but it was worth it. I was hooked. From then on, we charged for the shows, but paying three dollars was no big deal. I didn't keep any money ever, so it made sense. There were moments down there that were just magic—when there were two hundred seventy-five kids in the basement, other kids watching from the windows. There was sweat on the walls, condensation on the pipes. It was raining down on everyone.

"It was right around this time that I started realizing that punk was more about the way it was assembled and who it was assembled by than the content. It was possible to reject the tough-guy mentality. You can say something real. And just because you're real doesn't mean you're a thug from the streets. Because I'm definitely neither."

Rickly fell in with some local art-school kids who shared his expansive sense of punk and they started jamming together. "It all came from one song," he says. "They played me a song called 'This Side of Brightness,' and I just fell in love with it. I knew I needed to find a way to be able to sing it. And it's weird, before that I never really understood what singing was. I thought it was just yelling out whatever you were feeling haphazardly. But this song was so natural, it made me want to find a melody. I loved it so much I wanted to believe I was singing better. And when we went to record it as a demo, the studio guy was like, 'What happened? You can kinda sing now.' So I knew there was something really special the way we played together. Not like special it would mean anything to anybody else, but it would to us. I knew we had to stick together."

The young band was striking from its very first show, melding seemingly contradictory hardcore dynamics with dramatic, gothlike intensity. Songs veered all across the emotional map, and Rickly's newly discovered voice was clean and yearning. The songs took pieces of British pop and shoegazer and mashed them up with straight-faced emo fundamentalism. People said they sounded like Joy Division or a hardcore Smiths cover band. But people couldn't stop listening.

"The thing that tied together punk and the Cure was a real sense of urgency," Rickly explains. "Something more than the emotional content. The music being played wasn't incidental to what you were saying. The goth and British bands that I liked had the same visceral kick as regular punk but it seemed more like a place for me, a space you could inhabit. Something that was far away from reality. So I steered the band in that darker direction."

Much like Sunny Day Real Estate a decade before, Thursday didn't push listeners towards something as much as it enveloped them: kidnapped their fears and dreams all at once and whispered something that sounded like a secret. Thursday came out of the same basements that inspired Holtzman and Carroll, but followed its muse to a different end.

"Lyrically and conceptually, Thursday is about running away to a different place but simultaneously trying to make here more like that place. I'll be the first to admit that it's contradictory, but so are feelings. On the one hand I want it to be a place where people can go to escape the things that are bothering them, to rest and refuel. But at the same time I hope that the message is one of compassion towards everybody. One of the things we've always said is that there's no point in being a political band because most people in political bands are fucking total assholes. Activists in college could be monsters—all the kids who were totally into Marxism and pushing communism were also emotionally abusive to their girlfriends. At a certain point no matter what your politics are, every action you take is political. Making another human being feel like shit about themselves does more on a realistic level than any philosophical argument does. So what we are about is being compassionate towards others every day, in every situation. You can escape in the music but there's also things you really can do, change, and affect in the real world."

Rickly's politics are understated—the music comes first. But he's very outspoken when he wants to be. He seems to walk a fine line between punk's cocoonlike beginnings and its mall-bound future. He, like Holtzman and Carroll, wants to provide a safe haven for troubled teens, and he also believes in moving beyond the limitations of that introversion. Unlike anyone else in the often overheated world of punk, Rickly seems to possess both the widescreen perspective and the artistic sensibility that one more often finds in bands like R.E.M. or U2. Rather than run from the inherent theatricality of emo, Rickly embraces it.

"The first shows we played were really intense—the kids would come to the basement, everything was very spontaneous. Kids at other shows would ask us to jump onstage and play a song or two. So our philosophy was very circumstantial. Because of the way things were in the basement, we knew right away that we didn't want to be exclusionary. I have this really strong feeling if you're not doing it the way that you love it then you're betraying someone who can't afford to be betrayed by your music. If I had found out that a band I cared about so much was totally insincere I would have been crushed."

Moved by what he and his friends were creating, Rickly quit school to focus on the band full-time in 2000, and booked basement tours all over the country. When a friend passed Thursday's demo on to Victory Records's head Tony Brummel, he offered them a contract.

"The only reason we signed with them is because they wanted us to tour," Rickly says. "But the contract they sent us was the most ridiculous thing I've ever read. It was for seven albums and we gave up our publishing, our merchandise. It was a total major-label outrage contract. But Tony said that anything we needed outside of the contract would be taken care of on good faith, as friends. We figured we were getting screwed, but he was going to help us tour. Because without that, we might have broken up. While we were waiting for the album to come out, we booked another basement tour. Tony thought we were assholes for wasting our time being so small, but we were like, wasting our time would be sitting around doing nothing, we have to play!

"We did the whole country. We loved the new songs so much we decided to play every night like it's the last show we'd ever play; we played our hearts out. And the five or ten kids that saw us would tell their friends. So even though we were playing DIY places, the second time through there would be fifty kids and we'd sell out of T-shirts. There was one night in Buffalo when we played to five hundred people on a bill with pop/punk bands and we just did it like we were playing the basement. It was really visceral and really raw. I think that's when people started talking about us. Our record came out right after that, in April of 2001, and the first week it sold eight hundred copies. All of our shows from that point on were like real hardcore shows—kids up front pointing their fingers and singing along. There was a real unified energy. The kids were testifying to our music like it's a life-affirming experience. It was a massive response that I never ever would have predicted—the crowd coming up in a wave when we went on. It was so intense, so genuinely emotional. That's the power of music right there, to listen to a band and realize you're not the only one that feels something."

Thursday had little in common with the prominent emo bands of the day—they had no dominant pop hooks, no convenient anthems. Their accessibility and openness, coupled with the preestablished national touring network, connected all the dots that they themselves couldn't see. By touring with emo bands, by playing to young, hungry kids, Thursday brought their basement energy out of the basement. They became an emo band.

"Victory really wanted us to do a Saves the Day tour," explains Rickly. "We didn't think we were anything like them, but they're cool guys—they used to play our basement. At the time it seemed like they were the pinnacle of what an indie band could be. They had gone from our basement in New Brunswick to this impossible place. Even though we're coming out a similar tradition as a lot of these so-called emo bands—the lifestyle, the social aspects, the sing-alongs—I felt like we were quite different. Our intention is to try and find different textures, to deal with the collective conscious more than it just being 'I, I, I.' When we played to their crowds we got an amazing reaction. That was when we started to realize that maybe something bigger was going on. After that, when we went on tour by ourselves, our audience was a lot younger and a lot less familiar with punk. We had always hated the word *emo,* the condescending nature of it towards other music. It seemed so shortsighted. It's very possible that we're part of this thing that's bigger than us and we just don't see it."

I ask Rickly what it was that kids who usually sang about missing their moms found in his oblique lyrical visions.

"There's a real loneliness in our songs," he says. "Texturally, but also imagewise—like there's no sunshine in any of our songs, there's a lot of city streets with no people in them, gunshots with nobody around. Basically a lot of kids around the age that they're coming to see us it's simultaneous with the first time something hard happens in their lives. Maybe they feel very alone and alienated because of the things that are going on—even if they have nothing to do with what I'm singing about. There's a lyric in one of our songs, 'we all sing the songs of separation,' that really sums it up. There's a universal loneliness at play in our concerts.

"So it's a different generation of kids that comes to see us now. A lot of them tell me they heard of us from messageboards first. I guess it's like a fever, it catches. When we played our record release party in Manhattan, *Full Collapse* hadn't even come out yet, but the kids sang every word. It was cool; I'm glad they had it. Who cares that they didn't pay for it—they were having a great time and we were having the time of our life. It's also different that they don't have to do legwork to discover this music. I wonder if someone who's had it kinda handed to them can ever imagine how special it was to finally get something that you lost your mind looking for. There's a very information-age, disposable mentality about the punk scene now. I think it's too bad that there's a willingness to touch the surface without being part of the essence and understanding that it's the essence that makes things special. You combine that with all the money being spent on promotion now, you can really miss the real point of what we're trying to get at."

Rob is eighteen years old and a college student in New England. He approached me online to talk about how Thursday "totally changed" his life.

"Around the time *Full Collapse* came out, I lost a friend in a four-wheeler accident," he says. "I was very down on everything and it seemed like nobody cared at all. So I started listening to that record a lot and I found a lot of comfort. Afterwards I got a chance to hang out with Geoff for a little bit and I thanked him for playing those songs and told them how much they meant to me and what had happened to my friend. He just gave me a hug and told me how sorry he was and that he knows my pain. It was then that I realized that some people actually still cared. It made me want to care too. We've kept in touch and he recognizes me from all the shows I've been to. When you talk to him, you can just feel the honesty and sincerity. It's both comforting and inspiring."

One of the DIYers' biggest concerns about the rise of emo is the lack of politics, but Thursday is making inroads in that arena as well.

" 'Paris In Flames' made me realize that I'm sometimes not as sensitive to people as I should be," Rob continues. "The song is about alienation and homophobia. It made me realize how many negative connotations to homosexuality there are in our culture—everyone being like 'oh, that's gay,' or 'you fag.' I used to be like that too. The song definitely changed my way of thinking."

In his lyrics, in his stage persona, in the parking lot after the show, Geoff Rickly is therapist, psychiatrist, hypnotist, teacher, brother, friend, and idol.

"When kids come up to me and tell me what our songs mean to them, it makes me realize that no matter what happens we have to keep doing this," Rickly says. "I mean people get our dove logo tattooed on them, and it's not a band tattoo, it's a period in their life tattoo, remembering the period of life when our music maybe helped them change their opinion or perspective. I know what that's like. I have a tattoo of a Frail lyric, because the older kid who got me into punk, the last conversation we had before he killed himself was about one of their songs. We talked about how everybody was so focused on romantic love and didn't seem to care about love in general and compassion towards people who are unlike you."

"What is the tattoo?" I ask.

"It says, 'Love is love.' " He pauses. "It's weird. I think of music as a dialogue, one that's open for anybody to contribute. So we have a part in one of our songs where we quote the lyric because it's about him, my friend. It's a remembrance, an echo of that thing we shared in our lives. Of course, some people think we're just ripping off Frail. It's hard to tell them that subjectively I'm trying to close a circle on it. Most of our songs are about two things and where the two intersect each other. So we have a song called "Cross Out the Eyes" which is about losing your identity in other people but also about breaking down identity. Not making everything about I and ownership. So the song has a lot of lines from a book by Michael Palmer which I thought was perfect because the point of his book is that language is all recycled and metaphysical—that there's no ownership of it.

"So when kids talk to me it helps complete that same circuit. I was a little fat kid growing up and I got picked on a bunch. My social skills have gotten better because I force myself. I remember that this is me getting to do the other half of what I as a young music fan loved so much. Because I loved it when people in bands would actually speak to me like a person and not make me feel like they hated me. I forced myself to communicate more clearly because I don't ever want to alienate anybody. And that has made me such a happy person. I used to get so gloom-and-doom upset about things in my life, really fatalistic. Now, even if something crazy happens, I recognize that there's a sort of universality at play—even through ups and downs, I'm still tied to other people."

Eventually we both realize that the sun has long since set and there are precious few minutes left to return his overdue videos. So, tape recorder running, we hop back in the car and speed through the suburban summer night. We talk about the future of the band.

"The way we see it is, if we can be more of an honest band on a major than on an indie that's backed by a major then that's a step in the right direction. We were taking it to the next level already and it was completely out of our control and Island was the only one that said we want to give you total control. They knew we aren't elitist and that we want to have people find out about our band." His face is lit by the glow of the blinking turn signal.

"You guys are totally flipping the script," I say. "You're a young band and here you have the biggest company in the world coming to you, offering you freedom from an oppressive indie."

"I know it," Geoff says. "Sometimes I feel like they're making reparations or something. Look, I'm not really concerned about the cred aspect of it. But I am concerned about what I see as an important cultural shift—when a major company steps in and takes the power away from the kids in a scene, when they co-opt an established movement. I think you have to be pragmatic about things. I know for a fact that we did more for the DIY scene after signing with Victory than before. We've always tried to avoid Clear Channel and stick with indie promoters. Sometimes I feel weird about the fact that it's hard for us to play basements now, but the truth is we can't anymore because we'd shut them down. This band has exceeded any expectations I ever had for it and did so awhile ago. So at this point all I can do is try and figure out the best decision I can make for us in the moment. Do things in a way that seems right. Not limit anything, but always try to be honest and positive." He pauses. "Who knows where this can go from here?"

TAKING BACK SUNDAY

The first band doesn't go on until 8 P.M. but at ten minutes to seven there's a line of teenagers all the way down Leonard Street. People have stepped outside of their offices/lofts/gyms/orientalist furniture stores to see what all the commotion is about. Two chubby girls with glitter around their eyes are holding a ripped piece of cardboard that says "Anyone have xtra tickets?" and start to ask me the same question, before one of them says "No, we asked him already" and they move on, batting their eyes at other youthful, tattooed marks. At the door to the Knitting Factory a young woman is leaning out, leading an impromptu auction for her actual, not-made-up extra ticket. A skinny brown-haired girl is jumping up and down, offering $80. Then $100. Her arms are subsumed into the crowd. (I find out later that it eventually went for $130.)

The monthlong, nationwide tour of Taking Back Sunday, Brand New, and Rufio is winding down and the former two bands are home. None of the groups has ever been featured in the national press—only one (Brand New) has a video airing on MTV2. And yet the show is crackling with energy—it's the biggest thing happening in Lower Manhattan tonight, hell, maybe in all of New York City. No one in the crowd is over the age of twenty.

The scene inside is frantic. Kids are literally everywhere—if the show isn't not oversold, it certainly feels like it. There are short girls with low-riding corduroys flitting past, skittering like ants from the stage to the merch tables and back outside again, holding hands to snake their way through the ticket lines. There are clusters of clean-faced boys standing, cracking jokes in their earrings, full sleeves of tats, and black T-shirts emblazoned with band logos: From Autumn to Ashes, Coheed and Cambria, Midtown. I walk over to the front bar, which has been completely transformed into an emo Wal-Mart. All four bands performing tonight sport sales tables bigger than most Greenmarket vendors. Even the relatively unknown opener, Moneen, sports four distinct T-shirt styles and high-priced, stylish hoodie sweat-shirts. Rufio, the middle band, hails from California and has a huge selection of apparel, all emblazoned with its logo that spells the letter *o* as a grenade. But it's the combined Taking Back Sunday/Brand New corner that dominates the room. An entire wall is given over to their T-shirt designs—each band has at least eight. Taking Back Sunday's are relatively benign, but the sheer number has allowed the members to indulge their silliest late-night brainstorming. There's the blue one with the individual band pictures and the words, "¿Quien es mas macho?" There are straight logo shirts, album shirts, and ones that draft buyers into fictional, Long Island–based sports teams. Brand New has a more confrontational approach—one of its new mottos seems to be "Brand New Wants You Dead"—but the group also fills its quota of ironic (one shirt riffs on the Top Gun logo) and iconic (a giant "BN," which makes me think more of Barnes & Noble than Long Island punk). Both bands have stickers and patches by the drawerful and TBS even has an old-fashioned foam-style trucker's baseball cap. All of the varieties are selling briskly and the merch guys' tip jars are filling up.

When it's time for Taking Back Sunday to take the stage, the already thick air seems to double in density. The band members stand on the cramped stage, tuning for ages, while the kids in the front swell and teem like water over a hot stove. The stagelights finally go on, and singer Adam Lazzara appears. A roar is released. As the anthemic first chords of "You Know How I Do" ring out, the water boils over. "So sick so sick of being tired / and so tired of being sick," Lazzara screams giving voice to the innermost thoughts and frustrations of every member of the crowd. Suddenly, everyone in the room is sweating. The smell rises immediately to the balcony where I am—it's a high school locker room after dodgeball day. A lone fan circles pointlessly on the ceiling, trying to circulate air to the teeming crowd below. One buildup to the chorus and Adam is subsumed by boys clamoring for the mic. After those first few lines, Adam doesn't sing again for the rest of the song. Guitarist John Nolan picks up the backing harmonies/screams while a succession of audience members belt their living hearts out. The most surprising thing is how little it matters whose voice we hear. Some of them sound great—evoking credible screams despite the heat and the suddenness of their spotlight—but all of them sound appropriate. Eventually Adam lets go of the mic completely, content to raise his fist, flail around, and act as cheerleader for the fans of his band; as they surge and trample and scream, they *are* his band. A shoe appears on stage, then a dread-locked boy. There are two meatheads hanging out in the wings, happily waving their fists and singing along. "You guys," Adam swerves about the stage like a drunk, "you have no idea how much this means to us. No idea. This keeps our hearts beating." And another song, another succession of singers. Adam tosses the mic, spins it like a baton. I wonder, for a moment, just how he manages to avoid knocking his bassist's teeth out. Kids are crowd surfing now and so is Adam—a bouncer reaches into the scrum to pull him out before the second chorus of "Timber-wolves at New Jersey." Behind him, Nolan screams the words: "I've got the mic and you've got the mosh pit," but the divisions are hardly that clear anymore.

"Hey, can everyone take one giant step back please?" Adam asks at the end of one song. "Some people are getting really crushed up here." The crowd obeys, not that it makes much difference. "So, listen," he continues, "we were supposed to start the show a little late tonight because we were told that some folks from MTV were coming." Boos ripple through the crowd, a few middle fingers stand at attention. "Yeah, yeah, that's right. Because none of that shit fucking matters. We've been on this tour, and talking to all sorts of people from bigger labels. But all that matters is this right here. You guys. Thank you so much for being here for us." The band then launches into "Great Romances of the 20th Century," the ostensible single, and the audience's step back turns into two more steps forward. When people are held aloft by the crowd, Adam leans into them, cradles them. Shares the mic. Lets them have whatever it is they want to take.

Watching the total autonomy these kids feel, even here at this mid-sized club in Manhattan, it's hard not to think of the *Between Resistance and Community* documentary. The venue is obviously different, but the fourth wall is just as irrelevant. These are hardcore aesthetics, pure and simple, but taken out of the basement and writ large for everyone—for anyone—to take part in. There are scraps of all kinds of cultural detritus in Taking Back Sunday's songs—bits of hip-hop rhythms, heavy metal keyboards, Bon Jovi–worthy anthemic riffing. It's the sound of being young, being bored, being up late. Being touched by bands and not knowing anything about anything other than wanting to recreate that feeling again and again. Adam and John are the same, early-nineties recycling bins as their crowds, and they've taken the same catchall approach to the lessons and ethics of their Long Island home. It's approachable, immediate hardcore democratized (or gentrified, depending on where you stand) for the masses. The pierced, disaffected, anti-commercialist youths playing in basements for no one and for each other are still on the Island tonight. They have their salvation and are canny enough to know how to find it. This here tonight is for the other kids. For the kids like Ian Bauer—one of the Long Island Dashboard fans from the previous fall—who spent all day minding six-year-olds at a day camp and is leaving in less than a week for college; Ian, who fell in love with punk the first time he saw a mohawk in the video for Rancid's poptastic "Ruby Soho" but names Counting Crows as his all-time favorite group. Anyone can sing along with Taking Back Sunday because everyone can relate—it's a room full of young, teenage insomniacs, blissfully of the world, not willfully opposed to it, still reeling over getting hearts broken that they didn't even know they had. For the same reasons, anyone can sing *for* Taking Back Sunday. The Knitting Factory feels like someone's basement tonight, but the doors are left wide open. Everyone in here is speaking the same language and—oppressively—everyone is breathing the same air.

The sweat has traveled up all the way up to the ceiling by now. I'm dripping like everyone else. Adam keeps talking about how great it is to be home, how he recognizes people in the crowd, keeps asking certain old friends to raise their hands. The air feels like cake batter by the time the band crunches to a halt. But Adam isn't done with the gratitude.

"This means more to me than you will ever know. This is all my dreams come true. Don't forget you guys: friends are the only thing that's gonna hold you together for your whole entire life. We'll see you real soon." He throws the mic down to roars and applause.

It's all about to get so much bigger, of course. Taking Back Sunday's video for "Great Romances" is due to premiere on MTV2 within the month, a larger tour with major-label peers Midtown beckons in October. But tonight was an adreneline shot of what the band is about, and as they throw their instruments down, the band members applaud the audience right back. Tonight they got as good as they gave. As I turn to escape the sauna, the drummer throws down his sticks and dives head-first into the crowd.

At the end of 2000, Taking Back Sunday was playing its first-ever shows in and around the band members' Long Island home. In 2001, they had were playing to consistently enthusiastic crowds and shopping their demo. In March 2002, Chicago-based Victory Records released the band's debut album, *Tell All Your Friends.* From Long Island outwards, emo kids took the title to heart. When I interviewed the band in July, they were excited about embarking on their first-ever tour of the West Coast, but nervous about what sort of reception they'd receive out there. They needn't have worried. I was in San Diego with Dashboard Confessional just days after Taking Back Sunday played their first California show. The show had been sold out and I found myself surrounded by fresh-faced teens in freshly-purchased band T-shirts.

Taking Back Sunday is successful because the group is the sum total of its listeners' lives. Lazzara and Nolan are young, frustrated romantics with the attention spans of hamsters. They write songs about falling in love to other people's songs, about watching TV with your best friend and sitting around waiting for something to happen, though you have no idea what it is. Their success is the embodiment of modern emo—it exists in and of the moment and could only exist in this very moment. They are responsible for some of the most terrifically maudlin emo lyrics of all time ("and if you were to slit my throat . . . I'd apologize for bleeding on your shirt"), and some of the most clever ("so obviously desperate / so desperately obvious"). They write songs about nostalgia ("You're So Last Summer") and about fighting messily with your best friend ("There's No 'I' In Team"). They, like their audience, have an unhealthy fixation on high school ("Cute Without the 'E' [Cut From the Team]"). They have momentum. There's nothing artful about Taking Back Sunday or its music, it's all immediate—as quick to commit to a feeling as clicking "reply" on a heated email. Taking Back Sunday's flash of insolent, immature longing is instant-messaged across the country, relayed to the ears that most want to hear it. In any other era, the group would be stuck on Long Island—they wouldn't reach California until either the band or its listeners were too old to care.

Taking Back Sunday is the smashup of public and private music. The band transforms public clubs into basements, bedrooms into concert halls. More than any other band, Taking Back Sunday's success in 2002 was due to the new national subculture. Once one website listed the group as a peer of Dashboard and Thursday, everyone did. Taking Back Sunday was the next natural step, a vital piece of a movement that even its own members didn't even realize they were a part of.

Adam Lazzara is the healthiest, happiest, and handsomest looking punk you're likely to find. The only thing wider than his grin is the gulf between his ferocity onstage and his politeness off of it. His hair is floppy and hangs over his eyes in a manner that occasionally makes him look far too pretty and primped to do what he does. Mostly he exudes a boyish gentleness and calm. His onstage freakouts are soft edged—he throws his arms out to pull people in, not push them away.

Co-songwriter and guitarist John Nolan is equally friendly—a bit older, a bit less pretty, and a bit more serious than Lazzara. Behind his glasses his eyes have the charismatic gleam of a recent lottery winner. Maybe that's because everywhere he and Lazzara go these days seems to be a party—we almost missed each other for our interview at a Lower East Side vegetarian restaurant because the two happened to run into at least twenty black-clad tattooed friends and invited them to lunch.

Lazzara grew up in Greensboro, North Carolina, listening to his dad's classic rock collection, grooving on Lynyrd Skynyrd without ever wondering if there was something else out there. All of that changed with Nirvana. When *Nevermind* was released, Lazzara was only ten years old; his heart has belonged to punk rock ever since. His taste remained firmly entrenched in the mainstream underground—Green Day, Alice in Chains—until high school, when he met what he calls his "scene older brother."

"I never really fit in with the kids in my grade," he says, "so all my friends were older. One day I was sitting in the hall of my high school and this guy came walking up handing out flyers. He handed me one and said 'You should come to this.' From there I just latched onto him. The local scene was really more like a family. Everyone was into Lifetime and all the kids stuck together."

Lazzara spent the summer after graduating from high school "delivering Chinese food and dating a crazy girl." When he saw a young band from Long Island called Taking Back Sunday play a show without a bass player, he got to talking with its members. A few weeks later, Lazzara packed up his few possessions and moved up to Long Island to audition for the group's vacant bass slot.

"It was pretty shocking to me, yeah," says Nolan. "But there was also something pretty cool about a kid being into our band enough to drop everything and move out here."

After a few months, Taking Back Sunday's singer quit and Lazzara shifted to vocals. The change was electric and immediate.

"We'd only been playing about two months with Adam and we weren't sure where it was going to go," says Nolan. "Then we played one particular show at a club on the Island called Ground Zero. And for some reason, the kids just went nuts. They were screaming along with us, dancing, and pointing, and we had never had a reaction like that before with the old singer. It was amazing to see. I'd been in lots of other bands and no one ever screamed along to what I had to say."

Lazzara and Nolan were shacked up together in a one-room basement apartment, broke and living show to show. Without the benefit of sunlight, they'd stay up all night, writing songs and trading relationship war stories, shocked to find out how much they had in common.

"We'd both contribute lyrics," says Lazzara, "but they all seemed to be about relationships—dating relationships, parent relationships, friend relationships."

"You write about what you know," says Nolan. "I mean, that's about all we do know. If it wasn't relationships, all we'd have to write about is watching TV and drinking beer."

In the midst of their clever, best-friends-forever patter, it comes out that a prepunk Nolan used to be all about classic rock, jam bands, and guitar solos. This innate sense of over-the-top dramatics clearly reared its head in the late-night songwriting sessions. "Great Romances of the 20th Century" and "Timberwolves at New Jersey" struggle and soar against the innoculating boredom of dashed expectations—the titles, swiped from programming blocks on the *TV Guide* channel, are cloaked in a winning humility. Alone with nothing but their high school memories, their rock and roll dreams, their TV, and each other, Nolan and Lazzara wrote songs that, in their own way, are just as concerned with the numbing realities of Long Island as those of the DIY kids. It's just that Taking Back Sunday's proposed way out—through accessible concerts and the ecstatic release they provide—seems a lot more doable, if not considerably more pleasant, than forming an anticapitalist commune. Taking Back Sunday may not have played any shows there, but it too was born in the basement.

"I think it's very important to keep some amount of humor and sarcasm in lyrics," Nolan says. "Because you just can't be so serious about yourself all the time. I hate it when bands do that."

Taking Back Sunday's everyguy-isms translated across typical (and stereotypical) punk lines but, once hooked, the reaction engendered in kids was pure emo. Keith Colleluori was eighteen years old, a huge fan of Nirvana and Bob Marley. Even though he grew up on Long Island, his impression of punk was limited to the Sex Pistols and Green Day. During the summer after high school graduation, he broke up with a long-term girlfriend and was plunged into depression and confusion. "Right after the breakup I was online looking for friends that I could talk to, just to try and keep my mind distanced from it for as long as possible," Colleluori says. "I started to IM with my friend Ian, but he couldn't stay online because he was going to a concert and told me I should come along. I had never heard of Taking Back Sunday, but I told him I'd consider it. I had never gone to a concert by myself before, but I was desperate to get out and try and make something happen in my life at that moment—something other than sitting around sulking. The show was on Long Island and I got there right when the band took the stage. I went into the middle of the crowd and I saw the energy. I enjoyed what I heard more than any band since Nirvana. It got my mind off of everything and I felt like singing along but I didn't know the words. When the crowd squashed me into the person in front of me I understood that it was something that all the kids there were relating to."

Keith describes the kids who surrounded him as "kinda like me"—though he went alone, he was quickly enveloped by the instant community that Taking Back Sunday shows can create. "I would never go anywhere in my life by myself, but since that first concert I've gone to three others alone—even driven to New Jersey to see them a second night in a row when I had to be awake at 5 A.M. the next morning to work construction. I just stay in the middle of the crowd, getting drenched in everyone's sweat and not caring a bit." After spending most of his teenage years worshipping two untouchable, dead heroes, Colleluori is blown away at the accessibility of TBS's Lazzara. "Meeting Adam was so cool," he says. "I had never really had any living idols before. When I saw them at the Knitting Factory I saw him standing outside. I'm normally shy but walked over and said hi. He could have been like, 'What do you want,' but he was so cool. I walked away with a sense of him being exactly who I thought he was—polite and kind and similar to me. He didn't seem like a rock star. He seemed like the kind of guy that you would want to date your sister."

There is something universal and inspiring about Lazzara and Nolan transforming their ennui into anthems, stumbling around onstage, oozing with gratefulness for a room of kids exactly like them. Immediacy, accessibility, and empathy aren't just ideals with Taking Back Sunday—they are part and parcel to the band's appeal and success.

"Popular music has gotten to a point where if you're a disenchanted, angry young kid there's not a whole lot there for you," Nolan says. "There's always your Limp Bizkit, anger-venting sort of stuff. If you're smart enough to see through that, you're not going to be able to relate emotionally. So our appeal definitely stems from a lack of anything real in popular music. I think kids are making a point to seek out more bands that they can actually relate to and love, not just listen to. They're also realizing that there's something a lot cooler and more personal in finding a band who aren't superstars. A band where you can go to their show and then talk to them afterwards."

When Lazzara and Nolan titled their demo—and, eventually, their debut album—*Tell All Your Friends,* they thought it would be the only way to spread the word about their music. They didn't realize how prophetic a title it would be. "It was more of a hoax than a command," Nolan says with a laugh.

But the album, when it was released in March 2002, arrived at the exact right moment for its title to be taken seriously and obeyed to the fullest. Every person who heard the record passed it on to someone else, someone they cared about. *Tell All Your Friends* wasn't meant to be kept secret; it's not shy, retiring, personal emo. It's big, bold, and—above all—communal. Nolan and Lazzara are young and web-savvy enough to understand the way kids connect to music these days ("I can't go on AOL Instant Messenger anymore because if I do my life is just gonna get ruined," says Nolan. "It's like: once an alcoholic always an alcoholic.") and are therefore in a unique position not only to soundtrack that communication, but also to take advantage of it.

"Ten or fifteen years ago there's no way a band like us could've reached anyone outside of the tristate area so quickly," Nolan says. "When we signed with Victory, we already had somewhat of a following built in. It was definitely above and beyond what we could've gotten ourselves just from touring. It was solely due to kids' ability to download our music, go to our web site, and spread the word of mouth digitally."

"I first heard about them from a friend," says eighteen-year-old Iris Chi of Irvine, California. "He would IM me all the time about their great stage presence, so I decided to download a bunch of their MP3s and liked them. When I went to the show and I saw how out of control Adam was and how the crowd was totally into it I immediately became an obsessive fan."

"Almost anywhere you go now on tour, you can get a show and not have any idea where you are," Nolan says. "It's exactly the same at every show we play. The kids, the T-shirts, the style, the full-on reaction. It's pretty amazing, actually. From east to west, from north to south."

"We played a show in Anaheim," says Lazzara, "and it looked exactly like Long Island."

Taking Back Sunday has momentum unprecedented for a band so young, but it also has years of precedent to draw on.

"We called our manager today to check what our SoundScan is," Nolan says. "A year ago, I didn't know what SoundScan *was*. I had no idea. In a certain way, all of this attention is good because independent bands have been forced to think in a certain way. Now, I can't look at our band as a commodity or business. There is a reality to all of this that I can't ignore. We realize that when a manager or a label comes to look at us, they're considering how much money we can make them. We're not going to get suckered into thinking it's all about how much they love us or whatever. I want to have a career doing this, so I've had to learn a lot very quickly."

Taking Back Sunday tiptoes a tightrope of contradictions—a young band reaping huge national success, living in and profiting from a musical moment based on intimate connection and communication writ large. In their best songs, Lazzara and Nolan finish each other's sentences, answer each other's questions. Live, they give everything and get everything in return. On the same week that their first video premiered on MTV, the band embarked on its biggest tour to date. Three shows in, Lazzara leapt off the stage with his usual ferocity, but tripped on a cable on the way down. The result: a cracked skull and a dislocated hip. Two months later, the band played a triumphant homecoming show back at the Knitting Factory—acoustic this time, with Adam hobbling on a cane and seated onstage. The songs shone anyway, and the kids carried the day—so desperately happy to have their heroes back, they picked up the slack and drowned out the quieter sounds with their own joyful screams.

From the basement to the stadium, punk is about communication and community. Taking Back Sunday uniquely understands what that means in cyberspace and in real life—and how the two are inextricably linked.

"We get tons of email," Nolan says, "and when we're home I spend a lot of time responding to it all. The kids are totally shocked that we do that. Really, it's never been easier for a band to communicate. Writing an email isn't that difficult, and the kids are so appreciative of it."

"My thing is, I hated going to see bands that I really liked only pass the mic into the crowd once," says Lazzara. "It meant a lot for them to take the time to pass it to *me,* you know? I've heard people say that our shows are great but I pass the mic too much. I'm like, 'If you want to hear me sing, buy the record. If you want to see a show, then come to our show.' I do it because if it wasn't for these kids singing along, there'd be no reason for us to keep playing except to amuse ourselves. And we could do that without devoting our lives to music. I don't want anybody to feel like they're not cool enough, or they're not good enough to participate."

"All of our success goes back to the personal feelings that fans feel for our lyrics, to how much they get from the communication between the band and the audience," Nolan says. "Kids feel a lot more comfortable coming to our show or Dashboard Confessional's. They feel connected, closer, and not as inhibited. It's not like you're standing there watching this big huge band that you're intimidated by. It's more like you're with a bunch of people who feel the same as you do. Everyone feels comfortable—everyone feels like, in love in a certain way. That is very different than a traditional rock 'n' roll show."

It's also very different than a traditional punk show.

There's nothing traditional about it. It's emo.

PART THREE

DASHBOARD CONFESSIONALS

ELEVEN
DRIVING ON LONG ISLAND

(SavesTheDayfan85 signed on at 4:18 P.M.)

AGREENWALD: Hi, is this Anthony? This is Andy Greenwald—I'm the writer you talked to the other night at the Dashboard Confessional show at CBGBs. I was wondering if you and your friends are still up for talking with me.

SAVESTHEDAYFAN85: Absolutely. Howie and Ian are over here so we could talk now.

AGREENWALD: Great! Is IM ok, or would you prefer the phone or email?

SAVESTHEDAYFAN85: IM is better—that way we can all express ourselves.

AGREENWALD: OK. So who am I talking to?

SAVESTHEDAYFAN85: Anthony Lombardi, 16, student, Plainview, LI. Howie Kussoy, 17. Ian Bauer, 17. Justin Bolobanic, 17.

AGREENWALD: You guys seemed really into the show. What is it about Dashboard that you relate to so strongly?

SAVESTHEDAYFAN85: His lyrics touch you and you can relate to every word he's saying. Through anytime, good or bad, you

173

always feel like he's gone through the same thing and it's comforting. We are in the process of experiencing many situations right now involving love and life and the way he uses metaphors and beautiful lyrics to express himself is amazing.

AGREENWALD: Would you mind sharing something from your personal life that the music of Dashboard Confessional helped you with?

SAVESTHEDAYFAN85: This is Howie. I had a situation a month ago where I was in love with my best friend and was contemplating whether to tell her or not. I was in my car driving one day thinking about it when the Dashboard song "Living in Your Letters" came on. It hit me that I had to tell her—the lyrics spoke to me like a lifelong friend. I got extremely emotional.

AGREENWALD: What happened?

SAVESTHEDAYFAN85: Well, I took Chris's advice and told her how I felt.

AGREENWALD: Anyone else?

SAVESTHEDAYFAN85: This is Ian. Many little situations were stressing me out and as usual I was listening to one of my Dashboard CDs to help me cope. I've had a crush on this girl for a long time and we kissed about a month ago, but since then she's been acting stand-offish. One line in a song struck me differently than ever before: "and your taste still lingers on my lips like I placed them upon yours/and I starve, I starve for you."

AGREENWALD: How did hearing that line make you feel?

SAVESTHEDAYFAN85: It was comforting just to hear Chris sing—I was able to put out all of the emotions I had been building up as I sang along as loud as I could.

AGREENWALD: You guys certainly were involved in the concert. How would you describe a Dashboard show?

SAVESTHEDAYFAN85: Being in the atmosphere with Chris, listening to his music while seeing the emotion on his face really shows that the songs mean as much to him as they do to us. It's an experience unlike any other. Feeling all of the positive vibes that circulate through the air and the coming together of so many different types of people—it's just a remarkable thing and a great feeling.

AGREENWALD: You guys, I can't thank you enough.

SAVESTHEDAYFAN85: It's been our pleasure! We appreciate the chance to express our feelings about him.

(Agreenwald signed off at 4:37 P.M.)

To: IanBauer
From: agreenwald
April 1st, 2002

Hey Ian, I'm assuming you guys are going to the Dashboard show on Saturday night. Any chance I could come out to Plainview beforehand and then go to the show with you guys? Let me know, Andy

To: agreenwald
From: IanBauer
April 5th, 2002

What's up, Andy. We're cool to pick you up at the train station tomorrow. We don't really want to see the opening bands, so we don't have to head into Manhattan until 7:30. By any chance would you be able to coordinate us meeting with Chris? You seem to be pretty in touch with

him and I dunno it would just be so amazing! Alright, see
you tomorrow. Ian.

From the windows of an LIRR train window, Plainview, Long Island, is another anonymous salary-man town, one of dozens with cardboard names that dot the tracks from Queens all the way up to the Hamptons. The town was once the location of a pond considered holy by local Native Americans and was, up until the early twentieth century, one of the country's largest producers of pickles. These days Plainview is a stridently middle-class suburb with various housing communities bound together by wide commercial avenues dotted with fading small businesses, thriving chain stores, and car dealerships.

It's a surprisingly frigid day in April when I disembark at the rail station and go looking for the boys. I take out my cellphone to try and call them but quickly spy Ian, coatless and wearing a white baseball cap pulled low over his eyes, looking around the lobby.

"Ian," I say. "It's Andy."

"What's up, dude?" Ian is tall and solidly built with a thick, stumbling, yet sweet manner about him. "The guys are in the car."

There are two cars idling in the parking lot, belching white exhaust into the gray surroundings. I hop into Howie's car with Ian after giving a wave to Anthony and Justin in the other vehicle.

"How's it going?" Howie asks. "We're gonna head over to Justin's. That's where we usually hang out."

Justin's house is a modest cookie-cutter suburban home, located a few turns off the main roads in a neatly groomed community. There are shutters on the windows and the grass on the front lawn is making a valiant attempt to go green, despite the chill.

"Ma, this is the guy from *Spin,* we're gonna go upstairs and talk," Justin yells in the direction of the kitchen, already halfway up the stairs. A worried-looking woman in glasses emerges and gives a friendly greeting before retreating again to the unseen back of the house. There is a soft carpet covering everything downstairs; the colors are muted and nondescript.

Justin's bedroom takes up half of what is a tiny second floor—there's one large window and the ceiling slopes and gables around it. The walls are plastered with band posters—repeated images of Blink-182, Snoop Dogg, and, somewhat surprisingly, the thuggish rockers of Limp Bizkit. There are turntables buried beneath papers and CDs, ticket stubs taped to the wall, and a computer sitting patiently in the corner. High school bedrooms are like permanent snakeskin—unsheddable despite a rapid rate of turnover.

The guys crowd into the room with a chummy familiarity. Jackets—or what passes for them in a town where outdoors is just a place between the car and wherever it is you're going—are thrown down. Justin, a soulful, serious, and sad-eyed young man in jeans and a blue headband, cracks the window an inch, letting in a frigid blast, and with an expression of great relief lights an illicit cigarette. Ian settles onto a couch, picks up an acoustic guitar, and awkwardly begins fumbling with it.

I sit on the shag carpet in the center of them and turn on my tape recorder. "So," I say. "How long have you guys known each other?"

"I've known him since I was five," Howie says, pointing to Ian, "but we all really started coming together at the beginning of eleventh grade."

"We all hit it off really well in the beginning," Anthony says.

"We talked about shows we had gone to, and then all hung out together a few times," Howie adds.

"And then we became closer than anything," Ian adds, solemnly.

"We have other friends," Howie says. "But it's really just the four of us."

"Last night was a good example of it," Anthony says. "Everyone around here is very sports oriented, you know? So for them, it's always the same thing over and over again. But last night we went to a party and Ian was playing his acoustic guitar."

"Just rocking out," says Justin.

"Him and Howie have a little song that they actually made or whatever," Anthony says. "And we met these girls from Roslyn and they came out here. And they were like, wow, this is cool. We have guys around us but they're losers. You guys are cool. It was kinda like—"

"—They'd never seen real people that are emotional," Justin says, with a pause to communicate the gravity of the situation before stubbing out his cigarette. Ian switches places with him on the couch and lights one of his own.

"So when did you guys first get into punk?" I ask.

"I was really into classic rock when I was thirteen," Howie says with an embarrassed giggle. "And then in ninth grade I was all about rap. But I was becoming open to the punk scene. It's so different. It really opens you up to something new."

"Like what? The community aspect of it, or . . . ?"

"Nah," says Howie. "It was the energy. You can always rock out to it; it always gets you pumped up. Your first experience in a mosh pit at a punk show is like nothing else."

"I feed off of that stuff," says Anthony, whose first concert was Metallica.

"You just see the emotion," says Howie. "The singer is sprawled on the floor. He's hardcore, getting into it. You can totally relate to that."

"You go for different types of feelings in music," Anthony explains, "for different types of emotions. Like, if I want to hit someone, I'll listen to Limp Bizkit. I can still relate to 'Break Stuff.' But if something happens with my girlfriend, I'll listen to Chris [Carrabba]." Howie starts to add something, but Anthony talks over him. "It's all about the emotional intensity that turns you onto a band," he says. "I mean, you can have a good time listening to anything, but you might not get something out of it. And that's not what I'm looking for."

Despite their Long Island roots, the guys are worlds away from the politically charged DIY scene. Music to them is serious, but service-based. It's a gateway to specific feelings and emotions that are challenging, unfamiliar, or slightly out of reach. Hardcore isn't a message, it's a moment.

I ask how they first heard Dashboard Confessional.

"We were all really into Saves the Day," Howie says. "My girlfriend told me about them, like, two years ago."

"And last summer I was looking on Pollstar.com to see who was opening for them in New York and saw that it was this band called Dashboard Confessional," says Anthony. "So I went on Napster and downloaded 'The Brilliant Dance.' There was something about that song that just turned me on. So me and Ian drove and picked up his two CDs."

"The whole acoustic thing was really appealing to us at that time," Ian says.

Anthony nods. "There was a period when we were just loving acoustic. We would search on Napster for acoustic versions of songs by our favorite bands—just 'cause we were into that sound and liked those versions better."

"So they got the CDs and burned them for me," Howie says. "And then we went and saw him a week or two later opening for Saves the Day. It was—"

Justin gets up and checks his wall of ticket stubs: "July 14."

"I was weirded out at first," Howie says. "It was just a guy sitting on a stool, playing acoustic guitar."

Justin speaks up quietly, "I'll be the first to admit that I was shedding a tear during the last couple of songs."

"Yeah," says Ian, helpfully. "He was behind us, like, 'No one has ever made me cry by playing music before.'"

Justin sits up. "There've been times when I've listened to Limp Bizkit or Rage Against the Machine, when you feel that aggression and you just start to get it. But that was the first time . . . I mean, literally. Something sparked in my mind emotionally and brought it out physically. That was the opening, right there. I *had* to get the CD."

"It was a transformation for all of us," Howie says.

"We had never seen him before but suddenly we were all singing along right there," says Ian.

"Afterwards, I just played Dashboard in my car for three months straight," says Howie, reverently.

"We're the ones that turned this whole town onto his music because we're the ones that appreciate it," Anthony boasts. "Other people see our appreciation and feed off it. So they'll go out and download and burn some songs and take it from there."

"When do you listen to Dashboard these days?" I ask.

"Sometimes when we have nothing to do, we'll park my car in an empty parking lot, turn the stereo up, and just rock out," Howie says.

"We'll park and rock out and just do it," says Ian. "Have the time of our lives."

"No one else does that," adds Anthony.

"There are points in the day where you'll be upset and you just want to hear someone else," Justin adds quietly. "For you to vent and hear someone else vent helps you push on and cope better. It's not only sorrow and pain, but it pushes you." He pauses. "I know I do it."

"My favorite thing to do is drive," Howie says. "I go on random drives for hours. I also like to write a lot now, so I keep a notebook in my car. Dashboard is very inspiring. Chris will say one line and then it will give me a whole idea for what to write."

"He's got some great stuff written," says Anthony.

"When I write," says Howie, "I don't hold anything back. I just release."

"You guys certainly share your music with each other," I say, "but what about with girlfriends?"

The guys giggle.

"I think it's totally different," Howie says. "Girls don't listen to Dashboard like we do. They like it because it's catchy. I mean, I can sing along to it, bop my head and whatever, but we get the inner meaning, we get how it really relates to us. Like, I don't listen to any female bands—I turn away from them sometimes because I can't relate to it."

"Not to be sexist," says Justin, "but in a way you want to have companionship in music, that bond between another male that you can relate to. I don't think it could be such a strong connection if it was a girl."

"There's two sides to every story or whatever, but when you have a girl expressing her side of the story you really can't relate to it," explains Anthony. "Whereas, if you were in a certain situation and you hear Chris singing about it, you can relate. You put yourself in his shoes."

"It goes both ways," says Howie, helpfully. "I'm sure girls connect more to girls. Like Fiona Apple—she's like a Chris Carrabba for girls."

"My girlfriend actually hates Dashboard," says Anthony, shaking his head. "She has the feeling that every time I'm upset I'll throw on a Dashboard CD—which is true, but from the outside looking in, she sees it as a negative thing. Once I had a Dashboard lyric as my away message on AIM and she thought it was about her when I was just pissed off that day. It makes her upset."

"But Dashboard is just totally for you," says Howie.

"I was in a long-term relationship," says Justin, "and if we were in a car and there was awkward silence, I would have to hear Chris. She'd be like, what are you doing—it's just gonna make you more upset. Because they don't perceive it the way we do. Because what really happens is you get something back from it."

"But," I interject, "you were saying how some girls get impressed because you guys are so openly emotional."

More giggles.

"Yeah, girls like guys that are touchy," Anthony says with a confident leer. "Girls like it."

"We put on a show for 'em," says Howie. "They love to see us belting out."

Ian looks betrayed. "Fuck that, we're just having an awesome time."

"Like we said, you've got your sports-and-drinking people everywhere," says Justin, "and that becomes repetitive. Every night, it's us and it's music. And if it's not music—"

"It's always music," says Howie.

Everyone nods and murmurs their assent.

"I don't know what I would do if I didn't have Chris's music," says Anthony. "It's that much a part of me. When we walk around the halls at school, it's the way we're perceived through other people's eyes. And I'm not going to deny that. There's not one day where I don't talk about music or listen to music. And I don't know what I'd be doing with my time if I didn't have this to refer to or this to vent with."

"It's like a love," says Justin. "Music is an item to love."

"We wouldn't be where we are today without it," says Howie. "I think the four of us are closer than any group of friends."

"The music we listen to is so . . . *true,*" Justin says proudly. "It kind of reflects the way we are. It symbolizes us. We're true people. You're true to your feelings and true to your friends. You try."

"I can't stand people who say that emo music is pussy music," Howie says. "Everyone's got those feelings. It's whether you hide them or not."

"We've turned jocks onto Dashboard," Anthony says.

"The four of us treat girls pretty well," says Howie. "It just seems natural. We don't understand how someone could not be open about their feelings. What's the point? Why keep it inside?"

"It's true," says Justin, reverentially, rocking back and forth. "It's true. Everything is true."

I ask them what punk means to them.

"I don't even know anymore," says Justin.

"Punk was originally supposed to be away from the norm, but now it's become its own trend," says Howie. "Punk has lost a lot of its meaning."

"It's supposed to be about who you are and the individual," Ian says. "People look at us at shows and are like, 'You're not punk.'"

"He's wearing Abercrombie for God's sake," says Howie. "People like us should start developing the new punk."

"Do you guys ever listen to older stuff?" I ask.

"I have," says Howie. "It's just so different."

"It's evolved," says Anthony. "I can appreciate the Ramones or the Clash, but things are different now."

"I think emo is a better form of punk," says Howie. "Lyrically these bands can carry the style so much further."

"Emo may be marketed, but to us its fresh and it means something," says Anthony. "I define it as living your life and putting your experiences into music that other people can relate to and feed off of."

I ask if they've ever heard of Rites of Spring.

Blank stares.

Sunny Day Real Estate?

"We all downloaded a song after Chris mentioned them in an interview," says Justin.

The Promise Ring?

"I downloaded one of their songs by accident once," says Howie, laughing. "It didn't sound anything like New Found Glory!"

For a while we all talk about what's next in life. All of the guys except for Anthony are graduating in June—Justin is going to college locally, Ian is off to Albany, and Howie is straying the farthest, heading to the University of Maryland. They are, like all seniors, eager and nervous in equal parts. Everyone aspires to get off of the Island ("because there's nothing to do"). Justin is interested in business and Anthony is "looking towards accounting." It's hard to say if their passion for music, their friendship in general, is fleeting, but its effect is already profound.

"I'll probably do something with writing," says Howie. "I've always written but not this much. I'm very nostalgic so I started writing this autobiography. I started writing all about my life and I've got fifteen pages already. I'll see where it goes from there."

Suddenly someone looks at their watch and realizes that it's time to go. If we're going to make it to downtown Manhattan at the exact right moment (before Carrabba takes the stage, after the opening acts, yet with enough time to maneuver to the front of the crowd), we'll have to race to catch the right train. So with barely a shout to Justin's mother—still quietly toiling on something far out of sight—we race down the stairs and into the frosty, darkening evening.

The night is freezing but the guys don't wear jackets. Instead, all five of us pile into Justin's car. We have ten minutes to reach the train station. If I remember correctly, the train station is about twelve minutes away. Something will have to give—and within seconds I realize it's the Nassau County traffic laws. We peel out into the street with a throaty roar. I'm sandwiched in the backseat, grateful, for a moment, that I can't see the windshield clearly. Anthony and Justin roll down the windows in the front so they can smoke, and cold, nicotined air blasts back into our faces. Somebody leans forward to throw in the Thursday CD and the hopefully-not-prophetic opening chords of "Understanding in a Car Crash" blast out of the tinny speakers. As Justin speeds through yet another yellow light, I realize something: *it sounds fantastic.* The vocals start and all four of the guys join in in unison, belting out each lyric: "time runs through our veins!" Soon, some of them are singing the backup vocals, adding little flourishes of harmony here and there, while the guitars peal like church bells and we cut a quicksilver swath through suburban Plainview. Justin passes his cigarette back to Ian for a good-natured puff. I have no doubt we're going to make it in time when I realize this is every night for these guys—this is what they do: drive fast, listen to music, sing together. Listening to Thursday and then, when the song ends, to Taking Back Sunday in a speeding Toyota on a freezing April night in Long Island is like listening to Puccini in the Duomo or the Eagles while doing a coke binge in the Hollywood Hills: this is the right moment, the right time. For the first time, not a single note of any of these songs sounds forced or free-floating. This is beyond context; this is what these songs are about.

When we pull into the LIRR station at the exact moment our train is supposed to be leaving, an infectious giddiness spreads through everyone and we full-out sprint towards the tracks. It's a familiar high school confidence at work—we cannot miss this concert, so we *will not* miss it. The train will be there for us. There simply is no other option.

And, of course, it works out. As we skid to a halt, red-faced and gasping, on the platform we hear the familiar slow tolling of an approaching train. The rest of the waiting crowd—an assortment of young and very young adults done up to the nines in search of a flashy Manhattan Saturday night—gives us suspicious looks, all of which are deserved. When we pile into seats spread out over a mostly full car, it's almost a letdown.

For a while, the guys are silent, catching their breath, but as the train speeds up, talk turns to the concert we're about to attend.

"I'm really protective of Dashboard," Howie says. "It's so personal. It makes me physically upset when people tell me they heard him on MTV. He's come so far in such a short time."

"I'm trying to figure out how much farther he can possibly go with something that's so unique," says Justin, thoughtfully. "How far can it go in modern society?"

"He's successful, and that's great for him," says Anthony. "He made a career out of what he loves. But when it gets really big and you have all of Madison Square Garden singing the songs, it's not everyone living that experience or feeling that experience. It's just knowing the words and going with it. And that's what tonight's gonna be like. It will be people reciting words that they know as opposed to belting out the words that you feel."

"I don't blame him if he goes big," says Howie. "I wouldn't do it any different. But I want him to stay ours. I know it's selfish, but I feel like it's ours."

"It's like what happened with Saves the Day," Anthony says. "They played on Long Island a few months ago and now they're playing the Garden."

"It's like—what are you doing here?" Howie laughs "Where did you go?"

"There's no energy at big shows," adds Anthony. "No connection with the band. Taking Back Sunday at the Knitting Factory was the best show I've ever seen. It was no bigger than this train car, but I was *up there*. Adam gave me the microphone and I was singing with him."

"It's all about interactions," says Justin.

Anthony continues, "I'm making eye contact with the singer and we're feeding off of that. He keeps telling *us* that *we* rock."

"And this is a band we're listening to," enthuses Howie.

"But society tells you that it's a better show if there are more people there. That popular means better."

They all roll their eyes and laugh as the train enters another tunnel.

After a race through Penn Station, packed with passengers from the weekend rush, we hail two cabs and careen past blurring headlights towards Irving Plaza. The guys seem quieter, more focused. "All this talking has gotten me really pumped up," Howie says as we near the venue. When we arrive, I promise to do my best to introduce them to Chris, then push alone into the fray.

The place is packed to the gills and there's a palpable energy emanating out onto the street. Scalpers ask for extra tickets and mean it—this is not a no-show event. There are other bridge-and-tunnel teens clutching both their handbags and their boyfriends with giddy expressions on their made-up faces. I catch sight of a blonde wearing a baby-T with "Dashboard Confessional" emblazoned on it in bright gold glitter lettering. Everything has doubled since the CBGB's night just five months previous—it feels like a baby going straight from crawling to sprinting.

Up in the club's balcony VIP area there are industry vultures buzzing loudly, drinking, smoking, and laughing too forcefully. There are tables set aside for Carson Daly and for the lead reviewers from *Rolling Stone* and the *New York Times*. The table closest to the stage is empty, reserved for the Carrabba family. I meet a VP of MTV and a young NBC producer and his pretty VJ girlfriend. They rave about Chris and about how Carson's a huge fan. Fifteen minutes before show time Chris himself rockets out of the backstage door like a bullet, his tiny, black-clad frame cleaving through well-wishers like a car tire through wet snow. He greets everyone with a hug but his eyes are nervous, darting all around the club, and his blinking is rapid-fire. He moves on to second conversations before finishing his first. Apparently, he's desperately searching for his grandmother.

The show itself is rapturous and bighearted—but the guys were right, there are a worrying number of hangers-on hanging out in the back by the bar, neither participating nor listening. Howie and Anthony do their best to make up for them, though, singing loudly and lustily to every song—even providing harmonies and vocal counterpoints to the rest of the crowd on the most popular numbers. Every so often, the four try to move up to the lip of the stage but are rebuffed by the sheer volume of fans in front of them. They play it off, but seem slightly put out.

The show ends with an uncharacteristically rollicking version of an older Dashboard song, the self-punishing anthem, "Ender Will Save Us All." This time, instead of building to an introverted climax of frustration, Carrabba pounds on his electric guitar (a new addition to the Dashboard live show) and runs his tender voice to a harsh scream. As he crescendos with a savage yell of "try not to be wrong," he suddenly throws himself into the churning audience, fist raised like a championship boxer or martyr or both. It's worlds away from the intimate group therapy of previous shows, and is awkwardly strident.

The lights come on and the guys are smiling, but tightly, and it feels like ownership has been passed on. They wait for a while upstairs for Chris to come out and for me to introduce them, but twenty minutes later, when the bouncers tell us to clear out, it's evident he's not gonna show. Everyone's down, but understanding.

"I'd just want to thank him," says Justin, as he walks down the stairs. "Because he's gotten me through so much stuff. Just shake his hand, you know?"

"Yeah," Anthony says, "it's not about autographs."

We walk outside into the frigid chill.

"He's become one of us *to* us," says Howie.

"The love we all have for him is a common bond," Justin says.

"I mean, I've spent as much time with him as I have with these guys," says Howie.

There's a pause, some awkward shuffling. Ian kicks at the pavement. Justin is looking at the looming shadow of the deluxe tour bus parked in front of the club.

"You know what," says Howie. "I wish the four of us had gotten together in ninth grade and had the time and the money to start a band ourselves. Because we all have the desire and the passion. We would do it. But we're in April of our senior year—it's too late."

What I want to tell them as they hail cabs for the long commute back out onto the island, towards home, safety, quiet, and routine, is that they *did* form a band. With their heightened sense of drama, their dogmatic insistence on togetherness, on shared experience, on the validity of their worldview and an unyielding desire to spread it to others, they're no different from any young band playing at the Vanderbilt on Long Island, being traded on MP3.com, signed to Drive-Thru Records, opening for Dashboard Confessional tonight in Manhattan. They know what they want out of music, out of each other, and they have the ability to get it, whenever, however they want it. They stick together, they perform for others, for themselves. With graduation looming, their time together may be limited, but it's made that much more intense for it. Goofing on each other, arms linked, quick with insults and high fives, the four guys are living in their moment. Like any other emo band in America, the four are just, as Ian puts it, "rocking out, having the time of our lives."

TWELVE

THIS OLD WOUND

Chris Carrabba is an open book and he's begging everyone to read it. Since the year 2000, the twenty-eight-year-old punk lifer/special ed teacher has found a perfect way to meld his two callings. He performs and records as Dashboard Confessional, a self-lacerating public diary project that's required summer reading for every disaffected teenager in the country: those who are unhappy with themselves, with the opposite sex, with their parents; those who feel that they have hidden depths waiting to be explored; those who are bored, unappreciated, and misunderstood. Which is to say, all of them.

More than anyone else affiliated with the burgeoning emo scene, it is Carrabba who is the breakout star, a poster-boy combination of artistry, looks, and charisma. His music is stripped, direct, and painfully honest—informed by previous incarnations of emo and hardcore, but presented in a manner that is both original and timeless: comfortable folk/rock balladeering married to acrid, emotionally bulimic lyrics. His songs have titles like "The Sharp Hint of New Tears," and "Living In Your Letters." Fans have been known to sob and sing at his concerts. Girls want either to date him or comfort him; boys want to thank him or be him. His rise is both familiar and unique, but all can agree that it would have been impossible even five years earlier; call it grassroots .com. It is a success based on personal connection and word-of-mouth raves, just like hundreds if not thousands of underground phenomenons before him, and his work ethic is indie-rock through and through—during his first year of touring as Dashboard Confessional he played over 280 concerts in every town that would have him. He knows what it means to live your life in a rickety van, to eat three meals a day at Denny's. Yet his emergence also perfectly dovetailed with the proliferation of music on the web, not just as a delivery system but also as an aesthetic—a place where a best-kept secret can be public knowledge, where a random recommendation can, within seconds, result in a lifelong attachment. His fans know the words to his songs before they've been released, and his first-ever concert in California sold out two months in advance. He is the rare artist whose sensibilities and style perfectly mesh with a particularly appropriate cultural moment.

During his brief rocket ride into the national consciousness, Carrabba has been called both messiah and pariah—he's the singer/songwriter a generation didn't even realize they were hungering for, and he's the milquetoast balladeer about whom thousands of critics are cringing at the thought of covering. As with all true phenomenons, the Dashboard media experience has quickly overshadowed the music—he is a story, an avatar, a placeholder. To everyone, that is, except his kids.

Love for Dashboard Confessional spread across the country in 2001 and 2002 like mono in the '50s: an intimate interaction between mouthy teenagers. As Carrabba's popularity skyrockets, he brings elements of hardcore values into suburban bedrooms and major concert venues. For many young people, his concerts are the first time they've felt comfortable singing along, where they've been valued as equals of the band, not merely as consumers. He is the first pop star who's easily approachable, who makes himself accessible. By making his problems so public, he encourages others to do the same. He may not lead people to question authority, but he does make them question themselves.

Whether that's enough for some is a different matter. The brand of punk that Carrabba carries with him is a particularly egalitarian strain, one born more of suburban boredom than societal decay, and his fans tend to be more Abercrombie than anarchy. He makes no comments about world events or elections, he doesn't stump for Greenpeace or refuse to make videos. He has opinions, but he's very careful about keeping them to himself; he can barely figure out his own head, why try too hard to influence others? Unlike other genre figureheads or—gulp—generational spokespeople, Carrabba isn't a troubled genius. He's more of a troubled everyman, and he makes no bones about his deep-seated need for acceptance.

In this way, Dashboard Confessional concerts shatter boundaries between performer and audience, between artist and fan, and between complete strangers. There is a specific person onstage and specific songs about specific moments in one individual's life. But Dashboard concerts transform monologues into dialogues, secret thoughts into public statements. Everyone sings at Dashboard concerts—when Chris takes the stage his first words are usually, "Are you guys ready to try one?" and everyone sings loudly, passionately. They sing the words like they belong to them, but no one seems to mind that everyone else is claiming a piece of their property. There is an indescribable energy in the room; there's no shame, no judgment, and no restraint. Individual problems become group therapy; there is strength in numbers. Carrabba runs his voice ragged and lets a roomful of teenagers find theirs.

For a potentially limitless audience of confused teenagers, Dashboard Confessional is Fugazi—a vital trigger that, in one listen, can answer questions they didn't even realize they were asking. Unlike Fugazi, however, Dashboard doesn't push, doesn't demand, and doesn't challenge. There is no blueprint for better living, just a visibly bruised road map of one individual's emotional peaks and valleys. Yet there is a perverse strength in his community of doubt. Dashboard concerts are safe havens, full retreats from the world and into the self. Chris may be an easier sort of idol—musically nonthreatening to the extreme—but no less monumental. Fugazi wants to shake you until you wake up. Dashboard Confessional wants to hold you until you fall asleep.

Chris Carrabba is dressed in black, with a skate-company baseball cap pulled low over his huge, dark eyes and a hood cinched tightly around his head. You'd think he was safe. But not in front of these kids. They saw him coming a mile away.

"Chris! Chris!" they yell. A chubby boy asks for an autograph and two skinny girls, bordering on hysterical, tug at his arms. Soon he's surrounded. One cynic asks if Carrabba is in 'N Sync and gets quickly hushed. A boy with glasses says, "Chris, we have something to show you."

"What is it?" Carrabba asks patiently.

"It's a snake," says the boy, thrusting a wiggling green lizard underneath his nose. From the parking lot, the mothers of the eight- and nine-year-olds smile and laugh. It's like this whenever "Mr. Chris" shows up.

It's a November evening in Boca Raton, Florida, and Chris Carrabba is walking the breezeways of JC Mitchell, a special ed elementary school and after-school program where he worked in the days before he was known as Dashboard Confessional. Carrabba is preternaturally small and birdlike, yet he moves among the swarming children with confidence and patience. He remembers each child's name and never pulls away from any of them while he's speaking to his former colleagues about adult concerns (like mutual friends in rehab).

Though the cult of fans who live, die, breathe, make out, and IM to Dashboard Confessional's music are considerably older than those who surround him here, Carrabba's attitude towards them is markedly similar. "You should never ever talk to kids like they're kids," he says later, while driving in search of some coffee. "You talk to them like people. You think they don't know what's going on? Adults are so jaded by the world that we think we understand it. At least kids get the fact that they don't understand it yet."

There is, as always, an odd solemnity to the way he speaks, but also an undeniable charisma. At Dunkin' Donuts, Carrabba pulls out his wallet to pay and, along with the money, removes a thick wad of folded-up papers. They are notes, dozens of them, from fans. Letters, poems, thank-yous. "It's kind of ridiculous how much stuff I have in here," he says, unfolding one small piece of thick white paper with pencil scribblings on it. "I got into a brief conversation with a girl in Wooster a few months ago, right when we were just starting out. When we went through town again recently she had written this poem for me and I carry it with me everywhere I go—her name's Christine and she was at the CBGB show the other day because she goes to NYU now. I hold onto it. Kids don't need to write something for me to walk away with a great feeling, but I do hold onto all of it. You just don't know the power of your own words sometimes."

Carrabba is not at all the depressive his songs would make him out to be—he's constantly cracking jokes and laughs a lot, even at his own self-serious image (he once suggested filming a video dressed up as the "Visible Man," but lamented that "no one will realize that I'm kidding"). He has a well-publicized obsession with the television series *Buffy the Vampire Slayer*—and a huge crush on the show's star, Sarah Michelle Gellar. He is tightly wound, however—especially around those not within his carefully guarded inner circle—and tends to dictate the emotional stakes of whatever situation he's in. The notes in his wallet are a constant reminder of his chosen career path and the responsibilities he's taken on. Though they provide him with the creative fuel to continue, the expectations and hopes of his fans can weigh heavily on him at times.

Over the past two years, as Carrabba's popularity has grown, so too has the glare from the media spotlight. Magazines from *GQ* to *Tiger Beat* have given a considerable amount of ink to the young troubadour, usually focusing only on the more familiar parts of his history (sad breakup songs, fan sing-alongs) and casting him against his will as the ringleader of a national emo movement. When his critics cringe and dismiss his albums as self-indulgent whining, they're unaware that they're only listening to one side of the story. The purpose of Dashboard Confessional as a project comes from the completed circle, of the kids finding a commonality in the music and lyrics—a shared experience—taking in the bitter carbon dioxide that Carrabba spits out and audiosynthesizing it into fresh oxygen, into a fresh start both for them and for the rock star on the stage. It's understandable to become frustrated with the monotony, the relentlessness of Carrabba's recordings—it's hinted at in the name of the band. A Dashboard hears everything but gives nothing back. It's a one-sided rant and admittedly so. He takes his show on the road to find someone, anyone who will respond. Kids think they're going to a Dashboard Confessional concert to hear Chris Carrabba, but in all honesty he's going to hear them.

For all the talk of Chris raking over his exes in his music, the true constant is that he's putting the gun to his own head. There is an enormous amount of specific hurt that he has refused to talk about in public and continues to obsess over. There are things to be discovered about him that will only make his young fans want to care for him more, that will only make the trend-spotters sigh, crack their knuckles, and prepare yet another feature. Even his would-be enemies—Drive-Thru Records is one such example—praise him for always taking the high road and never discussing business difficulties in public. Call him a sucker, call him manipulative, but Chris Carrabba's entire existence seems to be about finding more people to give his heart away to. On one level, that's why he tours so extensively. Only the kids have never let him down. He gets onstage, rips his heart from his chest, and throws it out into the crowd, and he never ceases to look surprised when, lifted up by a thousand voices, it always manages to find its way back to him. "I'm open, but I'm not public," he said to me during our first meeting. "I made this music thinking only my close friends would hear it. I found out that there are more people I could trust with my feelings than I thought."

Most of those people, however, tend to be under the age of twenty-one. While the case could be made that any musician who gains new-found popularity via MTV or the radio will inherently attract a younger audience—and that it's teenagers who are perpetually those most fanatical about music—Chris's phenomenon is defined by its young adherents. He claims not to know why his crowds are always so much younger than him; why those who live and breathe his lyrics are often a decade his junior. "Maybe," he told me once, "it's because all the stuff that I keep buried is the stuff most people work through at that age." For all his emotional honesty, he's flexing muscles that are strained and atrophied. He's working over things from his own teenage years that he's yet to deal with while concurrently processing his life in a public, potentially unhealthy manner.

Since he walked away from college a few years ago, at the height of his own personal turmoil, he has lived the rock 'n' roll life—a blueprint that everyone from Mick Jagger to New Found Glory could tell you is predicated on the avoidance of reality, the perpetuity of adolescence. Teenagers are, by nature, "walking open wounds / a trophy display of bruises" they haven't yet learned how to let heal. But Chris is now caught in an emotional iron maiden of his own design. Every night he picks at his scabs until the blood flows again. The new batch of kids—bleeding for the very first time—have a new hero. But Chris has yet to heal. He doesn't have any scar tissue—he doesn't even have any scars yet. When I first met him he claimed that the songs were his way of "closure." When he pushes the problem out of himself it becomes everyone else's; he's free of it. But every night he lets the genie out of the bottle, then bottles him right back up inside of himself after leaving the stage. The moments that he shares are the worst moments. But they were still his moments, and now they're not even his anymore. When an entire phenomenon is based on the broken heart of one admittedly screwed-up young guy, is it possible to stretch it across an entire country? Across an entire career?

The older of two sons, Carrabba was born in Hartford, Connecticut, in 1975. His childhood was fairly typical by all accounts, his family both broken (he and his younger brother Nick were raised by their mother, Anne Dichele) and extensive (both Dichele and Carrabba's father, with whom he no longer has any contact, have deep roots in the West Hartford area). It was his Uncle Angelo who gave him his first acoustic guitar at age fifteen; it was his mother who instilled in him a love of language. "I have an incredible family structure," he says. "One where everybody's goals were touted as relevant and everybody's gifts were touted as extraordinary, no matter what they were." Following in his stepbrother, Bill's, footsteps, Chris became an avid skateboarder and a less than avid student.

"I was listening to pretty much whatever was on the radio and whatever my older brother thought was cool at the time, but he wasn't exactly a vast well to draw from. The Beach Boys, Metallica, They Might Be Giants. Anthrax. And then I heard Fugazi on a skate video and lost my mind. I realized, the rest of this stuff sucks. Where's the real deal? It turned me on. It lit me up."

It was around this time that Carrabba's mother, newly remarried, decided it was time for a change. Wanting to start a new life somewhere tropical, the family discussed moving to Texas before deciding on South Florida. Applying his newfound punk values to his situation, young Chris was furious.

"I didn't want to go there at all. It was terrible. I had my first girl-friend. I had my closest friends that I'd made. I had just turned sixteen when we moved. When you're an early teenager you feel like you've just made your first friends on your own merit. People are finally connecting with who you are or who you are becoming. It all felt new and didn't feel like this was something that repeated itself over and over in life. I was just young and stupid. And bitter. And angry. You know, a teenager. I didn't want to go at all. Of course, I lightened up about a month in. Made some friends and met a girl and realized I could skateboard all winter long. And that was it: I was in my glory."

Chris's tight posse of skateboarding buddies soon morphed into music-making mates as well. "The kids I was skateboarding with during the day went to shows at night, so I went with them. I remember thinking, 'Wait, people do this? They play guitar . . . together?'" Right from the start there was an appealing egalitarian aesthetic to the shows. The urgency that Fugazi communicated through headphones was suddenly brought to vivid life—there was no distance between performer and audience at those early Florida punk shows. The bands were people everyone knew. All of a sudden, music was no longer a one-way street.

"In terms of the music that we loved, Florida was about as geograph-ically isolated as you could get. For indie-rock and punk bands, traveling from Atlanta to Fort Lauderdale in a van to play for maybe twenty kids—that's a hell of a trek. So when you're there and bands won't come to you, you make your own fun. That's why there's such a healthy diver-sity in the music scene there. I mean, Marilyn Manson is from the same town we are—we used to see him at the local bar. So we all helped each other. The bands were all incestuous; I was in five bands at once and wanted to be in more. There was a time when my friends used to joke that I was in every band in South Florida. That wouldn't have happened anywhere else. In any other town it would have sufficed to be a fan and maybe noodled at home in my bedroom. I have incredibly bad stage fright and it would have been very easy not to get onstage at all. But when it was absolutely the most fun thing you could do with your friends, then why not? And everybody would go to everybody's shows. Partly because it was the only thing to do at night but partly because we wanted to support each other. In hindsight, it looks like we were trying to make a quality music scene. We just didn't know it."

The first band that Chris sang with was the Vacant Andys, a loose punk ensemble he helped start in 1995. When the band parted ways with their singer, Chris was named as his replacement solely because he could sing and play his instrument simultaneously better than anyone else. "The band was me, John Owens, who was one of my first and closest friends in Florida, Dan Bonebrake, my best friend, on bass, and Dan's brother was the drummer. So this was my family. We lived together, practiced together every night. I never felt like I was the focal point. Two days after we kicked out the singer we had a gig at this crusty, gutterpunk club right on the beach. And we were terrible. Yeah, I was nervous, but it was just so much fun. From load-in to load-out— taking so much pride in carrying your amplifier through the sand and over some rickety stairs. I fell in love with the whole process."

The burgeoning scene in Florida was the polar opposite of the earliest days of hardcore on the east coast, when every bit of progress wasn't just claimed but fought for, often bloodily. An aura of family, of friendship—perhaps fueled in no small way by the eternally beautiful weather—permeated the music that was made, transforming punk in the process. It wasn't oppositional, it was occupational. Bands that would later break onto the national stage would share gigs, meals, and drummers, and the support was evenly spread around, from the straight pop-punk of New Found Glory to the indie-pop of The Rocking Horse Winner and the unambiguous storytelling rock of Legends of the Rodeo. "You couldn't go to any show without everyone singing along," Carrabba says. It was exciting, thrilling, and expressive, sure, but it wasn't yet life or death for him. And that open-minded, lowstakes mindset profoundly affected his attitude towards his career. "I've never been a purist in any sense. Be on the radio. Music is for everyone. It didn't matter if you dressed like a hardcore kid or an indie-rock kid. Just go to the shows. There's no one you can't be at the shows. If it appeals to one type of person, why can't it appeal to others? Washington D.C. has always had a very heartfelt and unique music scene but there's an isolation there that's self-imposed. All the way down in Florida, their world always seemed kind of reactionary, like, 'We're doing things our way.' While we were just like, 'We're doing things!'"

At around the same time, Chris began college at Florida Atlantic University (helpfully located across the street from his high school), hoping to graduate with a degree in education. Since high school, he had been volunteering at JC Mitchell, a local elementary school and after-school program for kids with special needs, and had quickly found a professional passion to match the love he had for his recreational pursuits. While juggling classes and his various band commitments, Chris went from volunteering in the after-school program to becoming a full-fledged instructor. He kept an acoustic guitar in his office and often played music for the students. "I think I really thrived on it because you can have tangible evidence that you're affecting someone on a level that isn't nominal. Everything from helping them with their homework to maybe getting them to open up to you about something they wouldn't have shared with anyone."

Carrabba had a definite idea of the kind of music he wanted to be making—emotionally direct and musically expansive—but was unsure how to best realize it. Torn between professional commitments, the lure of being in touring bands, and personal upheavals, Carrabba left school for a time in 1996, returned, and then left again for good in 1998, determined to give music a serious shot. He spent some time as a second guitarist in a band called The Agency where he befriended the drummer, an infectiously outgoing Floridian named Mike Marsh. He tried starting a band called Red Letter Day with a friend from college named Jolie Lindholm. Brimming with songs but finding no outlet for them, Carrabba booked some studio time for himself and recorded three songs—"For Justin," "Drowning," and "Anyone. Anyone?"—by himself, alone in the studio with an acoustic guitar. Dismissed now by Carrabba as "an exercise," the songs, which would later form the first Dashboard Confessional release, *The Drowning* EP, were spartan, intimate, and richly emotional. "For Justin" was a particularly heavy listen that documented a cousin's drowning death. Though he claims to have been unaware of it, Carrabba wrote the song on the one-year anniversary of the event. (The title of the EP is always assumed, quite logically, to have emerged from that song, but Chris says that, in fact, it refers to drowning one's sorrows.) Carrabba gave a tape of the three songs to a friend named Chad Neptune. Neptune was playing bass with some friends with similar musical intentions and was looking for a singer. "There was something on that EP that sparked them," Chris remembers, "and so it looked like our ships were sailing in the right direction." The five-piece band was soon playing shows all over Florida under the name Further Seems Forever.

The group moved past the fun-loving sprawl of the Vacant Andys, crafting sweeping—some would say pretentious—soundscapes to complement the often bleak lyrical musings of Carrabba. Further was different outside of the music as well. While Carrabba was friendly with all of his bandmates, Further lacked the familial vibe that had been such a solace and strength to him in the past. There were plenty of interband squabblings, some of which turned physical. The stress was increased by the fact that the band's lead guitarist had a young family in Boca and refused to tour outside of the state, forcing a constant search for temporary replacements. For someone who had just left college and was living on ramen, the lack of dedication was frustrating. And yet, despite the stress, the band soon gained a rabid underground following. The songs were intense and intensely labored. Carrabba's life was in flux, and the lyrics he wrote and sang with Further wrestled with the same problems as on *The Drowning* EP, but on a much grander scale. Instead of questioning himself, with Further, Carrabba seemed to question the universe. This combination of the austere and the devotional led to the group being signed in early 2000 by Seattle-based Christian indie label Tooth and Nail (an act that would lead many writers and fans to assume—incorrectly—that Carrabba himself was a proslytizing Christian).

By that point, however, Carrabba had lost interest.

In 1999, Chris's personal life took one horrific blow after another, from the dissolution of a marriage engagement to an event in his family so terrible and personal that he still won't discuss it publicly. As he had done the year before, he sought solace in his acoustic guitar.

"I wrote the song 'A Plain Morning' at a moment in my life that was so horrible I desperately needed to feel something beautiful. I was in Connecticut and it's so damn cold there in March—that's where the chorus comes from, 'it's colder than it ought to be in March.' But it's also how I was feeling. It was the beginning of a crazy downward spiral that basically turned my life on its ear. What it did to my family. What it did to the relationships I was in. It basically ruined my life. And now couples tell me that that song is 'their song.' And I'm like, good grief!"

The lyrics do hint at a simpler sort of melancholy, of a lover on the road, anxious to return: "I've still got a day or two ahead of me until I'll be heading home and to your arms again." But the real subject of the song, often overlooked, is Chris himself and the loss of his happiness, of the status quo: "I'm glad you're not a part of this / there's parts of me that will be missed." The song's most lasting image, of a scented lover's note ("she wrote the words 'I love you' / and sprayed it with perfume. . . .") is also widely misinterpreted.

"I was sitting on a bed in Connecticut, trying to write that song, when my eight-year-old half sister walked into the room," he says. "She wrote that to me on a piece of paper and then sprayed it with her kiddie perfume and handed it to me. I immediately wrote it into the song and tried not to cry in front of her."

From that anguish, Carrabba crafted an eleven-song album. Since he considered the material far too personal for Further Seems Forever, in January 2000 he once again booked studio time and, with the help of friend and producer James Paul Wismer, recorded the album and titled it *The Swiss Army Romance*. He only shared the result with a few friends, but one of them was Amy Fleischer (the last song on *Swiss Army*, "Shirts and Gloves," was written for Fleischer when both of them were out on tour and were forced to miss their weekly *Dawson's Creek* party). Fleischer had recently started a fledgling indie label—Fiddler Records—and after much prodding convinced Carrabba to allow her to release *Swiss Army* herself.

Carrabba, very much involved with Further Seems Forever, felt strongly that the record was a side project made for his own sanity and as a way of explaining himself to a few close friends—one that could evolve to include other friends with hectic touring schedules and therefore shouldn't be credited to "Chris Carrabba." So, nicking a memorable line from one of the songs, "The Sharp Hint of New Tears" ("on the way home / this car hears my confession"), Carrabba named the project Dashboard Confessional.

Swiss Army, despite its unyielding Sturm und Drang, is a nuanced, melancholy album. The best songs evoke a fantastical teenage twilight—a world that's lost to memory that may never have existed or been as pure as it's remembered to be. A long-distance relationship haunts nearly all of the songs; we're privy to one side of cross-country phone calls and left to imagine the other side as only a dedicated romantic would. Underneath it all there's a real sense that the home Carrabba longs for so deeply isn't there for him the way it used to be. Hearts have grown cold, mistakes have been made. The album's soul is undoubtedly its center, where the forced smile of "A Plain Morning" runs into the wistful acceptance of "Age 6 Racer." The former begins with uncertainty ("it's yet to be determined") but the latter begins with a peaceful, utterly guileless farewell ("so long sweet summer"). With his close friend Jolie Lindholm singing with him, her sugarcane falsetto cheering his broken tenor, Carrabba sketches out a brief, bright burst of romance, snuffed out prematurely: "hey thanks for that summer / it's cold where you're going, I hope your heart's always warm." Eventually, to teenage ears, that song would become the perfect end to summer camp, an eerily accurate and haunting last song on side two of the high school graduation mix tape. But for its writer, it will always be painful.

"I was sifting through a lot of stuff that I hadn't dealt with on that album," he says. "One relationship had just ended and there was one that I had kept away, locked in a vault for much longer than was wise. It's all over the place because I was trying to capture such a long moment. It was a long healing process. I was so not happy and then I had to learn how to make myself happy again. That shows in the order of the songs. But I was really focused on one person throughout. And you can tell—the lyrics are really biting. What I was writing about her was so—I had to turn the eye inward finally, and become more self-effacing. That's where the title song comes from."

More than any other song in the Dashboard catalog, it's "The Swiss Army Romance" that seems to best capture what the band is about and what its fans clamor for. "The title referred to her—well, actually to people like us," Chris says. "Our relationship just got to this point where it was all . . . neutral. Totally neutral. Just like the Swiss Army." The song itself is anything but detached, taking a microscope to its author for the first time, locating the cracks in the public veneer, and then pulling out the blades and dissecting away. The first verse goes after the usual target: "you're not so happy / you're not secure / you're dying to look cute in your blue jeans / but you're plastic just like everyone," but the second verse is all Chris. While the recorded version is second-person all the way through, live, Chris switches to the first person: "I'm dying to look cool in my tattoos / but I'm searching just like everyone / I could be anyone." When translated to the Dashboard live audience, it's a rallying cry for a disaffected and profoundly misunderstood generation. "We're not twenty-one," the song continues, "but the sooner we are / the sooner the fun will begin / so get out your fake eyelashes / fake IDs and real disasters / ensue." The song doesn't judge the kids singing along for dressing cool, for wearing makeup, for trying to fit in. In fact, it empowers them by recognizing their secret depths. It quietly acknowledges the unshakeable uncertainty behind every one of those minute decisions, the daily choices that can ruin or save your life, when your life is only sixteen years long. Live, the end of "The Swiss Army Romance" is invariably a highlight of the show, as Chris's forceful strumming gives way to a roomful of kids chanting the final lines in perfect unison, "it's cool to take these chances / it's cool to fake romances," and Chris usually returns to the mic at the end, joining them as they all sing "and grow up fast / and grow up fast / and grow up fast." It's a powerful moment, caught somewhere between a desperate wish and a palpable fear, as an earlier lyric, echoing Minor Threat, declares, "youth's the most unfaithful mistress / still we forge ahead to miss her." It's not present on the record, but when performing live, Chris always ends the song with a drawn-out, heartfelt admonition: "don't grow up fast." It's the one moment when Carrabba reverts to his teaching days, placing himself, however slightly, above the audience.

"I wrote that song when I was twenty-three," he says. "It's about how normal it is for everyone to try and be something they're not. Why does there always have to be a golden goose? It's a chance to share what slim wisdom I have and say, 'Slow down. What's the rush?'"

But it would be the album's first song that would prove to have the most impact on Dashboard Confessional's career. "Screaming Infidelities," a letter to a betraying lover, is an unlikely breakthrough by any stretch. It's a three-minute wallow—self-pitying and generally humorless—though it does contain one of Carrabba's best lines: "[I'll] sit around and wonder / how you're making out / but as for me I wish that I was anywhere / with anyone / making out." There are three different melodic lines—generously, it can be said that there are three different hooks. But the entire effect of the song is more like an antihook—it lies down on the couch in front of you with a pained look on its face and more or less begs you to love it, or at least to listen to its litany of complaints.

It takes a hardened punk or a dedicated softie to sing the line, "I'm cuddling close to blankets and sheets / you're not alone, you're not discreet," but Carrabba, an avowed mama's boy, was never much of a punk anyway. The song is a baleful, puppy-dog stare and listeners were immediately drawn to it precisely because of its woe-is-me honesty. Everyone has, at least once in their lives, been betrayed, abandoned, or dumped, thereby leaving one utterly alone at the exact moment when another's presence is needed most. On "Screaming Infidelities," Carrabba builds a makeshift community out of the traces a relationship leaves behind—"the saddest songs," "the spots where we'd have to sleep," and, most memorably, "your hair," which is discovered everywhere. Just when he considered himself, finally, "alone in [his] defeat," Carrabba reached out to others. The song transforms into the anthem of a ragtag lonely hearts club band—a song to be sung by a group about being alone. It's the strangest hit single in quite some time—a slow-paced dirge that's fundamentally anti–slow dancing. "Screaming Infidelities" won't end any proms in the year of its success: it may be the perfect soundtrack for rocking back and forth with arms around you, but the only person you'll be hugging is yourself.

"I never intended to perform the Dashboard songs in front of people," Chris says. "I would play the songs for close friends who were familiar with what I was going through and, eventually, they would know the words and sing along with me. Not long after finishing the record, however, Chris was asked to join the bill of an acoustic in-store performance with Saves the Day at Blue Note Records in Miami. "It was in front of twelve kids and it was awful," he says. "I hated it. It was the scariest thing I'd ever done in my life." It all might have ended there had friends not begged him to join another bill a few weeks later, this one a charity benefit at a college in West Palm Beach. "It was a scene of kids who had never seen me before and I had never seen any of them. But they got what the songs were about, what they meant to me. They got it like *this,*" he says, snapping his fingers. The visceral thrill of having strangers not only empathize with but join in his musical healing process was addictive for Carrabba. Soon he was playing shows in Florida as Dashboard Confessional, a solo act with just him, a guitar, a stool, and a boatload of issues to work through. At the very first shows, Chris's friends would stand at the front, singing every lyric along with him, helping him get over his nerves, and reminding him that he wasn't really alone. Soon, entire crowds would follow suit.

Emboldened—and weary of Further's inability to motivate itself—Carrabba decided to take his music out on the road the the only way he knew how: by joining hardcore tours up and down the east coast. To keep costs low, and because there was no other logical way to present the songs, he played innumerable dates alone on a stool with an acoustic guitar sandwiched between crushingly loud and aggressive punk bands like Antiflag and Hatebreed. He also met, befriended, and opened for future emo success stories like Thursday and The Movielife. The surprise of seeing an acoustic balladeer in what was billed as a one-trick concert tended to mute the naysayers. Two songs into his anguish, a majority of the rooms was converted, and by the end of the set, the stage fright–riddled Carrabba had sent nearly everyone to the merch table to buy CDs ("nobody bought just one; they always bought an extra to send to somebody else who they felt needed to hear it") or straight home to their computers to search frantically for MP3s. "It was really scary playing those songs alone onstage," he remembers. "It was a real challenge. But that's where things started." And they continued online, where word of this empathetic troubadour spread like ebola. Dashboard Confessional was then, as it is today, the best possible kind of secret, one you want to share with everyone you know and care about. Links to MP3s of *Swiss Army* songs began popping up on the messageboards of like-minded bands—New Found Glory, Jimmy Eat World, Saves the Day. And in the summer of 2000, the Napster file-trading service was at its peak, allowing Carrabba's songs to crisscross the country like good-luck chain letters, spreading his legend and lyrics to places he'd never even visited, let alone performed in. Soon, Dashboard Confessional concerts would sell out weeks in advance and would be filled with kids seeing him for the first time, knowing every word by heart. "My music came at a time when Napster was really hot and so everyone in the audiences would know the songs before I got there," Carrabba says. "Kids would always come up to me and say, 'Man, I'm sorry I downloaded your music.' And I'd say, 'I don't care, you know the words! This is great! Tell everybody to download it!'"

With Dashboard succeeding beyond his wildest dreams, Carrabba's frustrations with Further Seems Forever reached a breaking point. After returning from a solo tour in August 2000, Carrabba informed the band that he was quitting. "I knew the only chance I had to make it in the music scene was to go out there and do all the legwork to push yourself and make yourself known," Carrabba says. "I was willing to do that and they weren't. They were playing music around their jobs, not as their jobs. I was like, if we're gonna be a band, let's be a band. This isn't going to happen by itself. No one hands you anything, you have to bust your ass for it." Carrabba still joined the band in September to record their debut album for Tooth & Nail, *The Moon Is Down*. The album is impressively overblown, filled to the brim with guitar theatrics and bombast, yet the results are first punishing, and then punishingly dull. Carrabba's voice is not well served by the intensity of the sound—the fragile cracks that make him human when he's singing about himself are lost in the swampy pomp. There is a veiled religiosity to the lyrics, but they mostly serve as nonspecific sketches of the personal turmoil chronicled on *The Swiss Army*. However, the album's high point, "Snowbirds and Townies," is one of Carrabba's most fully realized lyrics to date, illustrating a cross-class romance with a pleasantly light touch: "this winter is lasting forever / at least for tonight / and I know that you're never leaving / until your flight." (This sort of storytelling would reappear in Carrabba's songs for the third Dashboard album, as he let himself pull the camera back just enough to document the scenery, not simply his psyche.) The record didn't set the world on fire upon its release but has sold well since as word of it spreads among Dashboard fans. (Due in no small part to the increased attention, Further Seems Forever became more serious in a hurry in 2001. Even though only the original rhythm section remains from the group that recorded *The Moon Is Down,* the band frequently tours and has even opened for Dashboard Confessional on occasion, with a replacement singer voicing Carrabba's lyrics.)

Chris's goals of "pushing himself out there" were about to get a huge boost. In March 2000, Chad Gilbert, the guitarist of New Found Glory, heard a copy of *The Swiss Army Romance* and immediately called up Richard and Stefanie Reines, the brother-sister duo who ran New Found Glory's label, Drive-Thru. "Chad played us the album over his cell phone," says Richard. "He said it was his friend Chris. We were blown away by it." The two knew instantly that they wanted to release the record and contacted Amy Fleischer. Following some negotiations, Drive-Thru purchased the rights to *The Swiss Army Romance* (after allowing Fleischer to release 1,000 copies on Fiddler) and flew Carrabba out to Los Angeles, set on signing him to a long-term contract. Though Carrabba demurred on signing right away, Drive-Thru secured an opening slot on New Found Glory's east coast tour for Dashboard. Here the story begins to get murky and more than a little contentious. The Reineses claim that Carrabba was so thrilled about being affiliated with Drive-Thru, he talked about signing with them long term as a foregone conclusion, despite the fact that there was no written agreement.

"Chris was begging us to put the album out quickly," says Stefanie. "He was like, 'This is my livelihood.' So we pushed it through the system so he could sell it on that tour in November 2000. And we had to beg New Found Glory to take him out on that tour with them. Their booking agent, Andrew Ellis—who's now Dashboard's agent—told us that there was no way, that he'd get booed off the stage. We begged him; we were like give him fifteen minutes, no sound check, just him and a guitar. And Ellis told us he'd do it as a favor to us because New Found Glory are the nicest guys ever."

"Chris would say from the stage that he was in love with the label," Richard interrupts, "that his second album would be out on Drive-Thru sometime next year."

"People kept telling us not to do this. They said we were stupid for doing all this without a written contract. But we were like, he's signed to our label! He says it all the time!" says Stefanie, her voice rising. "We told the VPs at MCA [Records, the major label that had an option on bands signed to Drive-Thru] that we go on trust. And what do you know, we got fucked. Chris called us the day before Christmas and told us he had 'decided to pass' on our offer.' We were like, our *offer?* What the fuck does that mean? We were furious. This guy totally fucked us."

Perhaps not surprisingly, Carrabba remembers the events somewhat differently. "Amy had decided to sell the record to Drive-Thru first, then she told me about it and convinced me as to why it was a good idea," he says. "I was aware that it was going on, but I just didn't really care about Dashboard at the time. I was focused on Further Seems Forever, who were under exclusive contract to Tooth and Nail. But bottom line, I didn't like the contract they were offering me. It was only once I met Ellis and secured a booking agent of that caliber that I knew the stars were aligned for Dashboard and it was something I had to see through. As soon as the New Found Glory tour ended I went right back out on the road on my own."

While Carrabba was ratcheting up van odometers on a nightly basis, Amy Fleischer was in Los Angeles interning at Vagrant Records and spreading the word. "When Amy started working for me, right away she told me that she had this band that I had to hear," remembers Vagrant head Rich Egan. "At the time, I had just signed three bands and I told her, 'I don't want to like any more bands right now.' I just didn't want to hear it. She gave me a tape but I didn't listen to it for a couple of months. Finally, in November [2000], I popped it into my car stereo. And I freaked on it. I thought it was the most amazing take on indie-rock I'd heard in forever and a day. It was the same feeling I had when I heard the Cure for the first time." Overwhelmed by the music and with visions of the future dancing in his head, Egan booked a flight the next day to New Jersey, where Dashboard was opening a five-band hardcore bill in front of an audience of twelve hundred kids.

"It was clear that no one knew who the hell he was," Egan says. "Chris sat down with the acoustic guitar and the kids were talking all the way through the opening bars. But by halfway through it was silent. And by the end of the first song all of the girls had moved to the front of the stage. I was blown away by the sheer passion and emotion that he put into it. The honesty just floored me. After the last song he said, 'I'll be at the merch booth if anyone wants to say hi.' And he did four thousand dollars in merch sales that night as a band that no one had heard of before they got there. We had breakfast the next morning and really talked things over."

"I was listening to offers from all sorts of labels at that point," Carrabba says. "But when I met Rich I was so impressed by the contract he was offering and the dedication he had. It was too good a situation to pass up." After informing Drive-Thru of his decision in December, Carrabba flew to Los Angeles in January to sign a two-album contract with Vagrant and a management contract with Rich Egan. The next day he was back in the studio in Florida recording his second record. And the one thing everyone can agree on is that what happened next was ugly.

"We were all about revenge," says Stefanie Reines. "We went out and we talked a lot of shit. We said we were going to pull the album from stores. Rich Egan called me and was like, 'Don't be stupid; make money off of it.' I was like, 'Fuck money!' We were fucked and we wanted to fuck him over." She sighs. "We talked a lot of shit but we never actually did anything."

Carrabba disagrees, claiming that the Reineses engaged in a revenge campaign against him, even going so far as to reveal painfully personal facts about him and his family. "Everything was done the wrong way with good intentions. My take was, they bought this record from Amy, she made some money. Cool. I'm gonna go do my band. Then, wait a second, I got taken advantage of. But I still intended for them to keep the record. So one Dashboard record will be on Drive-Thru and one will be on Vagrant. Fine. I'll wash my hands of it. That'll be that. But then they started this slander campaign and it became a fundamental problem for me. I cannot allow somebody to make money off of my feelings while hurting them intentionally, as well as those of the people around me. But I never said anything about it publicly because I didn't want to stoop to their level."

Rich Egan, meanwhile, was thrilled and overflowing with confidence about the act that would prove to be his label's biggest success. Carrabba, in many ways, is Egan's perfect client: they share not only an aesthetic sensibility (love of Jawbreaker, loathing of punk orthodoxy) but also a crushingly serious work ethic. "He's the perfect balance of an artist and a

businessman," Egan says. "He understands his appeal without being calculating about it. He's a workaholic. And he's very, very honest—he spills
his guts every night. It's a dream to work with him."

Vagrant Records released the second Dashboard Confessional album,
The Places You Have Come to Fear the Most, in March 2001 with zero
advance fanfare. It had been just six short weeks since Carrabba had
inked his deal with Vagrant. As Rich Egan puts it, "I just loved it too
much to wait." Despite the rushed delivery, the record SoundScanned
over 5,000 copies in its first two weeks and made an immediate impact
on online reviewers, who raved about its honesty. The record got no
attention or mention from the mainstream or national press, but that
would change soon enough.

The Places You Have Come to Fear the Most is a wisp of a thing, with
ten tracks clocking in at only twenty-nine minutes. It was recorded, like
Swiss Army, in Florida, by James Paul Wismer. "Screaming Infidelities"
and "Again I Go Unnoticed" were re-recorded with friends and Florida
scenesters Dan Bonebrake (formerly of the Vacant Andys and then in a
band called Seville) on bass and Mike Marsh (also then of Seville) on
drums, fleshing them out and developing what had been one-sided rants
into multilayered pop songs. College friend Jolie Lindholm was again
recruited to provide backup vocals on a few tracks. Dedicated to an
assortment of familiar names—Mom, Rich, Amy, God—who "all take
on the daunting task" of keeping him sane, Chris also included his personal Hotmail address in the CD booklet. "The few people who were
gonna buy my record," he says, "I wanted to know who they were. Anybody that was touched by it should become a part of it. And if that
meant talking to me, then they should be able to. Now, of course, I can't
even keep the thing open 'cause it's always getting overloaded and shut
down."

From beginning to end, *The Places* demands that any potential listener check all irony and cynicism at the door. There is no subtlety to the
record—no artifice and very little art. The ten songs all express different
variations on the same, sullen and somber, mood. It's a much darker
record than *Swiss Army*—where that album occasionally attempted to
create light out of darkness, *The Places* seeks out the darkness, then sets

up camp. A relationship has broken apart—this album is the sharp shards scattered all over the floor.

"When I wrote that record," Carrabba says, "there wasn't much to draw on other than this is what I feel today and 'today' was a three-week period. I didn't change too much in those three weeks; I had some things that were weighing pretty heavily on me. I wrote it all pretty much in one go on my mother's couch."

The first track, "The Brilliant Dance," begins with some warm, minor-keyed strumming and Chris's voice at its most hushed and wounded, singing "so this is odd / the painful realization / that all has gone wrong / and nobody cares at all." It's the sound of someone with their hands covering their face, relishing the tactile specificities of emotional pain. By the end of the song, though, the agony is almost triumphal: "breathing is a foreign task and thinking's just too much to ask . . . / this is incredible / starving / insatiable / yes, this is love for the first time." It's the soundtrack to the moment after the tears have started, after the door has been slammed, the phone taken off the hook, and the face buried in the pillow. The moment when the rest of the world has been shut out and you, the listener, the eternal victim, are the only one left to document the drama in which you're perpetually cast in the starring role.

Despite the album's title, Carrabba's greatest gift as a songwriter is fearlessness, a willingness to throw himself into any lyric, melody, or sentiment, no matter how bombastic, traumatic, or corny. Many of his lyrics are cringeworthy on paper ("your taste still lingers on my lips like I just placed them upon yours and I starve for you"), but are delivered with such unwavering ferocity that they seem, if not exactly original or poetic, somehow necessary. Up-tempo numbers like "The Good Fight" and "Saints and Sailors" are still confessions ("no one should ever feel the way that I feel now"), but their strident tone demands an audience. It's as if the sinner has gotten lost en route to the confessional and delivers his litany of grief and guilt from the choir instead.

The sheer amount of verbiage weighs down many of the tracks, pummeling the melody and musicianship into submission, but the album is nothing if not consistent in its lyrical dominance. It's the sound of emotional bulimia, binging on depression and purging on the verbalization of it. "The Best Deceptions" raises the discovery of a cheating lover to

Shakespearean heights: "don't you see? / don't you see / that the charade is over . . . / so kiss me hard / 'cause this will be the last time that I let you." Though the song is addressing the sinner, it's also very much an act of refocusing. The protagonist has "heard about" the "cool guys" with whom the lover has been spending time. We don't get any other details, but his knowledge is damning enough. He desperately tries to reassert control over the relationship at the end by dictating the last kiss, by "ignoring the phone." Elsewhere he's "throwing away the letters" that he writes, thereby avoiding a second encounter with failure.

The album's first eight songs are a cry for attention, a cry for help. A main character has been written out in the first scene—it's time for him to write himself back into the thick of things. The attitude is that something terrible has occurred ("the painful realization that all has gone wrong"), but Carrabba seems powerless to stop it ("breathing is a foreign task and thinking's just too much to ask"). All he can do is "avoid the spots where we used to meet," "claim you as my only hope and watch the floor as you retreat." The action has happened off camera—we're left with an unwavering steadycam shot of loneliness.

The album's best song is also a prelude to its dark heart. The title track is a mellifluous dash of melody, a (mostly) calm and collected self-examination that hints at the disconnect between Carrabba's utterly composed public persona and his true self. His vocals on the track sound sober—it's the shot of black coffee after a night of tears dripping into beers. He sings:

> *Buried deep as you can dig inside yourself*
> *And covered with a perfect shell*
> *Such a charming beautiful exterior*
> *Laced with brilliant smiles and shining eyes and perfect posture*
> *But you're barely scraping by*
> *Well this is one time, this is one time that you can't fake it hard*
> *enough to please everyone*
> *Or anyone at all.*

Carrabba now addresses himself as he did wayward lovers on other tracks, implicating himself in the phoniness. He has reasserted himself only to find himself alone with his own flaws instead of everyone else's. The root of the appeal of Dashboard's second album lies not in the more superficial identification with playing the victim but rather in this inherent belief that the self is flawed and deserves the shoddy treatment described in the previous eight songs. Carrabba doesn't just announce that he has these places "buried deep"—he digs into himself and unearths them for all to see. The accomplishment isn't finding solidarity in common experience, it's unpacking the self like a novelist would a protagonist or a psychiatrist would a troubled patient.

"This Bitter Pill" ends the album and is, in fact, the place Carrabba visited to discover the title of the record. "There's a lot about that song that scares the hell out of me," Carrabba told me at one point, and with good reason. Though it begins calmly enough, it's the aural equivalent of self-mutilation—an almost pointless exercise in scarring. While in other songs, Carrabba seems to be beating himself up with a thesaurus ("this awkward kiss that tells of other people's lips will be of service to keeping you away"), on "Bitter Pill" all knives are out: "and you take this / this medicine is just what you deserve / swallow, choke, and die." Listening to the end of the song is almost unbearable; as Carrabba builds to a crescendo he lets his voice go, running it back and forth across a serratted blade until the sound is rough, ugly, lost somewhere between a sob and a scream: "this feeling of despair is never wearing out." The games have stopped, along with the distractions, the remembering, the excuse-building. "The bottle of beast," from "Screaming Infidelities" has broken and the "liquid diet" from "Standard Lines" has run dry. On "This Bitter Pill," Carrabba—and, by extension, the listener—is left with nothing to choke down but himself.

It's not a song that allows a casual listen—it's not background music and it's not suitable for a mix tape. It's purely music as a service, both for the singer and the listener. It's messy and unpleasant, and if you're not feeling that way too, there's little point in trying to listen to it. If you are, though, the song can be more therapeutic than a million hugs or well-intentioned advice.

When *The Places* was released in March 2001, fifteen-year-old Elizabeth* was drowning her depression in *The Swiss Army Romance*. As she explains in an email,

I would sit in my room, with my headphones on and just cry. I didn't think anyone else could feel the pain I was in. I was ready to end my life. Just because so much in it was so wrong. Everything I seemed to do backfired, and nothing was working out the way I planned. My home life sucked, school was nothing but another place to sleep. I cried every day of every month for four months.

When I grabbed the new album, I listened to it with my mom on the way home from the mall, and I started to cry. She didn't understand so she just left me alone. We came home, and it was on "The Places You Have Come to Fear the Most." When I got inside, I went to my room, Dashboard CD in hand, with a bottle of painkillers (my brother had gotten in a car accident and they were for his neck) and a cup of vodka. I put on number 10 (repeat was on). I started to listen . . . and I broke.

I was shaking so bad.

I spit the pills out, and I just . . . lay there. I was so amazed that someone could feel this way; the song made me feel like I wasn't so alone. Someone, somewhere knows how I am feeling and has lived to tell about it. The person Chris is talking about is someone like me. I've always wanted to tell this to Chris, and thank him. But it seems too "omg I love you, you saved my life . . ." and I'm not like that.

I'm so thankful for his words, his voice and the band's talent. I really think about if I had never heard "This Bitter Pill" would I still be alive? Would some other song have saved me? But that doesn't matter, because I'm glad I am alive right now.

When I tell Chris about Elizabeth he's speechless for three or four minutes and then whistles in disbelief. "I just can't believe it. That's amazing. . . . I guess it's like chaos theory, you know? When you do one thing, independent of the rest of the world and it sets off a chain of events that changes somebody else's minute. Or day. Or life. That's an uplifting story."

The Places You Have Come to Fear the Most isn't an abstract title. The moments captured in each of the songs really are the parts of Chris Carrabba that terrify him. *The Swiss Army Romance,* in many places, dealt with issues even more profound and affecting to their songwriter. But in that case, the bleakness of reality allowed him to seek the light in his songs, anything to create a moment more bearable than the one in which he was living. But *The Places* allowed no such indulgence. "Yeah, I was harder on myself on that album," he says. "Much harder. I don't know why I was tearing myself a new one, but I was. I guess I was in a lower place. I guess I just don't spend enough time trying to figure myself out."

It would be hard for him to have time to do that. For the twelve months following Dashboard's first show with New Found Glory, Carrabba played over 280 dates in every corner of the country. For those who first encountered Dashboard Confessional through those early live shows, the memories of their conversions smack of the religious. I encountered Mary Jane, an eighteen-year-old from Florida, on Makeoutclub.com where her username hinted at a love for Dashboard. Her first experience with Carrabba was in concert and she emailed me to talk about it.

> I saw him opening for Saves the Day in 2001. At first I
> wanted him to get off the stage because I had never heard
> of him and was really anxious for Saves The Day to play,
> but people around me seemed to know him and were singing
> along with this glassy look of awe in their eyes. So I
> listened to what he was saying and it was as if he was
> talking directly to me, as if he knew exactly how I felt,

especially since I had recently got thrown out of what I had expected to be an extremely long-term relationship. It was like he took all the confused thoughts running around in my head and put them into phrases that were so simple but powerful at the same time. I felt like I connected with him. It was like I could just listen and think, 'man I know what he was feeling when he wrote that.' After the show I downloaded some of his music and just sat there for hours listening. A few days later I bought The Places You Have Come to Fear the Most and just listened to it nonstop with my best friend. We would turn it up really loud and sing along until we collapsed crying all over each other. A few days later we drove up to Orlando to see him again and it was amazing.

Those who returned from the concerts, like Mary Jane, with the glassy-eyed look of born-agains, would immediately go online and talk about it. The concerts were such public acts of communion that the thought of keeping it a secret seemed not only inappropriate, it was downright blasphemous. The kids at the concerts were the first generation raised with the expectation of music as a free resource. And so, almost immediately, word of Carrabba's music spread like the inverse of the I Love You computer virus ("I Hate Myself?"), infecting messageboards, chat rooms, and countless private IM conversations. The moment of Dashboard conversion is almost always instantaneous—it's a form of recognition that's at once reassuring and startling. For many kids, listening to Dashboard for the first time on their computer speakers is like staring through a window and suddenly realizing that it's a mirror and has been all along. Danielle's experience, in that regard, is typical. She's a seventeen-year-old from Ontario and she emailed me to say that the first time she heard Dashboard, "It was like Chris was singing right to me about my life and me. It was totally different than most music I had ever heard. The lyrics are very easy to relate to. Everytime I hear a song it takes me back into my past and helps me to relive moments."

For all Dashboard fans, and especially those who first encountered the band when it was a Carrabba solo project, their loyalty towards Chris as an individual supercedes all else. The intimacy of the songs makes listeners feel like they've been trusted with something; to be fickle or fairweather towards Dashboard Confessional would be to trivialize it, to treat it like just another CD in the collection. This is serious music and should be treated as such. Carrabba engenders intensely strong reactions from all of his converts. He seems too selfless, like he's doing it all for them. And that creates a personal attachment that many of these kids have never experienced before and maybe never will again with an artist. One girl's post on a Dashboard messageboard was titled "Give Chris Money If You See Him." It continues,

> I've noticed that everyone I know who likes Dashboard Confessional just heard about it and downloaded the MP3s. Think about this. How many of you are here because this man's music helped you through a really hard time. You want to say it's not about the money, it's about the music. Tell that to a guy who gave up an opportunity to hold a real job and make lots of money in order to bring you his life in the form of lyrics. Next time you see Chris at a show, hand him a $20 bill. And if a new CD comes out buy it instead of downloading it. Chris, if you read this, know that when you come to Portland, I'll buy you dinner if you want it, and give you an extra $20 for the road. Thank you so much for all the music you've given me.

Major labels are afraid that file sharing will kill their profits, but Dashboard is a living example of how the Web can actually create, foster, and spread the one thing they can't buy: loyalty.

The Places eventually went Gold, but the center of the Dashboard Confessional experience remains the live concert. The shows create a safe haven—a space that is comforting, private and yet not private. There is a shared intimacy—every song is about you and for you but for everyone else too. No one asks or judges how you use the lyrics or the music to get through your day. It's enough to look into other people's eyes and recognize that you use it at all. It cuts across gender, across the usually strict social groupings of high school. Everyone raises their voices and sings together. And it's remarkable how good it always sounds—the voices are assured, confident, even if that's not the way they sound in real life. At Dashboard concerts, strangers can become therapists, shoulders to cry on, lovers, best friends, and soul mates. And afterward they can fade back into nothing at all.

"They get to share this together," Carrabba says of his young fans, "and they know it. So the heat's off. Because everybody wants to feel this right now, it's OK to feel this right now. And I don't have to be embarrassed about it. I watch people crying at the shows and no one's inching away from the cryer. They're like, 'Yeah, I've cried to this too.' And, you know, I listened to the Cure and the Smiths. I know how that feels. To be connected with something in that way. To hear somebody say something that you think but can't say."

"How could you not connect with these people?" Mary Jane wonders. "They are so passionate and when you're standing there crying with a complete stranger and singing along as loud as you can, it's hard to not get along. I'm one of those people who was brought up with the idea that emotion is a sign of weakness and should be avoided at all costs. So to be in that atmosphere was slightly awkward but extremely opening at the same time. To be with these people who weren't ashamed to cry in front of strangers was a huge emotional release. Something I haven't seen anywhere else among people my own age."

"The thing is," Carrabba adds, "I've allowed these kids to be in my band, not just at my show. That's why I always start by asking them if they're ready to try one, not that I'm going to play something. Right then, they're in the band. And when they're listening in the car later, maybe they're still in the band."

Indeed, the public foundation of Dashboard's music and the lessons it carries—that it's OK to feel things, that sometimes it's better just to let it out—does bleed over into private life. A little piece of the live experience is seemingly burned onto every CD, allowing it to act as a safe space to return to at the end of every difficult day. Song titles are used as emotional filters on web-based diaries, a way to understand, label, and interpret a rush of feelings on a daily basis. Happy-day entries often get the title "Hands Down" after Carrabba's most cheerful song, bad days are usually called "Again I Go Unnoticed." Most people listen to Dashboard after school, with the door locked and the volume up, or in the car with tempers flaring and the parking brake on. "Most of the time I lie on my bed and sing along," says Danielle. "A lot of time I listen before I fall asleep. Some of the time, I cry, depending on how my day went." Elizabeth tells a similar story: "I usually listen in my room with the stereo blaring. I cry and scream. And lately I've felt it so much more . . . just letting it cry out to my soul. I'm so corny!"

Though there's no way to prove that its results are lasting, Dashboard fans often claim that the lessons learned at Carrabba's concerts have changed their own behavior. "His music taught me to slow down and enjoy life," says Dulce. "It helped me to calm down and stop being mad about things that happened," says Danielle. "I can slow down and think about what went wrong and how I can make future relationships better." Shannon, a college student from Michigan, is more blunt: "I've honestly changed so much as a person since I started listening to Dashboard and in so many great ways. I'm more open about the way I feel and I feel comfortable about the way I feel . . . just because I know I'm not the only one."

Just as with their own diaries, listening to Dashboard's hyperreal emotions (where people "starve" for one another, where infidelities "scream") adds a touch of cinematic grace to the frustrations of everyday life, raising each feeling to global importance. If someone is singing about you, then your life is worth more than you realized it was—and having a soundtrack to it just crystalizes the drama. Melissa writes, "In many ways, Dashboard has changed my life. It's something I share with my friends so that now we have a Dashboard connection. There's nothing greater in life than sitting in a car full of friends and a Dashboard song comes on and everyone starts singing along. You kind of feel like a movie; it's a movie moment. And a thought comes into my head then that this is living."

Before heading out on the companywide Vagrant America tour in late spring of 2001, Carrabba spent a day sitting on his mother's couch in Boca, noodling on his guitar. "I'm very methodical," he says, "I have to sit on the same couch to write songs. It got to the point that I asked my mom if I could just buy her a new couch and take her couch to put it in my apartment. And I did. I mean, that's kinda stupid but it's this mental trick that I played on myself." On that particular day, his thoughts kept returning again and again to the girlfriend he left behind in Connecticut, the girl whom to this day he calls the love of his life. And in a span of about an hour, Carrabba had crafted four interrelated songs about young love, writing them in reverse order of the way they would appear on the record. The first song written, "Hands Down," was emotional, heartfelt, and inspiring. It was also . . . happy. "I jumped up and played it for my mother over and over," Carrabba remembers. "I was like, 'Ma! You've been begging for six years for a happy song. Here it is!'"

The four songs were pressed over the summer and sold on tour as the *So Impossible* CD. It would be the last new recording until the third album in 2003, and fans embraced it like a long-lost cousin. Though the songs are all acoustic they are more expansive and more complex, both lyrically and musically, than previous Dashboard songs. Opener "For You to Notice" is a winsome declaration of intent with charmingly low stakes (Carrabba dreams of coming off as "insightful or brave or smooth" with the sole goal of getting a phone call). "So Impossible" is a laundry list of adolescence—the phone call has been made and a date has been set. But in the world of high school, it's possible to know someone without knowing anything at all—and the things that you most want to learn can veer from the trite to profound and back again: "do you like dishing the dirt on the whole class . . . or wearing all of the latest fashions? / or bucking the trends and wearing your old threads? / or do you like coffee in the evenings?" "Remember to Breathe" throbs with a moody intensity that effectively counterpoints the lyrics about the moments leading up to a kiss. There's an inevitability and fear to the song that demonstrates more range than many give Carrabba credit for, communicating a theme without once again falling back on hoarse throat histrionics. And then there's "Hands Down." Carrabba has rightfully described it as a release, a gift to all of the kids who come to the shows and build up heavy emotions. It's giddy and up-tempo, the aural equivalent of standing up too quickly and feeling little black sparks explode behind your eyelids. It's a real-time rewrite of The Smiths' classic "There Is a Light That Never Goes Out," in which Morrissey imagined ecstatic death with a lover to be preferable to living. Here, Carrabba sings, "my hopes are so high that your kiss might kill me / so won't you kill me / so I die happy." While Morrissey saw suicide as the only way to indulge in physicality without eventual disappointment, Carrabba runs around begging for death and then begging to be resurrected just to do it all again. His love is storybook ("the streets were wet / and the gate was locked / so I jumped it / and let you in") and therefore rises above the mundanities of the party that's raging all around.

The EP is, in many ways, Dashboard Confessional's most popular and best recording. It's universal, as timeless as John Hughes's movies, as teen films of any era. But what separates *So Impossible* from the other teen romance fairy tales is its dependence on tactile details, on "the smell of your hair," the fact that she "always wore blue." For young listeners, the EP sealed the deal on Dashboard—here was a guy who knew them inside and out, sad *and* happy, and he had the guts to go onstage and make it something worth singing about. Kids love the way it mirrors the hopes and fears of their realities and their fantasies, but few of them stop to think that the person singing it is eleven years past the events described. The EP is a time capsule—a yearbook, an old photo album—but to Chris Carrabba, it really does describe "the happiest day" of his life. And so it is also draped in the same bitter regret and nostalgia as many of his more overtly painful songs. It's the moment he's always striving to recreate, a moment he carries with him as proof of his one-time success and his enduring failure.

In his typically self-deprecating, charmed and charming way, Carrabba made all the right friends in 2001, from myriad magazine editors to the highest echelons of power at the not-normally indie—not to mention new-artist-friendly—MTV. At thirty-eight, Alex Coletti is a fifteen-year veteran of MTV Networks. He's a small, soft-voiced, friendly guy responsible for every episode of the influential *Unplugged* show, as well as the producer of the MTV Video Music Awards gala. But when he talks about Dashboard Confessional, he comes off as another messageboard-scanning groupie. "Seeing my first Dashboard concert at Irving Plaza in New York was a life-changing moment, one of those nights you never forget. It pulled my head out of my butt—seeing thousands of kids in a sold-out hall knowing every word, singing their hearts out. And this was an artist without any radio support . . . it made me aware of this whole other world outside of MTV. I called Van Toffler [the President of MTV Networks] on my cell phone from the balcony and yelled, 'Listen to this!' He thought I was high." Coletti wasn't high—just enamored. His enthusiasm for Dashboard was infectious, and soon *The Places* was in heavy rotation in the MTV2 offices. "When I met Chris for the first time," Coletti remembers, "I told him that he was gonna do an episode of *Unplugged* and he just laughed. But a year later, there we were taping the thing."

MTV got behind Dashboard in a way that was unprecedented for a new artist. The video for "Screaming Infidelities" was unveiled in March 2002 as the lead single from an MTV telemovie about drug abuse, guaranteeing it heavy rotation; when the movie aired, the video—in its original version—continued to dominate the screen on MTV2. The song was included on an "MTV2 Handpicked" CD, and when MTV2 resurrected the long-dormant *Unplugged* franchise, Coletti made sure that his prediction came true.

On one level, it's very easy to be cynical about the relationship. MTV is nothing if not savvy—the channel has shown the tenacity of a cockroach in adapting itself to changing cultural trends and, above all else, surviving. With the *Total Request Live* bubble bursting, the network needs to keep itself fresh and relevant to a fan base tired of gloss and glam. Carrabba, with his matinee-idol looks and built-in, fanatical audience seems like a perfect fit—he's certainly an easier sell than some of his more aggressive counterparts. And in MTV-land it's a very short step to go from Carrabba's sensitive pinings to the equally fresh-faced acoustic musings of rising stars Avril Lavigne and Vanessa Carlton. The fact that the latter two are as prefab as Britney and that Carrabba has crossed over from a long tradition of punk and hardcore hardly matters. The artists provide the music but, as always, MTV controls the message.

That said, the network, though responsible for dozens of regrettable contributions to our culture, isn't nearly as Orwellian as its many detractors give it credit for being. At the end of the day, the decisions—especially with the nascent MTV2—are still made by people, and if one person is converted, it's not that big a leap to committed, on-air exposure. "There are a bunch of dedicated music fans here at the channel," Colletti insists, "and sometimes you hear something that just cuts through all the cynicism. And that's all there is to it, honestly. I don't think we can fuck this up yet. It makes me proud of my job."

Chris Carrabba taped his episode of *Unplugged* at the *Total Request Live* studios in Times Square on a warm, windy day in April 2002. Though few people realized it at the time, he was the first non-Platinum act ever to film an episode of the series. To make sure the right people were in attendance, Colletti passed out flyers at the Irving Plaza show a few weeks before and, to get the atmosphere right, the taping didn't begin until 10 P.M. Aware of what they'd be getting, Colletti cleverly set up the room in a unique way—placing three rows of risers directly behind the stage, thus making it impossible for any camera angle to avoid capturing the upturned faces of rapturous, lucky fans.

The audience selected by the network couldn't have been more perfect—dozens of teenagers, all between the ages of fifteen and eighteen, filled the surprisingly intimate room and seemed, generally, unable to believe that they were actually there. Since the show aired, some have complained that the crowd was overly preppie—there was no dark makeup, no punk accoutrements of any kind. This wasn't just the point, though, this was the truth. Other than your odd backpack pin and pair of vintage Converse sneakers, your average, dedicated Dashboard fan doesn't look all that much different than the all-American youth who fill MTV's studios every day for *TRL*. The only difference is their choice of hero and the fact that they greet him with rapturous attention and singing instead of frenzied jumping and hysterical screams.

As for Carrabba himself, he seemed, in a word, terrified.

Though the crowd erupted every time they caught sight of their hero, Carrabba stood stock-still at the mic, internalizing the stress of the situation. He tuned his guitar obsessively and seemed fixated on the earpiece that connected him to Alex Coletti in the booth. He needn't have worried. The crowd joined in on every song full-voiced, cheering wildly for the other members of the band when they flexed their chops on solos. The taping went on until nearly 2:00 in the morning—"Screaming Infidelities" alone was performed five times because Carrabba was insistent that the piano was out of tune. But the kids didn't mind. When the whole thing was finally over, they seemed just as fresh as they had at the start, bouncing around from nerves and excitement.

On TV the kids' singing seem almost too perfect to be believed—the camera shots reveal scrubbed white faces mouthing the words with an awestruck, obedient glassiness in their eyes. If the *Unplugged* made converts of the suits at MTV—which Colletti claims it did—it also no doubt made a few on the fence about Dashboard roll their eyes before rolling right off onto the bad side of it. As is usually the case, an organic phenomenon, once captured by television, starts to seem a whole lot less organic. The biggest mistake the producers may have made was in minimizing the shots of one rail-thin teenager who was seated just behind Carrabba's right shoulder on the risers. Throughout the taping, at the crescendos of certain songs—"Screaming Infidelities," "The Swiss Army Romance"—it was possible to see him actually break down—crumple at the shoulders and either cry or merely rest his head on his friend's arm. At first it seemed too much to be believed. But there it was. Of course, had they shown it, MTV would have been accused of crass manipulation of emotions, and maybe they'd be guilty. But it did happen, for one reason or another. In the same studio where Carson Daly informs a giggling gaggle of after-school girls about the Backstreet Boys's tour plans, one teenager had both an emotional breakdown and an emotional rescue. A show broadcast for millions still made one person cry.

MTV had caught lightning in a bottle—but as soon as it's bottled, lightning very often transforms into something else. As I prepared to spend three days with the members of Dashboard Confessional as they played their largest shows to date, opening for Weezer on the summer tour of giant, outdoor arenas, it was clear that the mainstream media, desperately in need of a hero, had decided to designate Chris that hero, but with reservations. It was easy to love the story but feel ambivalent about the songs. Hipsters still scoffed: Buddyhead.com—the Walter Winchell of punk—compared Carrabba to the Taliban; *Spin* asked if he was a cult leader similar to Charles Manson. But Chris Carrabba, like it or not, truly was the embodiment of the emo aesthetic—an immediate music that brought succor and strength to both musician and a specific type of teenage listener. His phenomenon was also different—it was even more personal than anything that had come before it, and it was mushrooming into something much larger. The Long Island guys had seen the sea change up close—they didn't begrudge him, but they didn't give their own hearts away as easily anymore.

Can something that begins with one person survive so many permutations? Can one heartfelt feeling be stretched far enough to cover the entire country? Dashboard Confessional's popularity is unique in its utter dependence on the fans, on the listeners. But while the faithful "kids" are the fuel that keeps the engine spinning, the machinery itself is still relegated to the churning, screwed-up insides of one young man. Thanks to the glut of articles, the videos, the tearstained testimonials, the Dashboard Confessional celebrity story was fully formed. The Chris Carrabba story, on the other hand, wasn't just unknown, it was unsettled, unfinished. The Weezer road show has been subtitled, "The Enlightenment Tour," and I guess that's what I went in search of in the first week of August. The view from the crowd was starry-eyed, positive, redemptive, and potentially limitless. The view from the stage seemed a lot lonelier, and I flew out to the desert to find out why.

THIRTEEN

When I arrive at the Cricket Pavilion—located just north of downtown Phoenix next to a gas station that my Eritrean cabdriver insists wasn't there last week—there is no one to be seen. The grouchy security guard sequestered underneath a flimsy umbrella informs me that the intense, none-too-dry heat has driven everyone into the relative safety of the dressing rooms. Because of that, I'm fetched at the gate by Dashboard's rock-solid tour manager Mike Schoenbeck (the tour, I find out later, has a preponderance of Mikes, so each has an officially designated, Carrabba-supplied nickname; Schoenbeck's is Mike D, after the Beastie Boy, for some inscrutable reason). Schoenbeck is a gentle, quiet type, large enough to be intimidating, sensitive enough never to act it. He welcomes me to the road with a wry smile—one of many that he dispenses per day—and leads me through a maze of eighteen-wheelers and steaming tour buses to the concrete-walled backstage area.

In the long white dressing room, the core constituency of the Dashboard Confessional touring machine is splayed out on a pleather couch and armchair, recovering in different ways from the previous night's end-of-tour-party. (The party was held in Phoenix with three shows left on the tour because it was the last free day that everyone had. Apparently all the metal gods retire to Arizona—and are buddies with Weezer—so a massive amount of drinking was coupled with an all-star jam session featuring Alice Cooper and members of Judas Priest. At least that was the story from those who could remember anything.) I say hi to Chris—he's sitting farthest away, idly picking on a black acoustic guitar—and Johnny Leffler, the floppy-haired guitarist. Mike Marsh, Chris's best friend and longtime drummer, stands up to shake hands. He's handsome, bright-eyed, and wiry, with antic, expressive movements like he's trying out for a Buster Keaton flick.

Seated closest to me on the couch is the group's newest member, bassist Scott Schoenbeck—Mike's brother and a former member of the Promise Ring. Schoenbeck has an unassuming manner, a brown mop-top, and dark sunglasses to help aid his hangover. Despite the anvils clearly bashing into the backs of his eyelids, Schoenbeck is unfailingly friendly. When Dan Bonebrake, Chris's close friend and Dashboard's original bassist, left the band in May, Scott—thanks to his pedigree and a hearty recommendation from his brother—got the call. He's in the unique position of having been around the hype track a few times before and having seen one almost emo-explosion firsthand, and he has used his low-key charm to quietly establish himself as an integral part of the group. Just a few weeks before he was sitting around on his couch at home in Milwaukee, wondering if music was still the right career path. Now he's backstage at an arena in Arizona, about to play for fifteen thousand screaming fans. Being a musician is like that sometimes, his still slightly bewildered (or queasy) face seems to say. Credit it to his being older than anyone else in the room, or a hardy liver, but it's immediately apparent that Scott has an innate ability to know when to join in the conversations and, even more important, when to keep quiet.

A short while later, it's time for lunch. The catering room at the Cricket Amphitheater is a bizarre cross between a high school cafeteria and a prison. The tables are uncomfortably crafted out of blue perforated metal and the walls are cement and bare. Chris helps himself to a turkey sandwich, some salad, and a large chocolate-chip cookie. He leans against the side wall when he talks. He looks tired.

"Emo," he says, apropos of nothing. "That word is gonna bury us. I'm really afraid of that."

"What makes you say that?"

"I don't know. It's just getting to feel that way. I'm not so foolish to think a career like this could last forever."

"Has this tour been rough?"

"I'm just getting burned out on it. We're never going to open for someone on this level again."

The high-stakes rock-star world of this tour is having a negative effect on Chris. When I saw him last, in New York, he seemed full of hope and energy. Now, he just seems tired.

"I mean, just because you're big doesn't mean you can't be normal. I

225

prefer the writers, the radio programmers, the people who are still invested in fandom. The people who are real people. . . . This cookie is really good. Are you sure you don't want one?"

The band spends the rest of the afternoon cooped up in the air-conditioning, listening to music, and bullshitting. Chris spends the rest of the afternoon deep in conversation with Katie, the high school–aged daughter of one of the venue's employees. She's a pretty blonde girl who admits to not knowing much about Dashboard, but is clearly thrilled to be around fame, in whatever form. Despite his preoccupation, Chris is eternally patient, asking her questions, playing her songs on his guitar and Jawbreaker favorites on the stereo. At one point, Chris fields an urgent cell-phone call from his grandmother, who is helping to organize a backstage visit for some distant Carrabba cousins tonight. At another, he announces, "Jimmy Iovine is coming tonight." Iovine is the legendary (and consummate) music-biz insider—producer of Fleetwood Mac, lover of Stevie Nicks, founder and president of Interscope Records, buddy of Dr. Dre and Eminem.

"Why?" I ask.

Chris looks at me with eternal patience. "Because," he says with a laugh, "I'm his new golden boy."

Ten minutes before show time, Chris decamps to the tiny bathroom and can be heard stretching out his voice via operatic warm-ups.

Five minutes until show time and I head out into the crowd. Arizona's (in)famous dry heat is nowhere to be found. On this night, the air is swampy and thick with humidity. Next to the various concession stands is a metal rig that looks like a tent without the canvas—in fact, each pole is a pipe, misting out cool water nonstop until show's end to help the kids survive. Passing the by-now familiar assortment of pierces, half shirts, and Saves the Day pins, I stake out a seat on the lawn—the farthest point possible from the stage. The seats below me are mostly filled or filling up—as the last bit of sunlight fades, there are still large pockets of empty space on the grass. Two guys with backwards baseball caps and a girl with cutoff jeans are seated just behind me. I hear them chuckling. "I really want them to start soon so I can have a good cry." Bright white searchlights pace back and forth across the moist evening sky.

Then the arena goes dark and the curtain opens, revealing a large black banner with the band's Don Quixote logo on it and the words "Dashboard Confessional—Fight the Good Fight." The banner is greeted with an energetic chorus of high-pitched female screams that erupt from all corners of the crowd—screams that double in intensity when Chris and the band emerge, looking like toy dolls from this distance.

There's a part in the second song of the night, "The Good Fight," where Chris always drops away from the mic to let the audience take the lead vocal. It's a very pretty, understated bridge and tonight, Chris takes a step back—testing the crowd's vocals—but doesn't stop singing himself. In the resulting pause, dozens of voices can be heard, but they're not singing, they're screaming like Justin Timberlake just streaked across the stage behind the drum kit.

The big dipper has come into view now, hanging low over the tip of the Pavilion. Chris steps forward as the rest of the band vacates the stage. Alone in front of fifteen thousand people, he strums and sings one of his earliest and most defining songs, "The Swiss Army Romance." It's a hypnotic moment. One tiny figure manages to hold an entire arena captive. "I'm searching just like everyone / I could be anyone." It's barely 8:30 in the middle of the desert and it's suddenly possible to hear the diehards singing along; from the skinny girls in Weezer shirts caught en route to the popcorn vendor to the cynics on the grass behind me, everyone seems shocked. Nobody's seen anyone ballsy enough to do a solo acoustic song at the Cricket Pavilion before.

When it ends, a giant cheer erupts. From behind me, comes a lone note of sarcasm: "Yeah, you fuckin' rule!"

This night, though, it seems that the band wins out over the venue. The changes made in order to better suit the cavernous performance space have actually helped the songs—the skeletons that the addition of a band helped to flesh out have now been placed on protein diets and are bulked up like Sammy Sosa's neck. "Remember to Breathe," a lovely, nuanced number, begins with Johnny coaxing a bit of abstract Radiohead-like business out of his guitar before giving way to the sullen undertow of the song. Chris introduces "Screaming Infidelities" with an odd caveat—"this song is on the radio; we're sorry"—but the song receives the biggest roar of the night anyway. All across the audience, lighters go up during the "your hair" refrain.

After a rousing "Hands Down," the set ends to much applause. Mike bangs the giant gong that he keeps behind his kit for no other discernible purpose than to end each night's performance. On the Fanavision screens, Chris looks like a prettier, punkier Edward Scissorhands, smiling shyly, eyes wary.

Backstage after the show finds the band sweaty but happy. Chris is breathless, saying it was so hot onstage he thought he was going to pass out on at least three occasions. He doesn't believe anyone who tells him it wasn't noticeable.

Rich Egan walks in with Jon Cohen, his partner in Vagrant, and walks over to Chris. Carrabba and Egan, when together, adopt a sort of creepy Vulcan businessman's mindmeld, sitting across from one another, knees touching, heads bowed, talking in intensely hurried code. Tonight's message is simple enough to decipher—the bigwigs are here and they'd like to come in and shoot the shit with their new investment. Chris gives the assent and soon all of the nonessential personnel in the room—every one of us except Chris and Rich—are transformed into bemused biz spectators. With a cursory knock, Jimmy Iovine sticks his small head into the dressing room.

"Hey, hey, is everyone decent?" he says, walking right in anyway. Iovine is a wiry, compact man in his mid-fifties, with a hunched posture and a baseball hat with strands of hair emerging out of it at all angles. His glasses are unobtrusive and very expensive. He's dressed down in a Hawaiian shirt and jeans with fancy sneakers that are worth more than Chris's guitar and Mike's gong put together.

"Hi, guys, great to see you again." Iovine is working his way through the room shaking hands of people he's clearly never seen before in his life. "Johnny? Great to see you again." He shakes my hand too, apparently under the impression that I'm a touring keyboardist or tambourine shaker. When he hits the back of the room he gives Chris a huge hug.

"Chris, it was great tonight. Really great. I loved it."

Chris remains calm. "Thanks, Jimmy. I'm glad you liked it."

Iovine is soon raving about one of the more polished new songs in the set, the epic rocker "Rapid Hope Loss." Soon, everyone is joining in, praising it with excitement. Iovine's enthusiasm for the song is apparent, but his rapid-fire, staccato speaking style makes it sound like he's talking about an IPO that he totally got in on early.

Rich, quiet up until now, pipes up: "Jimmy, we have a live recording of that we did on DAT. We can get you a copy."

"Oh, oh, really? Yeah, that'd be great, Rich. Thanks. That'd be great."

I look over at Scott, sipping his beer with a look in his eyes like he somehow stumbled into the carny funhouse. The boys in the back erupt into a cacophony of rich, male laughter.

Another knock on the door and suddenly the front of the dressing room is filled with wide-eyed, middle-aged yuppies wearing support-act backstage passes. Chris's family is here.

Excusing himself from the power summit in the rear, Chris expertly embraces and small-talks with a group of five or six relatives (with spouses) who he hasn't seen in at least a decade. There's a large, brassy woman in a sundress whose voice rings out over the others—this is cousin Lucille. She's playing the role of group tour leader to the other assorted Carrabba kin, who all are sporting shorts, high socks, and cell phone clips. All are red faced and absolutely thrilled to be there, to see their Chrissy in such a fame-drenched and evidently important context.

The volume in the room is considerable, but Chris handles it all, parrying family jokes and high-stakes industry shoptalk with the same calm demeanor. Rich gets up to get Chris a bottle of water and I ask him how he got here tonight. "We flew on Jimmy's private jet," he says, with only the slightest trace of incredulity.

When Iovine tires of the small talk, the entire party gets up to leave. There are hugs all around, one or two more raves about "Rapid Hope Loss," and then they are gone, leaving a gaping power vacuum behind. Chris turns to his family, relieved. "Those guys that were back there? They basically run the music industry."

"You want we should put the arm on 'em, Chrissy?" says cousin Lucille, to riotous laughter.

It's only at the end of the night—still sitting on the couch, hair still perfectly coiffed, still in deep conversation with a suddenly reappeared Katie—that Chris allows himself one beer.

That night, we drive to San Diego.

———

Morning breaks and finds the bus just outside of San Diego, parked on the edge of a highway next to a Howard Johnson motor lodge. Chris is up early—his hair is pompadoured before most of the band has even budged in their bunks. A black town car is waiting to take Chris, tour manager Mike D., and me to a radio interview. The driver is blandly handsome in the way that everyone in the service industry is in Southern California—he's an actor even if he isn't. "So, what band are you?" he asks me at one point in the ride.

"Oh, I'm not. He is. Dashboard Confessional."

The driver looks blank. "Huh. Have I heard him on the radio?"

Just then, Chris puts down his cell phone and suggests a coffee break. At a chain store in a mini-mall, he tries his first-ever scone, proclaims it to be "cake for breakfast," passes it off to the others in the car, and gets back on the phone.

When we get to the station—ensconced in an utterly anonymous strip of low office buildings, located, like much of Southern California, amidst some vague combination of palm trees, mountains, and express-ways—Chris is just as polite as he has to be. Making small talk with the DJs and station managers, picking CDs to play as "his" selections in between the on-air chatting, recording promos, call-outs, and photographs.

On the air, a caller speaks directly to Chris, "A lot of your songs are about girls screwing you over. I feel sorry for you. Are you ever happy?"

Chris: "Yes. I am. Those songs I wrote in a three-week period—everyone has times like that. You should come tonight. There's a lot of lighthearted energy at our shows."

When the DJ puts on a recording of "Screaming Infidelities" taken from the MTV *Unplugged,* Chris flinches and makes the DJ turn the volume down in the studio. "With that song, there's always something there to remind me. The girl it's about had beautiful red hair and no matter how many times I cleaned my car, I couldn't get rid of her."

The hour ends quickly and after some final promotional duties, we're back in the parking lot.

It's only then I notice that during our entire time at the station, Chris never once removed his sunglasses.

———

Canès is a bizarre place for a punk concert—it's built right on the beach, Hooters-style, with multiple levels, multiple bars, and multiple TVs all tuned to ESPNews all day long. Halfway through the sound check some workers show up to verify that no one will be needing the violet plush swing that can be dangled from the center of the dance-floor ceiling. While the band sound checks, locals in bikinis poke their heads through the open back door and random early fans walk right in to watch. The sound seems good enough, though distraction is rampant thanks to the beautiful waves and weather just beyond the club's windows. Still, Chris is more tense than usual. When Johnny muffs a few notes he gets an earful. When he and Mike can't seem to hit the right harmonies on the prettiest of the new songs, "As Lovers Go," he gets another. The band is clearly straining to get through it, but Chris has a new toy this night, a sound pedal that he crouches down to manipulate after hitting notes, thus allowing him to distort and recombinate any stray bits of noise that tickle his fancy. Ten minutes past the end of a song, he's still on his knees, twisting away at the sounds like some aural version of Space Invaders.

Finally, the troops are released. Chris is still twiddling knobs onstage and a dark mood is evident. Johnny and Scott walk by and ask if I want to have dinner. As we head down the boardwalk in search of food, Johnny is muttering to himself and Scott lets out a beleaguered sigh.

When we return the sun has started to fade and lower a bit in the blue-pink sky and the entire audience of the show seems to be patiently queued up in front of the door. Just when you think you've seen the end of the line, it curls around, revealing another cluster of kids drinking large Cherry Cokes and sitting cross-legged on the sidewalk. The T-shirts here are the same as at Dashboard shows anywhere in the country: Thursday, Midtown, Taking Back Sunday, Finch, Thrice, CBGB's. Nearer to the parked tour bus, I catch sight of Chris surrounded by girls in half-shirts and bright pink belts with star silhouettes seeking autographs, tipping nervously from tiptoe to tiptoe. A dour-looking goth chick wearing the shirt of arty metal band A Perfect Circle eagerly reaches for her camera. A tall, awkward-looking girl in a white tank top and braces stands nearby. This is a newer phenomenon, I think. Everyone wants a picture with Chris. They throw their arms around him, smile, and then rip the arm away, mumble thanks, and slink off. As the circle around him grows, one bearded guy snaps picture after picture of the scene. Chris stops him by asking if he just wants a picture for himself—muttering that those pics will be on eBay before the night is over. Just before the line proper catches sight of the star, Mike D. swoops down from the bus and makes a big show of collecting Chris and ferrying him safely back aboard. Once inside, his shoulders relax and he heads back to his bunk for a rare moment alone.

The bus TV is showing *Planet of the Apes* and a few members of the crew chew on turkey sandwiches (part of their backstage rider guarantees the Dashboard crew a plate of cold cuts, a loaf of bread, and some condiments every night; clearly unable to break from their hardscrabble van-bound tours of yore, every night's unfinished booty is dutifully collected and shoved into the bus's overcrowded fridges) and sorta-kinda eye the film. It's terrible. It's just another long evening on the road.

Eventually, Chris wanders back out. "Hey," he says, "let's go talk to some kids."

Looking withdrawn and remarkably tiny in an oversized sweatshirt, Chris maneuvers his way to the back of the club, the side facing the ocean. Most of the kids still loitering around the front (there's a strict no re-entry rule in effect) barely notice him. The larger a star is, the less likely people are to believe that he's short. Or that he'd be wandering around alone on the night of a performance. His mind somewhere else, Chris hitches himself up onto the cement wall, stares out at the moody, nighttime ocean, and waits for people to talk to him. And, slowly, they approach. Two Asian-American girls walk up nervously but talk tough—acting like this is no big thing for them, but their voices are high and skittish. Neither of them looks him in the eye.

"Hey, I want to ask for an autograph, but I'm sure that's so uncool."

"No," he says, "that's fine." He takes the ticket stub and scribbles on it.

"So, I was just, ummm, wondering . . . where do you get your material?"

"Yeah," says the other one, "did it, like, all really happen to you?"

"I draw on real life, yeah," says Chris in a monotone.

"Wow, that's cool. That's cool," says one.

"So, are you, like, OK?" asks the other.

"Yeah," says Chris with a half smile. "Things are getting better."

"Cool," they say, and wander off to inspect their autographs.

Another girl, clearly egged on by friends standing closer to the back door, approaches.

"Hey," she says.

"Hi," says Chris, looking her in the eye.

"Can I see your tattoos?"

Chris looks away. "Oh, sure." He rolls up his right sleeve.

"Wow," she says, appreciatively. "That's really cool."

"Yeah," he says. "But I wouldn't recommend it."

"What do you mean?"

"Oh, I just wouldn't do it again. I like them, though."

Eventually, she wanders off.

"What's different about these kids than the way it used to be?" I ask.

He kicks his heels against the cement wall. "It's like they're nervous. Too nervous to really want to be here or to look me in the eye."

"What is that, do you think? Is that celebrity?"

"I think it's that these kids are different than the original fans," he says. "They're just not used to being at shows where people are approachable."

The waves crash for a minute. The second band of the night, local indie-rockers The And/Ors, are starting.

"Let's go check out this band," Chris says. "The guy at the back door gave me shit when I left before about not letting me back in. Let's see what he does now."

He jumps off the wall and we head towards the back door, separated from the beach by a few concrete stairs and a porchlike entryway guarded by three giant-sized men in yellow "security" jackets. The one guarding the plastic velvet rope is a medium-sized older guy with a dirty-looking moustache. Chris walks right up to him.

The guy has attitude from the start. "I thought I told you you're not getting back in here."

"Dude," says Chris, "I'm going in."

"No, you're not," says the guard, tensing up and rearing back.

The few kids who weren't able to scalp tickets and are hanging around the back have noticed what's going on and massed around the stairs.

"I'm in the band. I'm going into the show."

The kids are starting to get involved. "Yeah," they yell, "this is his show. Don't you know who this is?"

"This is my show," says Chris, his voice rising.

"Who are you?" asks the guard.

"Who is *he?* Who are *you,* man?" scoffs a tall kid.

"I'm in the band."

"Which band? Let me see your ID."

Chris reaches for his belt and displays his Weezer support-act laminate.

The guy is annoyed, but relents. "OK, go ahead." He pulls the rope aside.

The kids are happy to have a cause and reluctant to let it go, so the tall one yells, "You're an asshole, you know that?"

The guy rears around. "Hey, I'm just doing my job."

Chris is at the top of the stairs now, but he stops and turns to face the guard full-on. "No way, man. That was just bravado and you know it. That was fucking ridiculous." His anger seems to be beamed in from nowhere, fully formed. It's sudden, violent, inappropriate. He's itching for a fight now. Was his daylong—possibly tourlong—simmer finally boiling over, or was it his own sort of bravado, a need to stand tall in front of his kids? Whatever the cause, the atmosphere has turned ugly, poisonous.

The guard reaches across Chris's body and snaps the rope back in front of him. "All right, that's it. You're not getting in."

The kids roar in disgust. Chris says, "The fuck I am," and, pushing his way under the rope, barrels towards the doorway.

A million things happen in a second. The guard lunges after Chris, ripping at his shoulders. Post abandoned, the ticketless kids hoot and rush up the stairs, hoping to take advantage of the melee. From inside the club, two enormous bald bouncers come sprinting towards us, pushing every kid in sight back outside. I see one engaged in a screaming match with Chris while another prowls menacingly behind them. It looks like punches are about to be thrown when suddenly it's my turn to be knocked off the porch and back down the stairs, along with a handful of kids who had tickets to begin with.

The original guard is refortifying the stairs when the tall kid, his hat mussed, leans into him. "You know what?" he says. "You're a tool."

The mood behind the club is jittery now. The ticketless kids have their story for the night and messageboard fodder for at least a week. I circle back to the front door of the club and push through the crowd, but Chris is nowhere to be seen. The room is packed—people sit on every available surface, stand two or three deep at the bars, against the walls. Things seem to have quieted at the back, but only just.

On the bus, most of the band is quietly lounging, watching TV. They're all eager to hear about what happened, though it's hard to tell why they're ultimately not surprised—is it because of the club's reputation for hard-assed, lousy security, or because they've seen this routine before? Soon, Chris, still fuming, storms onto the bus with Mike D. in tow. Everyone shuts up to hear what he has to say.

"Well," he says, "I got that guy fired."

He's still completely riled up, burning off angry energy like excess coal.

"Man," says Chris, "every time we have a headlining show these days some shit like this happens."

"What do you mean?"

"I didn't tell you about Pittsburgh? You should have been there to see the lengths I go to protect my kids. We headlined there and I almost got arrested. When the show ended, I had all the kids waiting for autographs lined up, totally orderly. And this cop shows up and starts hassling Mike D. about me starting a riot. I got into a screaming match with him—he was going to make me spend a night in jail."

I want to say that the stress of this tour is clearly getting to him, but it's more than that. Every kid deserves his moment—that's the central tenet of Chris Carrabba—but what happens when there are so many kids? Every moment—is it less and less meaningful? Chris is an emotion junkie, he feeds off of extremes in sentiment in a way I've never seen before. These spikes of anger, in a way, are like giant gulps of oxygen.

When the head of security knocks on the bus door to talk about what happened, Chris and Mike follow him outside to discuss it. A few moments later, and without any discussion, every other person on the bus makes his way outside and orbits, slowly, the heated discussion. The head of security is all apology and tact but Chris won't let him off the hook at first. He demands more of an apology, tells him the situation was bullshit, reminds him that he never wanted to play here again after their last, none-too-friendly experience there last year. The entire crew is pretending to talk amongst themselves, but everyone is listening. It's like an amped-up *West Side Story*—it feels like all Chris would need to do is snap his fingers and all of the assorted Jets (or Sharks?) would pull out penknives and pounce. But really, I think, most people are curious to watch the normally tightly wound Chris freak out.

But that will have to wait until another night. Tempers slowly cool until it's a virtual love-in of apologies and concessions on both sides. Chris even thanks the guy for the professionalism of the other guards who squashed the confrontation before punches could be thrown ("I thought I was gonna get tackled and flattened," he tells me later). And, before anyone knows it, it's time for the show to begin.

As soon as the lights go off inside Cane's, the now-familiar female screaming starts up. There's a group of young women behind me who are yelling, "Chris you are so fucking hot!!!" at the top of their lungs. Chris takes the stage alone, with his black acoustic strung over his shoulder. "I'm going to start with a brand-new song, if you guys will let me. It's really quiet. So . . . shhhhh."

The entire room obediently goes mute. The song is a simple plucked progression, notes descending in a manner familiar to anyone who has ever taken guitar lessons. Chris leans into the mic and sings, his voice choked up and hushed: "I've been bleeding well from this old wound / rubbing it with salt / so it will still feel new." It's an incredibly intimate moment—typically self-relexive for Dashboard, but the first time I've heard him comment on the odd nature of his fame and adulation. "And everyone watched me waste myself / And everyone cheered at last / And all of them found it comforting / It's better it's me than them." The hundreds of faces surrounding me are expectantly upturned, eyes shining, reflecting the lights, watching him waste himself, feeling comforted. The song is over five minutes long and never really raises above an anguished whisper, but no one breaks the silence. When it's over, Chris thanks the crowd and invites the band onstage where they break into "Saints and Sailors" and everyone is happy again.

For a moment, onstage, Chris has doffed his scabs and shown everyone exactly how he's feeling these days. It's an uncomfortable, swampy place. The feelings and situations revealed on the *Places* album are no longer his—they're out in the world, and he's got a roomful of teenagers crying out for them on the beach in San Diego. There's no shock value left in those songs—they're lyrics to sing along to. In contrast, "This Old Wound" is like a slap in the face preceding a comforting kiss. It's defiantly unanthemic; its melody is barely there, yet it stretches out and haunts for a good long while. The rest of the set is for the crowd; this one was for the guy on the stage. Chris tells me later that when he played the song for Mike Marsh and his wife for the first time, she ended up in tears. The next day Marsh came by Chris's apartment unannounced and asked him if, seriously this time, he was all right.

Still, it's nice to see the old Dashboard energy again after the antiseptic vacuum of the Weezer tour. Guys stand with their arms laced around their girlfriends' waists; every so often the girlfriends turn back to make sure they're both singing the right words together. There's a girl with long blonde hair gamely trying to stay upright as she sways back and forth on her red-glitter crutches, there are kids in Bauhaus T-shirts singing just as loud as their neighbors in clothing that advertises bespectacled singer-songwriter Lisa Loeb.

Actually hearing a crowd sing along with him seems to have cleared up Chris's gloom for the time being. As he scraps the set list early on, choosing to play "The Swiss Army Romance" solo, he is rewarded with a hugely full-voiced chorus. He steps back from the mic and lets the kids sing their heart out with a giant grin on his face.

It's a long set, with none of the old songs removed and all of the new ones tried out. "As Lovers Go," with its ecstatic harmonies, gets its second public airing, as does a jaunty acoustic number called "Carry This Picture For Luck." "So Beautiful" is introduced with the words, "This is a song about drinking . . . heavily." The song's logical bookend, "So Impossible," also has a regular introduction, where Chris dedicates the tender tale of a high school crush to "our friend Tony and his girlfriend." Hundreds of girls swoon, wishing the song had been written expressly for them. Little do they know that Tony is the name of a mentally retarded Subway worker with an unbeatable work ethic who the band encountered and chuckled over at a rest stop somewhere in the Midwest.

"Remember to Breathe" is realized to the fullest tonight. Always Dashboard's most atmospheric song, tonight it's positively claustrophobic. Where the refrain was once a gentle reproach, it's suddenly an ominous warning. Chris is testing the upper limits of his register, shredding the words a bit, and it feels like his confrontation with the bouncer all over again: intrusive, almost gaudily intimate.

Near the end of the set, Chris pauses to thank the security of the club and asks for a round of applause for them. There are scattered boos and a voice over my shoulder yells out, "Fuck 'em!," but Chris isn't kidding. "They've got a hard job to do and they do it well," he says.

At the end of the night, Chris tells the crowd that he'd like to meet each and every one of them, and he'll be outside after the show if they'd like to take him up on it. He introduces "Hands Down" by saying, "This is a song about the best day of my life . . . but today comes close." The crowd screams happily; more than a few girls murmur, "This is my *favorite* song!"

The performance follows the script right up to the end, with the crowd doing the lead vocals this time, leaving Chris nothing to do but to try and keep up. The song ends with a collective yawp: "hands down / this is the best day that I can ever remember / always remember!" But then, it doesn't end. Instead, the band opens up, extending the final chorus into a loose jam. The bass throbs, melancholy and Cure-like, Johnny's guitar nimbly picks lithe bits of jangle from the air. Minutes pass and Chris falls to his knees, twisting the knobs like he did in sound check, manipulating questioning feedback from the monitors. It's an uncharacteristically arty interlude and kids begin to shift on their feet. Every time Chris goes down to his knees to play with the effects pedal it's as if he's going down in search of himself, in search of inspiration. But nothing seems to satisfy him. The rest of the band is trading looks, wondering how long this is going to go on. When the beat has once again stripped down to its essence, Chris returns to the mic, eyes closed. His voice sounds choked, thick. With a pained look, he whispers some lyrics from "Shirts and Gloves," a relatively inconsequential song from *The Swiss Army Romance:* "when I'm back from the road / and you're out on it . . ." Suddenly his voice scales to the top of his register and he's screaming: "how dare you leave me here to drink alone?" His voice is going places no one has ever heard it go before. A few people hoot dumbly at the drinking reference, the rest stare. It seems like improv but the words are coming too easily. "I find out that I am so alone . . . / but I'll take it / and I'll take it. . . ." Hands fluttering protectively to his head,

Chris tears into the refrain from his most visceral song, "This Bitter Pill," a song that collapses into sobs on record and one he's labeled "too difficult" to play live recently. His voice is shredded, he's turned the words in on himself, replacing "you" with "me": "this bitter pill is leaving me with such an angry mouth / but I'll take it / and it swallows down like chalk / and it's bitter / so unbearable / and it makes me feel all fucked. . . ." The veins are swollen in his neck, the entire top half of his body is bright red. He's left the band in the dust now, and most of the crowd too. "I swear! / I lied! / I swear!" he's leaning onto the micstand like it's a best friend's shoulder. The entire concert seems to be wavering, teetering between sane and insane. I feel queasy and nervous. The whole thing seems like too much. This is Dashboard Confessional turned up to eleven—Chris is bleeding but the kids aren't there with him this time to provide bandages. He's pushed himself past them, taken one step too many out over the edge. The crowd is silent, watching. He's out on his own again, where it started. The old wound bears fruit—and if it doesn't, he's content to cut himself all over again.

Then, out of nowhere, it becomes "Hands Down" again, but rushed and giggly with phony happiness. The relief in the room is palpable. "Always remember," he sings, "always remember."

When the lights go up and people clap and realize that it's over, they become fans again, no longer part of the band. The entire audience is quickly ushered outside by security, but they all gather out on grass, in the parking lot. I look around for Chris and run into Rich Egan, standing on a rock, smirking slightly.

"Hey," I say. "Aren't you the head of that red-hot media darling record label?"

"Yep," he says. "I'm the president of Sub Pop."

"So where is he?" I ask.

"Right there." He gestures below him to the center of an enormous galaxy of teenagers. Sure enough, Chris is standing there—completely subsumed by taller fans and outstretched arms with cameras. He's patiently waiting, signing, smiling, hugging, posing while literally every one of the hundreds of kids who was in the show lines up patiently for his or her moment to shine.

The yellow-shirts are wary of another confrontation, but they're clearly not happy about the situation outside of their club. Occasional police cruisers stalk the outskirts of the parking lot like barracudas, slowly marking their territory. I fear a repeat of Pittsburgh, but things stay calm. For one hour, then two, Chris stands patiently. Rich dispatches his assistant, Ryan, in search of a bottle of water for his young star. But other than that, not a word of complaint as boys and girls, preteens, teens, and twentysomethings all receive their personal interaction. So many cameras flash I'm afraid Chris will develop cancer of the retina, but he provides each and every flash with the same warm, worn smile. He's a pro, a professional interactor. A girl is pushing up behind me, camera in hand. Every few minutes I offer her a chance to cut ahead, to get closer to her hero, but she nervously giggles and demurs every time.

I lean over and ask Rich how the flight back home was last night on Iovine's private jet.

"Short," he says. "They wanted me to go with them to the Irvine show tomorrow night in a helicopter. I said, no. I'll drive. Can you imagine me helicoptering over my wife while she's stuck in traffic on the highway below me?"

When the last ticket has been scribbled ("I'm doing my best to completely devalue my autograph on eBay," he tells me later), Chris and Rich wander off in search of Taco Bell.

Chris wants to be friends with the entire world—he searches for meaning in quotidian interactions that most of us expect only from our family and loved ones. It seems the only people he truly trusts, at the end of the day, are the kids. Because they are there for him, night after night. They don't ever let him down. They don't ever betray him, or ask him for too much, or give too little. But the more famous he gets, the less these kids want to be friends with *him*.

The more famous he gets, the more split up into little bits he becomes. He's not *yours;* he's *everybody's.* He belongs to your friends, to the people in your school who hadn't even heard of him three months ago, to *Teen People,* to MTV. The more casual his fans become, the more they think that they have him already—every piece of him. Meeting him in the flesh becomes more of a summation—*look, here is this person I know and he's exactly the way I knew he'd be!*—than an opportunity for further development of what had been a one-sided relationship. The irony is, the more dissipated his celebrity becomes, the more desperate for these quiet moments Chris is. It doesn't take much to satisfy him, just an honest word or two about who they are, an interest in him as someone who would care about their job, their breakup, their parents' divorce—someone connected with the world, not driving through it nightly on an impenetrable tour bus. A lot of his bedrock faith in what he's doing comes from them, from "the kids," from their support. From their just being "cool"—supportive, physically there night after night. After Weezer, after Jimmy Iovine, after the groupies, suck-ups, bouncers, DJs, and hangers-on, they have heard the worst aspects of his personality and burned it onto mix CDs. They've seen the worst parts of his personality and still bought two posters.

Every night Chris throws himself into the crowd like this, desperate for the connection he needs, a service that many of the picture-takers and well-wishers don't understand they're responsible for. The kids come to his music fresh, find what they need in it, experience the raptures of the concerts, and their own experience is completed. They've adapted the songs to their own situations, hopes, fears, and tears, used them as they saw fit. For them to be able to do that, Chris has to dig up things for them, painful things that should be kept buried, things that led him to seek their help in the first place. While they go home satisfied, he's left with handfuls of dirt. Chris still provides everything the kids want, and then some. What happens when they no longer satisfy him?

"It's probably not as important to them anymore as it is to me," he says. "Maybe it never was. I couldn't care less about giving my autograph, showing off my tattoos. It doesn't make me feel good. It makes me feel like a showpiece. I mean, I'm grateful. It's nothing compared to talking to somebody. The kids seem to want to do that less and less."

As soon as the tour bus pulls out of the parking lot, Chris disappears into his bunk, headphones on, Discman working overtime. That night, the bus returns to the Howard Johnson on the side of the highway and parks until morning. While most of the crew retires, I go out for a late-night bite with Johnny, Scott, and MP, the engaging veteran drum tech. After the eggs have been eaten and the clock nears 3:00 in the morning, we walk back in pairs. MP tells me about his sudden shift from unhappy bar manager in Los Angeles to drum tech on the bus of rising international star. Though he's the second oldest in the crew and, in many ways, the most independent and roadwise, MP also has the best perspective on how lucky everyone involved is. Just how lucky he feels is evident in the way he's still guilt-ridden about a drunken incident from the month before. During a crew member's birthday party backstage in Texas, MP—who personally hired the dominatrix to spank the birthday boy—and a few others left the dressing room covered, floor to ceiling, in chocolate cake. Hardly *Spinal Tap* material but, for this tour, more than rowdy enough. Through the following morning's hangover MP knew he was in trouble.

"As soon as I woke up, I felt terrible," he says. "So I walked straight to Chris and was totally up front and apologized for it. It was wrong, it was my fault, and I would make sure something like that never happened again. His point was absolutely the correct one. That when things like that happen, it's his name that gets dragged around. So we have to comport ourselves the way he would."

There are crickets singing in the Southern California night and we stomp through three motel parking lots en route to the bus. Solitary drivers whiz past. A billboard advertises cheap home refinancing.

Right before we climb aboard, MP stops. "Something truly magical and wonderful is happening to this kid right now," he says, gravely serious. "It's amazing to be around to see it happen."

On that note, everyone retires to sleep on the parked bus, listening to the traffic just outside the windows. It's been a long day and a longer night.

At dawn the bus rumbles to life and heads north on the interstate towards Los Angeles. This being the wonderful world of arena tours, however, our final destination is about an hour's drive away from the city, in Irvine. The Verizon Amphitheater (the umpteenth Verizon Ampthitheater of the tour) is located on a swampy-looking patch of grass behind a water park. As the crew members stumble out of the bunks, Chris is already perfectly coiffed—once again, no one has ever seen him with his hair down—dressed, with sunglasses on. Once the bus is parked, everyone heads out in search of coffee and a shower.

The backstage area at Irvine is like a trailer park inside the Astrodome. An oddly rickety tin ceiling shields the individually air-conditioned dressing room/trailers from the already punishing sun. Each trailer has a '70s rec-room vibe to it, with antiseptic bathrooms and prickly, tacky couches. There are also windows—replete with venetian blinds—overlooking a large common area between the trailers that has a few wooden benches and some metal folding chairs. Mike D. is tense this morning because Chris has an interview to do with the frothy syndicated entertainment show *Access Hollywood,* but they've just called to say that the interviewer is going to be late. Fed up with waiting, Chris grabs me and we head to the back of the bus for an on-the-record chat.

The bus's back room is messy—the three-sided couchlike seats are covered with random objects: socks, extra cords, a guitar tuner, an enormous, blue-toned portrait of Chris, replete with giant, soulful, watery eyes that a fan handed him in San Diego. Before we sit down, Chris picks up a backpack and pulls out a red-white-and-blue sweatband.

"This beautiful girl gave me this yesterday." He holds it up close to his nose and inhales. "And it smells like a girl. She was like, 'I noticed you didn't wear one today, so . . .' I'll save this." He pauses. "She was like eighteen!"

"Tsk tsk," I say, pointing to the tape recorder. "Be careful!"

"Oh, yeah. That's bad." He laughs. "I don't want anyone to know I'm into hot girls." He quickly throws the backpack into his bunk and settles back into the couch.

"So," I begin. "What happened last night?"

"Well," he says, "there are some songs where we give ourselves a lot of freedom, songs where we just let go. Last night we really let go. My goal is to use that moment to tie a bunch of things, a bunch of stories together. I tie different moments from different songs into one story that can tell more, that better captures the range of emotion that life gives you. So I start at one place, which is 'Hands Down,' which honest to god was the best day of my life. And inevitably I bring it way down to a really dark place." He straightens himself out on the couch. "It's improvised, but there are lines that pop out every time, but I don't know what the pattern is going to be. But I always try my best—for my own self-preservation, really—to slowly get it to a really hopeful place. That way, hammer it back into 'Hands Down' and back to what that song really means to me. Last night, I couldn't do it. I let myself get so down, so dark that I couldn't get myself back to the point where it . . . it was weak. I brought it back and all with the lyrics and maybe it came off. Maybe people in the crowd were like 'Wow, he did it. Everything was all right in the end.' The truth is, it wasn't all right. That's why I went to bed so early last night. It wasn't the standing out there with kids getting pictures taken, or the long day. It was that moment onstage, I felt it go. I felt it all go. You have your reserve of energy and mine was gone in those moments. I just couldn't do it anymore. It induces nightmares and shit like that. I think it's bizarre to let yourself do that. I was hurting so much afterwards, emotionally. For some stupid reason I keep doing that to myself. Like a moron." He pauses. "That shit could kill me. I gotta cool off. I have to find a balance. Maybe some nights we could do that song in that way and have it just be about the music. Instead of just, let's see how much I can salt my wounds."

"What lines are the ones that you keep coming back to?"

" 'Bitter Pill' seems to find its way in every time. Which makes sense considering how hard it is for me to perform that song. Those lines about medicating myself and 'you' coming back to me. The first time I went down that road, it was an eye-opener for me. I was onstage and I was shocked; it hurt so badly. I thought: Why am I doing this? Why do I sing about needing to get better so she'll come back? That's a real problem that I have. I don't need to get better—I need to find someone who likes me the way I am, someone who finds Chris desirable. My self-esteem is so low that I always think that I need to change, that there's something wrong with me." He rubs his hands together. "I'm actually honest in that song. The first time we did it that way, there was such spontaneity. I now have this world to play with that I can go back to on a nightly basis. But it's a dark place to carry with you all the time."

Chris sighs and debates something in his mind.

"I wasn't singing about a lover last night. I was singing about losing a friend that I value, that I love so much. That I want to love me so much. Someone who I felt like was my sister who now feels like I owe her something. It's just . . . really disheartening," he says, infusing the word with all the tragedy of the universe.

"There were moments last night when I felt almost uncomfortably close to you as a performer," I say. "Like with 'Remember to Breathe,' it was so queasy—it all felt very personal."

"Someone said to me recently that they thought this was like performance art. I didn't really know what that meant because I'm very stoic on stage. Physically. In those moments when I'm really giving myself up, I don't move much. Which is true in my own personal life as well. If I'm in a situation that I'm uncomfortable in, I'm stuck. Then I realized what he meant. I'm performing, but there are these other guys in my band and the audience as a whole who have a very textured awareness of what I feel. It's like they're appendages. They're just going off what I'm feeling. It's putting myself on display in a way that I don't do in my life. I'm too guarded."

"Why?"

"I don't know why. It's so stupid. I can't tell you how many people who are close to me say, 'How can you feel so much onstage and let yourself feel so little in real life.' But, hey, that's my protection. That's my armor. I've probably failed at more relationships by being guarded than by being an asshole."

"Well, I think that guard has served you very well recently, just in terms of the constant demands on you personally. The touring, the press, everything being so focused on you."

"Well, now we're getting to the meat of the matter," he says, cracking his knuckles. "There is this new heightened sense of guard that's serving to freak me out a little. All these people know something so personal about me. They don't know me, but they know these personal things about me. They own it. It's theirs now, it's not even mine. It's my worst moments—and my best moments. Like 'Hands Down.' I'm not lying— that was the best day I ever had. My watermark. It could get better and if it does there will be a new song then. But it's not mine anymore." He straightens himself and smooths out his pants. "OK, maybe everybody feels these things because we all only really feel one strain of emotion, or whatever. It still felt like mine before."

"But doesn't it help you to share that in a way? Isn't that what this is about?"

"I never don't feel the emotions that I'm singing about. But, yeah, there are moments when I feel that this is *our* problem. When I say that, it could mean me and the girl I'm singing about, or the friend I'm singing to. Or ours like this is our band's gift to you. Or this is your gift to me because the crowd is as much the band, if not more." His voice peps up and he's speaking faster now. "Like last night, 'Swiss Army' was not on the set list. I have no idea why, but I was just hating playing it. Then I got onstage and it was the song I wanted to play the most because something in the crowd was giving me the vibe that it was necessary to play that one song. It was a highlight. The crowd swelled at that moment in a way that was so amazing. They were phenomenal. There's a moment when I think you can see it get sucked right out and there's no one else in the room. I'm stuck right where I was, stuck in my head. That's where I was at the end of the night. Back there. There was no one else in the room at all."

"Wouldn't it be better for you to leave a show feeling part of a community? Feeling less alone?"

"Well, yeah, but you know what? Someone walked away feeling good. I felt those kids; during 'Remember to Breathe,' during 'Swiss Army.'" He looks out the window thoughtfully for a moment. "You know when you're in a movie and you don't know anybody else in the theater and the most beautiful thing happens on the screen? Everybody there feels this overwhelming sense of whatever that emotion is? You're surrounded by strangers but you're all feeling the same thing. The feeling is intensified because its being shared by three hundred people all at the same instant. That's what we try to do too. I mean, we'll never, ever be as good on record as we are live because we're not a full band unless those kids are there. We ride the ripples of that emotional tide like at a movie theater. If there's any artistry to what I do, any gift that I have, it's that somehow I've been able to tap into that. People have told me that I guide it. I don't think so—I think I ride it." He looks at his hands. "That's what I'll miss most when it's all over. But maybe I'll just go to more movies."

This is a new obsession Chris has acquired since I last saw him—his humor has always been self-deprecating, but he's taken to sprinkling his most serious thoughts with references to his career's mortality. It's not self-important or tragic; it's matter-of-fact. He seems to be eyeing the finish line like a toll plaza—bureaucratic, clinical, inevitable. Sometimes when we're sitting in the back of the bus reflecting he talks about this stage of his life like it's already over, as if he's glimpsed an expiration date and is trying to make sense of it all while he still can.

"You seem so sure that this is going to be over," I say.

"Well . . . no. I'm not really sure."

"It just begins to sound like you're preparing yourself."

"Well, I assume it's going to be over. Because why wouldn't it be? I'm aware that this is a flash in the pan and it isn't going to be cool forever. If I survive this hype machine it's because my fans have given me a wide berth to be everything that I want to be. They still see the same things in however it's presented. So maybe I can survive it."

There's a burst of laughter from the front of the bus.

"I don't care if I'm cool or not," he says. "I've always been an awkward person anyway. There are some people who are dying to be famous because it's the only way others will pay attention to what they do. In my case it's just the way for them to pay attention to me. And I don't want them to pay attention to me—just what I do. There are kids that do care and that will still care ten years down the road. I hate to sound stupid and idealistic but it's never been about money or success. I just love connecting with people."

"But the press is . . ."

"We're not a one-hit wonder, you know? We're a no-hit wonder. It's kind of like the Grateful Dead in that sense. There are people who have connected to this on a really base level and they see that a hype machine didn't do this and a hype machine couldn't do this. So this is the flash part of it. I just don't think the people in the press realize that what they're doing ruins everything in the long run."

There's a knock on the door and Rich Egan walks in. "Hey bro," he says. "You spilling your guts?"

"You know it."

"*Access Hollywood* is ready for you."

"Oh, great," Chris says, rolling his eyes. "Tell them I'll be right out." After Rich closes the door, Chris speaks more quietly. "Look, I say all this but I would really like to eat my words. It would be great, after all of this, to know that we're still relevant. I'd rather be relevant than cool any day of the week." His voice drops to a whisper. "I never really felt cool anyway."

He stands and moves to the door. I ask if I should leave him alone.

"No, you should stay and watch. Watch my face when he asks me the same old questions. It should be good. I have no poker face."

He may not have a poker face, but he definitely has a game face. When we leave the confines of the back room, Chris immediately turns himself back on, and the front doors slam shut behind his eyes. A slick Hollywood type with an artificial tan and an expensive V-neck sweater is sitting on the bus's front couch; he introduces himself as the interviewer. The cameraman and producer are sitting opposite. The camera starts rolling almost immediately and I crouch next to the driver's seat with a random assortment of handlers and hangers-on: Jessie Tappis, Vagrant's publicist, is there, along with Lori Earl, Chris's new rep from Interscope (Earl also does press for Guns n' Roses).

Mr. Hollywood phrases every question as if he and Chris are old pals, pretending to mock the idea of an emo phenomenon but still asking about it. Chris is a pro and he parries every thrust like an Olympic fencer. He keeps his voice measured and speaks in full, considered sentences, sticking to his own situation, refusing to be drawn into a debate about whatever musical moment he's a part of. Next to me, Lori Earl pumps her fist and mouths the word 'Yes!' after every answer.

With the interview winding down, Mr. Hollywood pulls out a doozy: "You're becoming more and more successful. Do you think it will be hard to find something to sing about when you're flying around on your private Gulfstream jet?"

Everyone's jaw hits the floor except Chris's. He's not an agitator—it's as if his brain is computing the end result of every potential answer, considering and rejecting a scenario where he laughs and sneers due to an innate understanding of how that would come across on TV. America doesn't like people who don't play the game, and Chris plays the game. Yet just as he can subtly alter the mood of an entire room, he can also tweak the rules, and he answers a stupid question with a brilliant answer.

"Well, we're a far cry from having a private plane. . . . I saw a documentary on Bruce Springsteen the other day and he's incredibly successful and wealthy. But he still sings about the working classes and the issues that were ingrained in him and that he still passionately cares about. I don't think your situation should change what you believe in."

Mr. Hollywood nods sagely, then glances over at his producer. "We good, Jerry?"

Jerry strokes his white moustache. "Ask him more about the concerts and the kids singing."

Mr. Hollywood obeys.

After the crew has shut down, shaken hands, and laughed loudly at a few more of their own jokes, Mike D. ushers them off the bus. Chris sighs, opens a bottle of water, and beckons me to follow him. "What did you think you of that *Access Hollywood* business?"

"Well," I say, "I was impressed at your patience. I think it's big of you to honor bad questions with serious answers. Why? What did you think?"

He pulls his black acoustic out of his bunk and collapses back onto the couch. "I think I just lost a whole lot of cred."

Back in the dressing room, Scott and Mike Marsh are eating baby carrots from the spread and Mike the merch guy is complaining about the assholes in catering. Mike D. is, as usual, somberly plugging away on his iBook, plotting out the flights home and to Europe for all eleven members of the crew. The tour ends tomorrow night, but right now it's still humming along at a full clip. Giant productions like this don't cruise to a gentle stop. They go flat-out one hundred miles per hour until the very last moment, when they just shatter. No one talks about it much, but everyone is anxious for that moment to hurry up and arrive.

After sound check and after a shower, Chris seeks me out and asks if I want to talk more, and we decamp once again to the back of the bus. He assumes his standard position, reclining on the couch, hugging a pillow to his chest and staring at the ceiling. I sit across from him, notebook on my lap balancing out the psychotherapy cliché.

"You look tired," I say.

"Yeah, I am," he says. "We're really excited for this tour to end."

Again and again, Chris speaks in the first-person plural, using the royal we both as a reflection of his desire to be a part of something larger than himself and a defense mechanism to shield himself from the glare of the celebrity spotlight. He tried to make Dashboard Confessional a band once before, in the fall of 2001. His offer to make the then-current lineup of the group the official entity was rejected. Guitarist Mike Stroud quit to join former Dashboard opening act Ben Kweller's band, and bassist and friend Dan Bonebrake quit to rejoin his old Florida band, Seville. Only Mike Marsh accepted and is considered a full-time member. Chris was crushed by the rejection but quickly refocused and now talks frequently about extending the same offer to Scott and Johnny. The heat on any solo artist is always a few degrees hotter than on a full band, but Dashboard takes that to unenviable extremes. Chris is the songwriter, singer, star, and subject of the Dashboard Confessional machine. Everything—from the bus we're sitting in to the dozens of teenage girls lined up in the parking lot—sprang from his mind. He responds to pressure the same way he responds to everything when he's on the clock: calmly, seriously. The cracks are beginning to appear and the word "I" is slowly disappearing from his normal conversation, as if he's saving it only for special occasions.

"Is this a lonely life?"

"Oh, like, 'woe-is-me?' The lonely guy who made it out of the cramped van and got to ride on a plush tour bus?"

"You know what I mean."

"Well, I'm incredibly lucky and I love what I do. I got the brass ring. Whatever, yeah, it's lonely. It's isolating. Nobody really wants to. . . . Like, people are always saying, man, you must get so many girls. None of these girls really want to talk to me. They almost want to talk about me while I'm there. The simple connections are so hard to find. But I'm lucky—I've got a pretty good support structure."

"It seems like you've had family in every city I've seen you in."

He laughs. "Everybody in my family goes to great lengths to be wherever I am. It's incredible. My seventy-four-year-old grandmother will drive to Manhattan to watch me tape the Carson Daly show. That's amazing to me. I had some reservations about being on this Weezer tour and mentioned it to my brother. There are no secrets in my family. You tell somebody something and, ten minutes later, all eighty-nine of us know what's going on. My aunt once said she had to leave the house to finish a sentence. So anyway, I tell my brother, and the next thing you know—and nobody said anything about it outright—but there hasn't been one week on this five-week tour where a family member didn't come to see me. They keep me from getting homesick. Or getting down.

"But then I have a surrogate family here. I don't know any other band that has kept the same crew for so long. There's this loyalty that we have to them and that they have to us. I think of them as family and they think of each other as family and we will go to great lengths to support each other. I tend to foster that attitude wherever I go because family is what makes me who I am. It's not even like this us versus them attitude. It's more like, 'it's us!' That's it. We're together. And that's enough."

Chris picks up his guitar from the floor. "Do you mind if I do this? I sometimes feel more comfortable when I've got it in my hands."

I think of the grizzled road vets on the bus, how the sarcasm melts away from them when they talk about Chris. How MP winces at the mention of chocolate cake like he's just cut himself. "It seems like courtesy is just as important to you, doing things the right way," I say.

"Yeah, of course. There are ways that you should. . . ." he catches himself. "No. There are ways that I should behave. And I look at the world through that."

"Even so, it was pretty huge that you thanked security last night after what happened."

"Why is that?"

"Well, you *could* look at it like you were trying to avoid getting your ass kicked, but . . ."

"No, I wasn't. There was one knucklehead who had something to prove. The other guys made things right and that was impressive. Whatever. They did a good job at the job they did. And so why not say good job? Courtesy is important because there's nothing more memorable than somebody being a dick to you. I mean, sometimes I'm gonna be a jerk. Totally unintentionally. And because every interaction with me is heightened, that could ruin somebody else's day. So I try my best. Plus, I genuinely like people to feel good. So we try to do that. Which is ironic since my music makes people feel maybe not so good. Although in the end it does. There's a purging of evil spirits kind of thing."

I try to engage him more but he's lost in his own world now, his fingers slowly picking out the melody of "This Old Wound" over and over again.

Attempting to ride out the silence, I flip through a scrapbook that a fan handed Chris in San Diego. It's an amazing project, dozens and dozens of handmade pages covered with magazine collages, printouts from messageboards, pictures, and envelopes containing private letters. The book allows Dashboard fans to reveal themselves directly to their idol, a chance not only to explain what he's meant to them, but to show him. The book was made by Melissa Chavez, who later told me, "I wanted him to have something of mine because I figured he's given us so much with his music." It's funny, moving, and incredibly alive—a physical reassertion of the fans' equal footing in the band's existence, a fact easily lost in the hollowness of the Weezer tour. A few weeks later, I'll get a cell-phone call from Chris late on Sunday night saying, "I've been looking through that book I got in California and it's making me cry. I hope I'm not bothering you; it just filled me with all of these feelings and I feel like I ought to share them." But for now, he's lost in his own world.

Putting the book aside for a moment, I try to draw him out by asking who he thinks these kids are, the ones who made this book.

He lets out a giant sigh and doesn't answer for a while, his fingers still tracing the simple descending pattern of the song. It seems like I've asked the wrong thing, that there's something he wants badly to say but won't offer it up unrequested. Eventually, the tape runs out and there's silence.

I watch Dashboard's set from the side of the stage with Rich Egan and his assistant Ryan. Rich scowls through the whole set, seeing things in it that no mere fan or mortal could ever divine. It's numbing to look out into the seething sea of blackness that is the crowd. Tonight's attendance is over fifteen thousand—Weezer is an L.A. band and this is reportedly their biggest show ever—and though not every seat is filled, it's getting closer and closer to capacity. The sound is tinny from the monitors but the set is smooth and professional. Mike Marsh has developed all sorts of little fills and trills to plug up the cracks between songs and during the times that Chris probably should be bantering but doesn't feel like it. What's most noticeable is the darkness and the moments when it lifts. When the spotlight suddenly turns on the crowd it's a reality check. There are hordes up on the lawn who remain faceless, but the entire front of the house is suddenly granted a personality. Girls in the front are staring at Chris like he's the pope, swooning and rocking on their feet. At the end of "Swiss Army" I catch sight of one girl almost fainting, collapsing into the arms of her equally young, equally enchanted friend. When the band launches into "Remember to Breathe" I spy them leading their row in an impassioned sing-along directed at the stage, and then to each other, holding hands, toothy smiles bright. Later, Egan and Chris dismiss the show as sub-par, saying the crowd was "typical L.A.," meaning cooler-than-thou and dispassion-ate. In reality, though, the show was just fine, one of those rare nights when the Dashboard machine operates flawlessly on a large scale. No one's life was saved, but those watching on TV at the back had a per-fectly nice show. During "Screaming Infidelities" the air was filled with cigarette lighters, not a youth chorus.

After the set the number of people in the backstage area seems to triple. Opening act Sparta's party is raging in their dressing room and out into the common space. Jimmy Eat World's tour manager and guitar tech are there. So is Rich Egan's entire extended family, including his very friendly wife and his sister Maureen who, along with her partner Matthew Barry, directed both Dashboard videos. There's a hail-the-conquering-heroes spirit in the Vagrant camp tonight. I duck into the dressing room to pick out a new pen and see Chris talking to an older guy with thin facial hair and long black locks.

"So, what'd you think?" Chris asks the guy.

"What do you mean?"

"Of the show?"

The guy looks pained. "Don't tell me I missed the show. It hasn't hap-pened yet, right?"

"No, dude, we just got offstage."

"Oh my god! Fucking kill me right now! The traffic was a night-mare."

There's a pretty-looking girl in the room too, sitting on the opposite couch, eyes never leaving Chris. But he's ignoring her.

Outside the dressing room door, Scott Schoenbeck is sipping a Corona.

"What's going on in there?" I ask.

"Oh, it's a big meeting. That's Jack Joseph Puig." The name is vaguely familiar and with good reason: Puig is low profile but has had a hand in many of the most influential modern rock albums of the last ten years, including Weezer's *Pinkerton* and albums by Belly and the Black Crowes. His signature style seems to be never making you notice that he's there.

"Is Chris considering him for the new record?"

"Yeah."

"Because he missed the show tonight."

"No way. Are you serious?"

Just then, Chris appears at the door and whispers me over, "Hey, can you go get Mike D. and tell him I need him to get this girl out of here?"

"Sure," I say, and wander off.

Chris and Mike Marsh talk to Puig intently for over three hours, never once emerging from the dressing room or letting anyone else in. It's serious business. Outside, Weezer's afterparty is raging in the catering area. There are plenty of stereotypically hot, blonde SoCal girls present, most of them spending their time running away from the frequent hugs of over-anxious, over-forty record executives in tracksuits. I meet two girls who have flown all the way from Japan to see Weezer for the eighth or ninth time this year. Despite the free light beer and giggling groupies— or perhaps because of them—most of Dashboard chooses to spend the aftershow ensconced in the bus, drinking Maker's Mark and watching MTV. At around 1:30, Chris and Mike Marsh return and the bus grumbles to life and steers northward, beginning the all-night drive to Concord, California, the last stop on the Enlightenment Tour.

That night, after most of the crew retires to their bunks, the band stays up late talking. Chris is hopped up and excited from his talk with Puig and an encounter with an old friend. He's chattering away like he's got a Red Bull IV stuck in his arm. Intense in-jokes rattle around the bus like pinballs, followed by serious concerns about the future.

At one point Mike Marsh mentions he had a dream the night before where they began each night on the fall headlining tour with the entire *So Impossible* EP, track for track, telling the story in full. Chris loves it, then realizes that "Hands Down" couldn't end the show then. "That's OK," he muses, "maybe it's time for a new closer anyway." He told me once that he lies awake at night sometimes, either in his bunk or at home in Boca, dreaming of set lists. "No band cares as much as this band does," he says to sleepy, nodding assents. Scott is disappearing into the couch, listening intently. Johnny looks nervous. But for this night at least, the boss has shaken his blues and wants to talk, so they're talking. It's almost 3 A.M. when I turn in. The rest of them are still out there.

Saturday breaks beautifully in Concord, California. It's just south enough of San Francisco that the weather is summery, just close enough that everything looks like a postcard. We're surrounded on all sides by burnished gold mountains. By noon the temperature is already well over eighty degrees. I find Chris sitting on a wooden bench in the shade of the Amphitheater's medical tent. The tour buses and semis are parked and rumbling anxiously just to his right. He's wearing his dark shades and a tight blue T-shirt. He's all right angles and seems to disappear into the building behind him. As crew members traipse back and forth, unloading, none of them seem to notice him at all. He beckons me over and I sit down. He's silent for a moment, then lightly punches me in the arm. "It's really good to have you here, homes," he says.

"Why is that?" I ask.

"This has got to be strange, right?" he says. "Like I know the way that we've come to be known is not normal. And I just . . ." Mike the merch guy walks by and waves. "So much time is lost now, I can't remember details. I would have liked to know more about what really happened. It would be so neat to have somebody to tell as things happen so that later on, for me and for anybody that's interested. . . . These kids are so invested in it, they should know more. They should know more about what really happens. About how hard it is. And how uplifting it is when it works. And why I have this undying dedication. And why that makes it feel so hard on days when it just doesn't feel like it works. Why the highs are so high when I do get to do something like *Letterman*. Why that means so much to me from coming from a place where, it was better to walk a mile to use the bathroom at the gas station than the one in that club 'cause you'll definitely catch diseases just walking through the door. So. I guess that's why."

We talk about business a little more, about how he always wanted to be on Interscope Records and that, in a short time, Jimmy Iovine has become a mentor to him. With the heat rising, we head back to the spot on the back of the bus.

Months back, Chris had copped to a serious crush on *Buffy the Vampire Slayer* actress Sarah Michelle Gellar. I ask if he's met her yet.

"Oh, god no. She's gonna get married soon and I don't want to be an adulterer."

"I think you need to steal her from Freddie Prinze Jr."

"No, no. I've done a lot of thinking on this subject. She'd be so creeped out by me talking to the press like this."

"She must have heard about it by now."

"I doubt it. I'm a peon. A peon."

"Well, maybe things will change if you win that MTV award." A few days ago Chris found out that Dashboard was up for a trophy at this fall's MTV Awards. The category is voted on by the fans and Chris is up against some of the hottest—and coolest—bands of the year.

"Oh, nothing will happen. In all honesty, I can tell you that I'm not going to win that award."

He drifts into silence and begins plucking at his guitar. I ask a few more questions but his mind is lost somewhere. Eventually, I turn the tape off and flip through the book that the kids gave him the night before. All of the pictures and email addresses and hopes and fears and dreams. Chris is picking at "This Old Wound" again. He motions for me to turn my tape player back on.

"This . . . this is pretty much exactly the place I'm in right now."

Staring at the floor, Chris plays and sings "This Old Wound" for me and for himself. His voice is high, slight, and wounded and when he runs up against certain line-ending words—"salt," "black," "tracks"—it seems to retreat from him, like a boxer's wobbly knees in the eleventh round. On the chorus, his strumming is slightly off, the sound discordant. But he plows through anyway. Again and again the lyrics allow him to set himself up and knock himself down: "I believe in luck / I think I do," "a blind belief in goodness / that doesn't seem to show."

When the song ends, it remains slightly, hanging over the room like a veil. It's a silent, nearly creepy moment. Chris puts his guitar down and lies back, defeated.

"That's the one that Mike had to make sure I wasn't suicidal after hearing it." Even his speaking voice seems different now, worn out and hollow. "The lyrics are about as literal as a metaphor can be, I think. Remember what I told you once about keeping things surface level and never letting yourself really heal? That's what I was thinking about. I was having a day where I was like, how am I ever gonna get over this stuff? It was a particularly bad moment and I wrote down those words. I just had this image of . . . ," he rubs his arms fiercely, "scouring, you know?"

"So you're afraid of not getting over the stuff you sing about every night."

"Yeah. Or the specific things that cause those songs. The strange feelings that they conjure up that no one should rightly feel on a nightly basis. No one that's not being punished."

"Because you're not getting over them?"

"In doing them I'm not getting over these things or I'm finding new things to not get over. It seems really stupid sometimes."

"It wouldn't be so rough if you weren't so serious about performing them," I say.

"Sometimes I envy pop bands a lot."

"Do you ever find yourself retreating in a song?"

"Meaning, do I ever let myself live a little? Do I not punish myself so much?"

"Well, yeah. Every song is so intensive."

"I never let myself off of the hook . . . but maybe a lot of people are like that. I know so many alcoholic songwriters that write the best songs I've ever heard. I have friends that are addicted to drugs who I actually envy. Because they're so talented and it's so richly derived from the punishment that they give themselves on their arm or up their nose or something. I don't have those things, that's unappealing to me. But I've often wished, often thought that it might even be easier to do that than to do what I do. Which sounds really melodramatic when I say it out loud." He laughs and rubs his head.

"Kids are always asking you how you're doing and you say you're fine, that singing these songs is part of how you deal with things," I say. "In many ways, it's like the people online who make their diaries public."

"I hear that and I think to myself how could you do that? How could you possibly do that? And then I realize that's what I do too. And maybe it's human nature for people like us. And not everybody's like us. But there are these people that need to air it out in some way. I used to write long letters and just make them undelivered. It's probably better just to do that."

"But that's kind of a retreat, isn't it?"

He stretches, sinks further back into the couch. "Yeah, that's true. But . . . I didn't write any of these songs with the intent of sending them out to who they're for." He's silent for a time, staring off at nothing. Suddenly, he says, "I would hope that she would see this as a letter. When you're holding your CD-R in your hand from the studio and driving by her house on the way to yours and thinking to yourself, I've got two copies here. I could put this one under her windshield wiper. But that wasn't the plan." He sighs. "Do you see the mood that song just put me in? That's what it's hard to walk away from. I'll shake it off in fifteen to twenty minutes. That's usually the max if it's one song. But 'Hands Down' the other night really put me in a spiral."

"Well, it didn't let up."

"Yeah. And it's usually the vindication moment. I hope I didn't rob anybody of that."

There's something different about the way Chris is answering the questions now. He's resigned almost—the security guards have abdicated their posts behind his eyes and he's talking freely. But their coffee break has a time limit. One has to grab all the goods in sight and get out of there before the gate slams shut. So I ask a question from yesterday again.

"What was it that set you off last night?"

"Maybe it was the physical altercation. Maybe it was being on the beach all day, and having specific memories of certain people. Maybe it was such a release from doing these Weezer shows. I ran this huge spectrum of emotion; I was all over the board. That's not always healthy. It's like people who are manic-depressive have extreme highs. I could understand that. I don't suffer from that, but I think I get a quick insight to it once and awhile. There was—somebody had insulted me. Somebody I respect had said something fairly insulting to me earlier in the day. Then took it back and said they never meant it but they were just angry. But nonetheless . . ."

I wait for him to say who had done it, but he moves on.

"There was a moment where I didn't think I was going to make it through the rest of 'Hands Down.' I didn't think I'd get back even to finishing the song the way that we have to end it."

"The songs seem to come out of you—both in terms of writing them and performing them—in these huge emotional spikes."

"Yeah, it's true. It's a weird channeling thing. 'Hands Down' kinda freaked me out, though. It was so happy!"

"It is a change. You've had all these songs which are upset, very pointed letters and now . . ."

He sees where this is going. "I hope every girl I might fall in love with listens to that song and says, 'OK, this guy isn't lost.' Because otherwise, what kind of catch am I? Why would girls want to be with this horrible, morose guy who will probably write horrible songs about them."

"Oh, I'm sure there are plenty of girls who want to be the one to fix you," I say, "the one who you'll write wonderful songs about."

"Wonderful songs?" He laughs. "Yeah, maybe. Maybe now that they've at least seen the potential for it. But that's why I named the EP *So Impossible*."

"You told me once that the night you talk about on that EP happened when you were sixteen."

"Yeah. It's an ever-evolving story, that one. I don't want to give too much away. But it's someone I've stayed close to. And she might be the one, y'know? I was reading this report that the general advice twenty years ago was never to marry your high school sweetheart. But then, when I was in college, I read about current opinion that said you absolutely *should* marry your high school sweetheart. What's the quote? 'We love but once because only once are we truly equipped for loving?' Maybe that's true. You only have your full capacity—total trust, complete love and surrender—once in your life."

"Like a stinger on a bee."

"I need to let some of this stuff go." He sighs. "Stop living so behind myself."

Off the record now, Chris spins tale after tale of his romantic history—girl after girl who betrayed him or he disappointed. Most of them he's still friends with and most of them seem to live in New York and be friends with each other. When he's talking about his own drama, without the benefit of art obscuring it, he's not depressed. He's excited. "You know that movie *Can't Hardly Wait?*" he asks, referring to the "last night of high school" teen movie from 1998. "I've had that day. It's so crazed and desperate but there's a big kiss at the end. I've had it and it's one of my favorite movies because of it. I'm a sucker for that '80s shit." He's had more serious relationships in his twenties then most people have in their entire lives, and the drama of it, the sheer romantic hopelessness of it all, seems to swell him with a perverse pride. The love he believes in is so perfect, so impossible, that it's as if he's proving himself right with every wrong turn his personal life takes. The night may end with the kiss and the music may swell, but the credits don't roll. It's in those moments afterward that life starts and Chris retreats, and that's where his own songs come in.

"The girl I wrote 'Screaming Infidelities' about called me after the headlining shows in the spring," he says. "She said she really wanted to see me. So I went to see her—I owe her that much. She said she was so happy for my success. Then it slowly crept into, 'Do you think about me?' I do, you know? Then it turned into, 'I'm thinking of breaking up with my boyfriend and I really miss you so badly and I know that I fucked up.' This is the guy that she cheated on me with. It's like this whirlwind of emotion, really negative and really positive. All I said was, break up with this guy. Don't worry about me, but break up with this guy, because you're talking to me right now. She called me when we were in Detroit last month and said, 'So . . . I didn't want you to hear this from anybody else, but I'm getting married.' What? This is three months later. Jesus Christ."

"So it never ends. In life or in the songs."

"See how much more to the stories there are? That's what I think about when I'm onstage. That's why I can never get over it."

There's a knock on the door and the young guitar tech that Chris has named Novice (though after this tour he's considering upping him to Sophomore) appears.

"Just to warn you," he says, "there's a group of fifteen sixteen-year-olds standing outside of the bus."

Chris is nonplussed. "How'd they get back here?"

"I don't know."

"Well, don't get rid of 'em."

"They're just standing there with tickets. Waiting for you."

"Let 'em wait. I'll go talk to them in a minute."

There's a pause, Novice and Chris look at one another.

"Should I go get you a Sharpie?" asks Novice.

"Hell, yeah," says Chris, laughing.

The last show of the Enlightenment Tour goes off without a hitch, but Dashboard's set is lackluster. Chris's voice seems worn out and he looks dwarfed by the crowd, not lifted up by it. The teenybopper screams are louder than ever here, though there are at least two occasions when big fratty dudes in baseball hats look at their eye-rolling friends, say fuck it, and stand up all alone, belting the words to "Swiss Army Romance" with all that their muscled lungs can muster. During a version of "Ender Will Save Us All" that never takes flight and merely seems to circle back in on itself, Weezer's crew plays its tour-ending practical joke, letting loose with dozens of paper airplanes that spiral and crash all across the stage and into the front row of the audience. It seems wildly out of place—the communal, "Hey guys we did it" last-night-of-the-tour gesture by the crew, which goes unacknowledged by Chris, only serves to heighten the disconnect of the moment. Playing arena rock games at a Dashboard show is like a whoopee cushion in church—it may help break the mood but, really, the mood is everything. In San Diego Chris fed off of his frustrations and exhaustion and turned it into something bleak, potentially cathartic, and undeniably powerful. Tonight it all just seems lost.

After the set there's more relief than anything else in the dressing room. Chris hangs with Sparta for awhile, trading war stories and making plans to tour together again sometime. The merch guys trade concert shirts with the other crews and Mike D., happier than anyone, allows himself a healthy splash of bourbon in a wine glass.

In the Weezer afterparty area, the usual girls crisscross the tables, searching for drinks and a moment alone with Rivers. The air is lovely and soft, the end of summer in the mountains. Chris sits to the side on some equipment boxes with Scott; like everyone else they've got their digital cameras out and are snapping away. It's the last day of summer camp and Chris is folded up like origami—cataloging each piece of himself and consigning it away to storage just like the crews are doing out on the empty stage, making sure he knows where everything is for when he needs it again in Europe, ten days from now. My friends are waiting for me outside by the tour buses where a kooky old man on a golf cart will drive us out to the parking lots and back to real life. I say my goodbyes and walk away, thinking of the last thing that Chris said to me as we went in search of autograph-hungry teenage girls this afternoon: "I'm just one of those hopelessly romantic people so I don't think I'll ever run out of stories. I'm always looking for love. But I'm afraid now—by doing what I do—I've missed my chance to ever find it. That I'm destined to get burned again and again."

He couldn't have been more wrong. A month or so later, Chris wins that MTV Video Music Award live on international television, shocking the hell out of everybody, especially himself. The award was, of course, voted on by the fans. Onstage at Radio City Music Hall, the blonde actress who announces the winner looks confused and says "the winner is Dashboard Confessionals." Co-presenter Anthony Kiedis of the Red Hot Chili Peppers furrows his brow. There's a strange rumble in the massive auditorium—a cheer that rises not from the industry seats in the front, but from the bleachers, the nosebleeds; all the hidden pockets in the back where the real fans sit. And all of a sudden, all of the stress, all the misery—both self-imposed and otherwise—seems to dissipate from both Chris Carrabba and Dashboard Confessional. He had driven himself to the breaking point over the summer of 2002, and now the fans had banded together and given him something back. The award—though relatively unimportant—was tangible proof that it had all been worth it. Onstage, Chris and his bandmates look shellshocked, appreciative. They crack self-deprecating jokes and smile big for all of the cameras.

On my computer, an IM screen blinks open. It's Ian Bauer from Long Island. "Dude," he writes. "Did you see that?" A pause. "This is crazy!"

Upstairs in the balcony, unseen by the cameras, Rich Egan jumps out of his seat with his fist in the air, testifying back to the stage with his mouth hanging open, just like he did at the earliest punk shows of his youth. The first thing he thinks is, "I can't believe we won." The second thing he thinks is, "It's all over." The third thing he thinks is, "Well, what a way to go."

It was an ending, but it was also a beginning.

Later that fall, an article appears in the *New York Times Magazine,* a starry-eyed puff piece about another young, tortured singer/songwriter—Nebraska's Connor Oberst—whose grandiose, theatrical musings on love and art have made his band, Bright Eyes, a critical darling. The purpose of the article is to position Oberst, who has recently taken to singing slightly more political songs, as "the new Dylan," mostly because of his opposition to a war in Iraq. But the article misses the point entirely. The baby-boomer generation—always so quick to anoint successors to their own cultural heroes—is the one that needs a new, political Dylan, not their kids. In a complex and tumultous decade, Bob Dylan helped map out a sensibly conflicted path through a convoluted and frighteningly large world. A true twenty-first-century Dylan would map out the terrain that is the most compelling, confusing, and necessary to today's kids; he or she would try and sketch out a map of the inside, of the heart.

I reach Chris on his cell phone a week after the MTV Awards. He's in Connecticut for a few days, visiting his family and relaxing. But he doesn't sound relaxed. He sounds giddy.

"It's not real!" he exclaims. "It's not real! I mean, what planet is this? But really, Andy, why shouldn't the Olson twins come and say hi to me backstage? Why shouldn't Kirsten Dunst come over and congratulate me. This is happening, but it's not happening. It's like a dream. When they said our name, I didn't know what to do. Thank god Marsh was there. He was the one who shook me and started yelling, 'We won, dummy, we won!'" He laughs and keeps talking. "I always knew the kids cared so much about us, but how unusual is this? I mean, we're nowhere near as big as those other bands. But it's a fan-voted award. They made it happen. That's how much they care. I don't know if they'll ever know how much we appreciate it. I have to let them know. I'll figure something out."

He pauses, then starts up again. "Did I tell you that Triumph interviewed us?" He is referring to the Insult Comic Dog puppet that sparked controversy at the awards by provoking an ornery Eminem. "It was the highlight of the night. We walked over to him and he was like, 'Tell me . . . are you Dashboard Confessional?' And we said we were. And he said, 'So, then . . . will you confess to SUCKING?!'" Chris laughs his short, loud laugh.

"How is it being in Connecticut?"

"Oh, man. It's been so good. So wonderful. I have to tell you . . . I'm thinking about making the move."

"Really? Leaving Florida? The beaches?"

"Yeah . . . oh, god, it would break my mother's heart if I did that. But it's so wonderful to be up here and be surrounded by family. There's this house up here—it's the house my grandfather built. He was the typical hardworking Italian immigrant and it's the house my entire family grew up in. All my cousins and I used to play there. When my grandfather died we couldn't afford to keep it anymore. We assumed we'd have it forever. But now, there's a rumor that it's going back on the market. All the cousins are debating . . . should we do this? As a family? Should I just do it? I don't know. I've had such a wonderful time I'm seriously considering it."

He sounds better than he did when I saw him last, more grounded. Healthy. There's no more mention of it all ending soon. Far from it. He talks a lot about plans to record the third record, about messing around with pop pastiches and techno instrumentals, just because he can. About making sure that from now on people realize that Dashboard Confessional is a vehicle for *all* of the songs and moods that come out of Chris Carrabba—it's not a code word for a depressed guy on a stool pouring his heart out. He talks with genuine excitement about Jimmy Iovine's plans to make him a "career artist." He's beginning to look ahead and move forward. The old wounds are finally starting to heal.

And I think: in some small way, it's already past him. Dashboard Confessional was an emo moment, not an emo career. Carrabba may have many more years and songs ahead of him, but those frustrated, tormented ballads will live on. His worst moments may well outlive his best moments. He has pushed the punk/emo model as far as it can go—a personal, private hero to an ever-expanding (and ever-demanding) public of individuals from CBGB's to Radio City. It can't stretch forever, though—no one could survive that. The time we spent together on the Weezer tour proved it. Emo acts, by definition, don't fade away. They burn up. No matter how much the kids love Chris, they will get older, they'll get disappointed in something, and they'll move on. But will he?

Talk eventually turns to an old girlfriend, the one he's carried a torch for since childhood. She's coming back to Hartford that night for a holiday.

"I'm going to get her to hang out with me," he says matter-of-factly. "And I'm going to tell her how I feel. I've carried this around for twenty years. It's time I did something about it, and stop pussyfooting around about what I want in my life."

"Wow," I say. "Good for you."

"Yeah, well, we'll see. I can sort of foresee how this is going to go, but who knows. Maybe it'll work." He sounds down for a moment and then perks back up again. "And, hey, if it doesn't, maybe I'll get a good song out of it!"

PART FOUR

LOST & FOUND IN DIARYLAND

FOURTEEN

NOWHERE TO GO—GO NOWHERE

Wilkes-Barre, Pennsylvania, is pretty barren these days. A once-proud mining town nestled cozily between the Pocono Mountains and the Susquehanna River, Wilkes-Barre fell victim to the same blight that affected all of America's midsize towns in the latter part of the twentieth century. Neither urban nor suburban and stripped (strip-mined) of its main industry, the town greeted the new millennium as a relatively anonymous shell: home to a crumbling downtown, a shared triple-A baseball franchise, 1,001 doctors' offices, and a disaffected generation of young people bored out of their collective skull.

I feel fairly confident making these statements because Wilkes-Barre is where I'm from. My parents were born and raised there—I made it until just past my first birthday before moving to Philadelphia. But my grandparents and extended family all stayed in Wilkes-Barre, and I return a number of times a year. There have been two constants during my visits. One is that there is nothing to do. The other is that I never see any kids. I know they must be there, but it's impossible to find them. Almost all of the town's movie theaters have been shuttered; not even Starbucks has dared to lay down a franchise. One day, when driving in for a family event, I was forced to stop at the Wyoming Valley Mall, located at the top of a street filled with chain stores and restaurants that slopes down into the valley, a first (or last) watering hole of commercialization before the town-proper's spartan half-sprawl of decrepit mom-and-pop stores and decrepit moms and pops. It was 7 P.M. on a spring evening when I parked my car and attempted to duck into whatever cheap shoe outlet I could get in and out of in ten minutes. The parking-lot entrance to the mall opens into the food court, and it was overrun. There were dozens of teenagers, ranging in age from eleven to twenty, swarming, teeming. They bounced and buffeted from one seemingly random grouping to another like bubbles in a glass of Mountain Dew. There was a desperation to their socializing—laughs were loud and sharp, gestures were dramatized one hundredfold. The styles ranged from thoughtlessly preppie to more familiar blends of mall and skate punk (Marilyn Manson T-shirts and attitudes, dyed hair, intentional-unintentional butt cleavage). Mall security guards played their Keystone Kops role to the fullest, rounding up the loudest kids, becoming distracted, and letting their harmless perps slip through their grasp. It was like being dropped into the feeding end of an overstuffed fish tank. The targetless desperation was palpable and pathetic.

It is precisely this sort of hopelessness that causes hardcore scenes to sprout like so much acne—similarly fueled by fierce teenage apathy and equal parts attention-starved, angry, and noticeable. Indeed, central Pennsylvania has long supported an intensely political and loyal indigenous scene. Which is more than well and good for a certain type of teen—it's positively lifesaving. But what about the other kids—those stuck, lost, and bored in malls of their own making? The answer is rooted in the ultimate escape hatch of the twenty-first century—the web. When there is truly nowhere to go, you go nowhere, but when the entire world can come to your bedroom, that suddenly isn't such a bad thing after all.

Kate Flannery grew up in the town of Pringle, a tiny suburb of Wilkes-Barre located in the shadow of the "back mountains," a sector clogged with the ghosts of a Waspy past long buried. Her parents—a successful lawyer and a registered nurse—are part of the last generation of upper-middle-class professionals to stay and make a life in the Wyoming Valley, and though happy at home, Kate chafed under the limited circumstances and unlimited boredom of her hometown.

"Wilkes-Barre is so antiyouth, it's ridiculous," she says. "There are anticruising laws, so kids can't drive around. They can't loiter in the mall. All there is for them to do is hang out in people's houses and smoke pot or congregate in parking lots. The biggest hangout in the area is the Gateway Center—an abandoned shopping center off the highway and across the street from a family restaurant. And that's where they park and meet other kids. That's what they do. There's nothing there."

But Kate was born in the '80s, and at the age of twelve she discovered something else, something that took her far away from the parking lots and shopping centers of home.

"My parents got AOL when I was twelve," she remembers. "And I was hanging out in some teen chat room—because what else do you do when you're twelve in Wilkes-Barre. And there was one kid who started talking to me who was like, 'I'm a punk. Punks wear leather jackets.' And I was like, 'Weird!'" She laughs. "My brother is thirteen years older than me and I remember he had some Sex Pistols and Ramones LPs in the basement and I thought, 'Is this really happening now?' So this kid started making me mix tapes and talking about his drug addiction and I thought it was the coolest thing ever. Of course, he was fifteen and lived in Illinois, but it didn't matter.

"Through him, I got into messageboard culture, punk rock, and zines. It was amazing. You're twelve or thirteen in middle school, and get made fun of because you're dorky. And all of a sudden here's this little movement that fits you perfectly. You can be a cool kid, and feel important. It was all I needed. I didn't have to worry about being called ugly in school anymore because I could just retreat into this other world where I had friends, even though I didn't know what they looked like. It didn't matter. It was possible to have intense relationships solely throught the written word."

In the early days of the web, Kate found the same solace that teenagers have sought in emo music for two decades—the ability to gain both community and self-definition. She started a zine called *Sneer* that combined poetry, collage, and diary and gained fans across the country (eventually triggering national press in magazines like *Seventeen* and *Newsweek*). She transformed herself from "the straight-laced preppy smart girl" into "a freak" but, armed with a virtual community of peers, she relished her outsiderness. Instead of stymieing her individuality, Kate's teenage years were about developing it.

"You're creating a persona for yourself and your zine is reflective of that," she says. "It's the most base form of: Look, this is me. It's their function, to relate to other people and figure out an identity."

Through the web, she was able to find like-minded souls in Wilkes-Barre—something she never would have thought possible—as well as to foster and become a vital member of a burgeoning national scene.

"There were these chat rooms on AOL," she remembers, "hardcore chat and punk chat. And that's where everyone congregated. It was a tight-knit scene but widespread—you knew kids but only as their screen names. I guess there was a real romance in it. We all came from small towns where there wasn't much to do, and so you go to an online forum and talk to people from all over. You go from a small community to a much larger one. There's nothing to do outside so you sign on and talk to your buddies and make plans to meet them.

"I spent all of my free time online. All of it. That's just what you did. It was eternally gratifying. I would go from being teased and picked on at school to this little community where *I* was popular and everyone thought what I said was smart or funny or clever. It was an escape. It was fun. When you're hanging out in a parking lot in Wilkes-Barre, you're still hanging out with football players. Online, you're hanging out with kids who are into the same music as you, that have the same feelings and outlook."

In other words, you go from a small parking lot to one that is infinitely bigger.

Kate Flannery found an escape hatch early and followed it as far as it would go—from being an internet "celebrity" to national press, from being physically in Wilkes-Barre to being culturally miles beyond it. Today she is a savvy graduate of Bryn Mawr College who has lived in New York, Boston, and London. But her ability to transform herself was still relatively limited and depended largely on her own legwork and sensibility. Though her friends were virtual, her zine was still paper— the work she put into it was still flesh and blood. It would take a friend of hers, a bizarre modern combination of hardcore punk, dot-com bubble surfer, and old-fashioned snake-oil salesman, to craft a centralized vision of the web as solace. Where previous generations' dreamers had started bands, labels, and zines, Gibby Miller took the tools available to him and crafted the greatest venue in the world—a virtual safe haven, club, and coffee klatch rolled into one and available to all at the click of a mouse. If a combination of emo and file-sharing technology gave even the most unpunk young people something to feel, Miller's creation,

Makeoutclub.com, gave them something even more vital—somewhere to *go*.

"I was visiting a boy I was dating that I had met over the internet," Kate Flannery says. "He was living in Boston. One night this tall skinhead-looking guy came storming in, totally drunk, covered in tattoos. I was like, 'Ew, who is this?' He was so rude, so obnoxious. That was the first time I met Gibby."

Miller, in the summer of 2000, was twenty-two years old, a design student at MassArts, and generally notorious for considering himself notorious. He was cocky, omnipresent, and intensely, intensely social. He fronted a series of highly (if locally) regarded hardcore acts and maintained a website to display his photographs. Even then, though, he had the inklings of a much bigger dream.

At that point—with the web dominating the news as well as the day-to-day lives of virtually every teenager in the country—there were a few websites that offered what some would call community-building tools and others would label glorified singles ads. One was a feature of the website for the tiny Philadelphia-based indie label Trackstar. Kids would send Trackstar boss Bryan Poerner (Flannery's roommate) photos of themselves, which Bryan would then post with an occasionally flattering but usually viciously insightful description he had written. The other, larger, site was the cheekily titled sexyscenesters.com that allowed users to post a picture, some contact info, and their own list of biographical details and preferred bands. Though joking in tone, the sites' blossoming success was serious business. Teenagers were, as always, hungry for an opportunity to escape their surroundings and meet like-minded peers, and the allure of persona-creating—now freed of the staples and papercuts of the zine generation—was overpowering. Both sites were divebombed with applications and hits in their first few months of creation, so much so that their founders—short on resources and vision—were overwhelmed. When sexyscenesters' server crashed midway through the summer of 2000, Miller, entranced by the social possibilities of the sites, stepped in.

"I had reserved the URL 'Makeoutclub'—from the great Unrest song—earlier that summer with the idea of moving my personal stuff there," he says. "But when sexyscenesters went down, I thought it could be something really great if done properly, with the focus more on music and less on, well, sexy scenesters. So I threw it together with some friends. One of them wrote an automated system to make the workload easier, and we put it up. It was really just me picking up on a great idea that a few kids couldn't handle."

Makeoutclub.com—or "MOC," as it quickly became known— launched in July 2000 and spread through the online world like syphilis through a GI barracks. The site both simplified and expanded the prem- ise of sexyscenesters. Accepted applicants gained a profile on the site (helpfully divided into searchable "boys" and "girls" categories) that was wholly modifiable—the picture, contact information (a username, location, email, AOL instant messenger name, personal Web site URL), and "interests" box were accessible for personalized updates 24/7. The searching function was completely automated and smooth, allowing users to look for new friends by town or interest. There was also a mes- sageboard for constant, hormonal chatter. Within weeks, Miller was beseiged with applications.

"I think loneliness had a lot to do with its success," Miller says. "If you're in the middle of nowhere or don't know anyone who shares your tastes, it's a great thing to see a response to something you wrote, to go online and have people to chat with. I'm more interested in people meet- ing each other, forming bands, finding roommates, or starting mix-tape circles. I can't ignore the fact that people find potential love interests on the site—and it does bridge distances. But that was never the point."

Upon hearing this, Kate Flannery—who in 2000 became one of MOC's first members, its "staff" zine reviewer, and was briefly romanti- cally involved with Miller—laughs. "Gibby can swear all he wants that MOC is 'an internet community to find like-minded people and find out about events in your town.' But that's not what it was and that's not how it started. It's called *Makeoutclub*—you're never gonna get over that— and it is a total singles page. That is what it is. You search for boys and girls in your area, you see who's cute and you email or IM them. Yeah you can find out what's happening in your area, but the purpose of it is mating. Gibby can say he didn't know it was going to blow up, but he knew what he was doing. Oh, yeah."

Kids heard about it from other kids, from the media, from happy accidents. They joined to escape their limiting homes and lives, to meet people, or to score. People in bands joined, so did indie-label heads. Virginal preteens and skeevy adults submitted their pictures and profiles for consideration. They joined as jokes and they joined as dares. No matter the reason, they joined.

Within a month, the site had close to one thousand users. One year in, it was at ten thousand. After laudatory write-ups in *Spin* and references in other media, Makeoutclub hit twenty thousand. By the beginning of its third year, MOC was at thirty thousand users and growing at the rate of one hundred new kids per day.

It was, as Kate Flannery puts it, "the future of things."

Gibby Miller was born and raised in St. Louis, another of the small/big places in the country—one filled with people but bereft of choices. "I had a great childhood," he says, "but all I remember about it is sitting around and not knowing much of anything." A camp counselor turned him on to elegant and elegaic British bands like the Smiths and New Order at a young age, and he spent his early teens as the youngest person crouching nervously in the corner of local hardcore shows.

Unlike most people, Miller got a taste of the social potential of the web early on. "There was one website in St. Louis in 1990," he remembers. "There was a semicelebrity college radio DJ in town who ran a really primitive bulletin board system—it was thirty-three phone lines, thirty-three robotic modems, and only thirty-three people could be on it at a time. I didn't have internet access of my own until I was living in Boston in 1996. In St. Louis, though, all these kids would sign on late at night and have conversations. You'd meet people and then make plans to meet at the mall on weekends."

The power and reach of this sort of community building was never far from Miller's mind when he moved to Boston to attend boarding school at the age of fifteen, and it still crackles from him today. He's a thoroughly modern type—part social gadfly, part charismatic huckster—whose entire existence seems to be defined by getting groups of people together. To spend time with him is to get the creeping suspicion that you're being *played*—that Miller is searching you out for ways you could benefit him or participate in a scheme—but that you also don't mind. He's a web-savvy punk, one who believes in the unlimited power of *the message* but has no shame about doing whatever it takes to communicate it. One whose music tastes look backward, but who is so future-soaked that he gets the jitters if more than a few hours pass without an ethernet connection.

To log on to Makeoutclub today is to see the national subculture at its horniest and best. As Miller puts it: "All of my friends make fun of it, but they're all on it." From day one, the interests window became a canvas for a list of preferred bands—the more obscure the better. Kids have always defined themselves through music, and here was yet another way to make it public. Other artistic-leaning teenager standbys also dominated—poets like Anne Sexton, hobbies like photography, printmaking, and drinking. Boys usually declared their boredom, girls usually ended their list of dislikes with the damning/beguiling tease of "boys like you." Usernames tended to dabble with straight-edge constructs ("xbluestarsx" or "xjaggedlittlerazorx") and pictures were usually arty and obscured.

If the constant hum of online traffic had created an emo matrix of bands—once a band was accepted into the stream, they were cleared for commercial takeoff—Makeoutclub helped codify and spread a very specific oppositional teenage aesthetic. Instead of just a primer for listening, the mass individualism apparent from the beginning provided a virtual how-to guide for teenagers who were off the cultural grid. Kids in one-parking-lot towns had access not only to style (e.g., black, black glasses), but also what books, ideas, trends, and beliefs were worth buzzing about in the big cities. If, in the past, one wondered how the one-stoplight town in Kansas had somehow birthed a true-blue Smiths fan, now subculture was the same everywhere. Outcasts had a secret hideout. Makeoutclub.com was one-stop shopping for self-makers.

And as tastes change in the sped-up reality that is essential to both teenagers and the web, so too does the online profile. MOC users are not only given control of their entries, they are given control of their public selves. If one's own particular subcultural slice becomes too familiar, one can update it, embellish it, expand, and dramatize it. Yesterday's Dashboard Confessional fan can become tomorrow's Nick Drake enthusiast. A Wes Anderson advocate can easily morph into a dedicated follower of Truffaut. If someone else's profile turned you on to the fiction of Haruki Murakami, it's all too easy to absorb that knowledge into your own. Makeoutclub provided a public forum that could keep up with the constant flurry of self-definition and redefinition that mark the teenage years. Don't like the way you look? Take a flattering webcam picture with your bangs in front of your eyes. Don't like the books on your shelf? Pick different titles. Don't like your name? Boyfriend? Life? Everything is malleable. Version one of your subcultural self is easily transformed into self 2.0.

Teenage life has always been about self-creation, and its inflated emotions and high stakes have always existed in a grossly accelerated bubble of hypertime. The internet is the most teenage of media because it too exists in this hypertime of limitless limited moments and constant reinvention. If emo is the soundtrack to hypertime, then the web is its greatest vehicle, the secret tunnel out of the locked bedroom and dead-eyed judgmental scenes of youth.

Makeoutclub.com is that secret spot inside every individualistic teen's brain where they are king and queen and everyone else isn't disdainful—they're jealous. "MOC is a place where you can totally build your own personality from scratch," says Kate Flannery. "You can be portrayed as you want to be portrayed and that doesn't happen in real life. And that total control makes you feel good."

If the directories are the well-apportioned menu, it's MOC's vibrant messageboard that provides the entrée. Says Sarah Cairns, a charismatic Canadian college student and recovering MOC addict: "The board is the heart of the site. When you're on there it's a whole different perspective. You can use it for dating, but the people who frequent it are more friends than anything else. Whatever you want to use it for, you can; it's up to you." Bristling and bustling at all hours of the day, seven days a week, the messageboard is where makeout kids from all over the world gather to discuss issues that range from the sartorial ("Bandannas as Belts") to the scatological ("Butt Sex") and from the savory ("Is Beef Vegan?") to the sadly self-aware ("Why Can I Only Talk to Girls on the Internet?"). The dialogue (if one can call it that) is pure chaos theory in action—somehow, amidst the general cliquiness, disdain for newcomers, and uniformly juvenile attitude, resolutions are, if not gained, closed in upon. The sheer volume of posts suggests a chattering class enthused with the power and breadth of its own voice more than one with a realized agenda. The no rules, no grown-ups context is contagious and exhilarating. One youth-minded adult—K Records founder and Beat Happening main man Calvin Johnson—even got himself caught up in the fray, posting his profile, befriending the kids, and even writing a song about the frequent posters. No stranger to youth movements, Johnson proclaimed the MOC messageboard "better than TV," and cannily used it as a peer-networking platform to convert hundreds of teenagers into fans of K recording acts.

Though political debates are surefire attention-grabbers, conversations on the messageboard are often about subgrouping, defining borders—not just in terms of individual tastes (although there are always plenty of chances to do that), but in terms of your peer group and your place within it. Towards the end of 2001, as the site's popularity continued to increase exponentially, the biggest trend on MOC was "teams." Taking the by-now familiar inside jokery to a new level, users would post bold statements of intent, declaring the formation of a new breakaway group without any information on how one could go about joining it. The intended subtext was, of course, that you couldn't. Team names ranged from the specific ("Team Vegan," "Team Jesus") to the aggressive ("Team Elitist Fucks") and the trash-talking between groups was both heated and clever. Those on the boards who complained about the silliness and the exclusivity of the team concept misunderstood that the entire goal of the exercise was fragmentation. Grudging respect was afforded those unaffiliated souls who chose not to mock the teams outright, but rather form their own team—in many cases, a team of one. It was both a recasting of the tedious and degrading color wars and dodgeball games of summer camps past (finally basing success ratios on more competitive categories like style, music taste, and individuality) and yet another reenactment of the self-building that MOC was created to engender.

Another popular trend is rating users based on an infinite number of invented (and inventive) scales. At any time during the day (although frequently very late in the night) a male or female user will begin a post with a title of "I WILL RATE YOU BASED ON '80s SITCOM CHARACTERS" and then the kids are off to the races for hours. Sometimes the rating scales will be more personal (on girl/boyfriend potential, on looks) but more often they will be willfully obscure and pop-culture referencing—yet another multifaceted and ultimately insightful way to dance around sex while also dancing around.

The MOC messageboard is also where the battles over the present and future of the site are waged. People flame and rage against the "emo" tag, tripping over each other to make fun of the word, the media, and the bands it describes. Instead of being forced to the sidelines of the debates and pronouncements about their generation, kids on MOC are thrust out into the battlefield and allowed to fend for (and defend) themselves. Music tastes on the board tend to run more in the direction of indierock and punk than emo, but emotional involvement with the music is no less immediate or vital.

Needless to say, the most popular topic in the board is sex. Throughout the day bored and horny boys and girls—at work, in dorm rooms, or home sick from school—post willfully outrageous comments about sex acts, fetishes, and preferences. Gay or straight, male or female, the only constant is frankness, but it's a refreshing and ultimately healthy release, because if the boys control the bands, the girls rule the boards. Stripped of their one-sided soapboxes, the boys are revealed to be nervous, stammering simpletons, laughing at jokes they don't quite get, desperate for action they don't know how to handle. In other words, they're boys. Online, female voices can be just as loud, if not louder. They're not up on a pedestal, they're down in the trenches, slugging it out and usually winning. The result is a sex-positive dialogue that's raunchy on both sides of the ball.

Out of this hectic, shrieking, lewd, and crude cacophony can come genuine community—as Miller himself has repeatedly said, "distance doesn't mean shit online." Love has indeed sprung from the nonstop heavy virtual petting of the site—Gibby claims that at last count there were two marriages (one a "Canadian punk-rock couple") and countless cross-country hookups, and he currently reels at the thought of the now inevitable first MOC baby. Douglas Rainwater, a twenty-six-year-old Chapterhouse fan, moved all the way to Manchester, England, to be with his true, online love. "Makeoutclub is a great way to get to know a person on the inside," he says.

Twenty-one-year-old Jeralyn Mason agrees—she once traveled from her New England home to Cincinnati just to see a boy she had begun "dating" through Makeoutclub but had never actually met. "You can be a lot freer with people online," she says. "Because your personality is all you have to draw the other person to you. So you share so much of yourself in the hopes that they'll like it and then share themselves too. This leads to a really intense closeness that could take much, much longer to develop with a person that you casually see in real life." Though the relationship fizzled, Mason's belief in the friendship-building abilities of the internet have only grown. "I've 'met' so many people in the last few years, from all over: California, England. Places where it would have been impossible for me to know someone without the internet," she says. "They've changed me in the same way any real-world relationship would—they've taught me things about myself and the world that I wouldn't have been able to learn on my own."

Beyond romance, Makeoutclub kids look after one other in the way that they would want to be looked after themselves. Early in 2002 a shell-shocked twenty-two-year-old posted in the wee hours of the morning: he had just learned of an ex-girlfriend's death at the hands of her current boyfriend, who then killed himself. What followed his post was an outpouring of anonymous support, ranging from respectful silence to advice and offers of help. Mercifully absent in the comments was any trace of self-righteous lecturing or self-important grandstanding. It was perfectly appropriate, it was peer-to-peer, and it was immediate. An instant therapy group convened across state lines in the dead of night. After reading through the responses, the twenty-two-year-old typed,

> By the way everyone, thanks. I really don't know many people at work I can talk to about my personal life. MOC, for all the criticism levied towards it, has been a great experience thus far for me. I'm glad to have met such nice people here.

Problems are forced into the public eye on MOC, and the reactions to them are just as personal and undiluted. There's a popular acronym on the site: IRL, which stands for "In Real Life." It pops up a lot—in reference to meet-ups or parties—the differences between friends out in the world and those on the computer. But the most common usage of it— and the most lasting—is in reference to differences in the self. Because in a very legitimate way, people are often *realer* on MOC than they are IRL: less inhibited, wittier, wilder, more serious, and more fun. They are more outrageous, certainly, but also more tolerant, sensitive, and caring.

As 2001 became 2002 and MOC became flooded with more and more people from increasingly obscure locales (from Akron to New Zealand and back again) with radically divergent tastes and agendas (incorporating everyone from self-deluded emo boys who claimed they weren't emo while clutching teddy bears, to pierced goths, mall rats, and born-again Christian Saves the Day fans) many of the original kids grew disenchanted. As the second generation emerged and asserted themselves, older users realized that what once made you special can easily make you commonplace—especially online. While some succumbed to work (school or otherwise) and faded from view, many more took center stage on the messageboard to declare their exit from the site with as much drama and élan as possible (indeed, on MOC, all high schoolers are theater nerds). One fellow took the more sensitive and self-serious latecomers to task in his profile, declaring, "After I finish my steak and have a beer I'm going to fuck your girlfriend you straight-edge piece of shit." Eventually, many of the original, northeast-corridor MOCers created a similar site that was more suited to their flashy and exclusive tendencies called Lipstickandcigarettes.com. Others wandered onto regional permutations (like pahardcore.com) or dabbled in the burgeoning for-profit emo/punk online porn scene on sites like suicidegirls and supercult.com or tongue-in-cheek-yet-still-compellingly-sexy versions like the aptly named onlyundiesclub.com. None of these sites had the range, the stability, and the fanatical messageboard of MOC, though, and most dissenters eventually came grumbling back into the fold.

"There's posts all the time about people being mad about MOC getting so big," says Sarah Cairns. "It's just the same thing that people say when a band they love gets popular. Personally, I'd go kind of crazy without it! People get bored and they need something to do—that's pretty obvious from what's on the site."

Gibby Miller, after wrestling with the changed reality of the site for a few months during which he considered selling it, moved to New York in 2002 and fully embraced his role in the online monster he had created. Living in a tiny apartment in Williamsburg, Brooklyn, Miller made his income through DJing in Boston and Manhattan and found enough record company advertising dollars to keep the site on stable servers. He spent his days sleeping into the afternoon and then fiddling with the site, updating profiles and IMing friends old and new. Whether he intended it or not, the internet—and, more specifically, the aesthetic of MOC—had infected every aspect of his being. He was as likely to shut down the site as to go a day without email.

"It's lost its innocence in a lot of ways," he says. "It's like it went from a photocopied zine to a glossy in two years. But it's changed all of my interactions away from the computer. Now, when I'm waiting for a cab, or trying to go somewhere, I get so impatient. I'm so used to getting things fast."

Content to let the site grow and evolve, Miller has decided to pour money back into it, to add features that other web destinations brag about in an attempt to establish MOC as the hub of any emotional teenager's internet experience.

"I'm going to add options for online diaries, secret messages, private messageboards, locked sections of profiles," he says, grinning. "All because it's mine and I want it to be the best."

These additions may make users more loyal, but they can do little to add to MOC's already timeless appeal. The reason? All of the enhancements Miller talks about are things to make the site more personalized and, ultimately, more private. Teenagers already have enough private spaces—most of them are trapped in said places when they log on in a desperate search for freedom. It is the interaction, the freewheeling controlled anarchy of the place, that fills it with joy and makes it essential. Makeoutclub.com, like emo, takes essential elements of teenagehood and punk rock and rewrites the rulebook for everyone. And at its tortured and dirty-minded heart, Makeoutclub *is* emo, because it is both a tool and a mirror for vital acts of self-discovery and definition.

Makeoutclub succeeds precisely because it is never too much of anything. Gibby's true success is realizing that the battle isn't won when you create the world's greatest venue. It happens when you turn over the guest list to the guests and let the lunatics run the asylum. MOC is more than a genre or a moment because it collects new moments and recreates itself to suit them. It—or at least the media movement that it best represents—is the first step in a more sustainable teenage hyperreality.

Makeoutclub isn't a record label, a band, a genre, or an ideology. Makeoutclub is a safe haven and it reinvents itself nightly. There are no limitations of temporality, no outdated battles over cred, because the site itself is a constantly mutable battlefield. The site's value as a vehicle for self-definition is well captured by one user, whose profile is located deep into the site:

> oops..forgot my black rimmed glasses today..guess i dont fit in.
>
> im melanie. i dont fit into a label. i think they're pointless and not worth the effort to 'be.' the music i listen to does not affect the way i look, dress, act, or the way in which i view things. i dont care if you dont think things i do are cool, that's your opinion. i'm not in a band. i have dreams. unrealistic ones, they make me happy. boys also make me happy. nice ones..hard to find and easy to keep. im not fake. i am also not 'hot or sexy or bangin' or any of those other lovely words. im just me. my beauty is in my creativity..i sing. i write. i do artsy things. im not here to impress you. im here to make friends, and maybe learn something.

Melanie is aware enough to defy some cliched expectations and yet embrace others. Makeoutclub may be silly, it may be crowded, cacophonous and indulgent, but its users know it and they still feel comfortable using it as a homebase for whatever they want to do and for whatever they want to become. When the media glare fades, teenagers become adults, and Dashboard Confessional becomes a footnote—that's what emo is anyway.

"It's always just been a place to go," says Gibby Miller. "What you choose to do once you're there is up to you. My dream for it is to be insanely huge, like make it the *only* place. I just want to make it the fucking best place to go ever." He pauses. "And I can't do it alone. . . ."

FIFTEEN
MAKE YOURSELF

"There's no such thing as shyness on the internet," Kate Flannery says. "You can say whatever you want, you can leave whenever you want, you can be nasty to whoever you want. You can be whomever you want."

There's no such thing as shyness in emo songs either, but they eventually end or get popular or get far too linked to one specific time and place. On the internet, the constant blur of opinions, attitudes, feelings, and identities never ceases, never bogs down in the mail or in print. It simply exists, and when it doesn't, something new has long since taken its place. "Free beer tomorrow," says the sign in the bar. "No shame today," says the computer monitor. In a world supposedly desensitized to extremes of sex, violence, and media, teenagers online immerse themselves in a heightened reality, one where emotions are currency and instant messaging means never having the time to say you're sorry.

If Makeoutclub.com gives young people a venue to perform their own youth, LiveJournal.com has given them the tools to make themselves rock stars. Instead of taking their emotional succor and community from someone up on a stage—even if the stage is as communal as a basement—through personal websites and online diaries kids can now get all of this from a peer. Instead of becoming a fan of Chris Carrabba—a man a decade older than most of his fans and, despite his best efforts otherwise, generally unknowable and unreachable—it is now possible to become a fan of a girl your age, in your town or, better yet, a hundred towns or miles away. Online, it's standard behavior to help and be helped—to create a watchful and caring dialogue in real time and in a thousand tiny ways, one that far outstrips any band/audience dynamic anywhere.

The only thing as old (and established) on the internet as pornography is the personal website. Often called weblogs (or blogs), these constantly updated sites are private soapboxes, places for an individual to build a small, expressive shrine to themselves. That alone isn't shocking—the old joke about there eventually being a cable channel specifically made for every person in the country comes awfully close to reality online—but the rise of slightly organized, free, and easy-to-use diary sites has caused what once was a trend to coalesce into a social movement. A conservative estimate would be that, in 2003, over a third of all high school students with consistent access to a computer maintain online diaries. This is relatively shocking, unknown, and unimaginable to the public at large—and the kids want it to stay that way for as long as possible.

Brad Fitzpatrick is a twenty-four-year-old computer science student in Seattle. In the summer of 1998, he decided he wanted to maintain a journal online, but one that would automate and simplify the updating process. In a fit of boredom, he created a rough, but certainly usable, template. When he arrived at college, his roommate expressed interest in having his own journal too and Fitzpatrick obliged him. Soon interest spread down the hall of the dorm, then throughout the dorm, the college, and, eventually, the country. LiveJournal.com was born. As word about its ease of use and services spread, the user base grew exponentially, from fifty users (mostly Fitzpatrick's close friends) to five hundred and eventually to five hundred thousand and beyond. (As of this writing, the site has over one million registered users.)

The appeal of the site was, at first, its ease of use; later its dominance became a selling point. All one needs to start a free journal is an access code, something given to every new user when they begin, meaning that it is impossible to launch a livejournal alone; new users must procure a code from an established user. This simple action encourages community from the start and immediately links your journal to someone else's. Unless you begin with a paid account (a much less popular feature that, for a nominal monthly fee, offers more versatility and options), a new journal is never born into a vacuum. It is immediately linked to the push and pull of an enormous community. Free journals have a number of preset design options (all of which are modifiable) and allow users to update quickly and easily from anywhere—the web or their own computer desktop. Once a journal is begun and a username chosen (unless it's already taken, user names often dovetail with AOL Instant Messenger IDs), each journal has a hard-to-forget URL (http://www.livejournal. com/~username) to pass out among friends.

Aspiring livejournalists fill out a list of user interests (don't worry—they can be changed at any time) that usually focus on bands, but also authors, food, people, and, of course, sex (flirting and fucking are two popular entries). Each item listed under interests immediately cross-references you with everyone else on livejournal who shares your taste—finding the eighteen other people who enjoy The Shins or "falling asleep on the F train" is only a click away. There is also a list of friends' journals and a separate list of the journals that list you as a friend, so you can keep track of your amigos as they update their own journals, or people who have grown to like your writing can further explore your world.

LiveJournal, like Makeoutclub, also has mutable "posses"—it's possible to link your journal with friends or peers or start a group journal (one in which all members can post) based on musical obsessions, hobbies, afflictions (drug abuse, anorexia), race, religion, or more whimsical flights of fancy (the "dear you" journal, which allows users to post blind letters written to anyone in the world or imagination).

Perhaps the best and most compelling aspect of LiveJournal.com is the comment feature. On every journal, at the end of each entry is a place to leave a comment or read previous comments (like most aspects of live-journal, the word "comment" can be changed—some of my favorites have been "magnificent liars," "new bruises," or "crush me baby I'm all ears"). While the entry is the definition of monologue, the comments prove that the words do not disappear into cyberspace. If you are feeling down, friends (represented by their livejournal user photo and a link to their own journals) will add a few words to cheer you up. So too will anonymous lurkers, web-only acquaintances, and total strangers. Of course, there are always enemies who might mock you, but the livejournal community is not very forgiving of hostile flames and/or intolerance. A tearstained post is a breakdown, while the comment screen becomes the virtual shoulders upon which to cry. Each entry is a starting point for chaos and consensus—usually both—and it's often quite uplifting to watch a mood unfold over a night.

"The reason I got one was because I liked to write," says Whitney Borup from Utah, "and I liked people to comment on my life. It makes me feel special or something. And I use it to vent and write cryptic messages that no one ever knows are about them. But it helps me be more open with my life because, for the most part, I'm pretty private. It helps you either get closer to the friends that read it, make new friends, or just be like . . . relieved of all that pent-up tension."

The comments enraptured LJers leave on each other's entries read like adolescents playing dress-up. The language is inflated, coded as "adult" and "poetic," which often translates into affected, stilted, and forced. But if one can accept that, there's a sweet vulnerability to it. The world of LiveJournal is an enclosed circuit where everyone has agreed to check their cynicism at the sign-on screen; it's a pulsing, swoony realm of inflated emotions, expectations, and dialogue.

It's also addictive: one wrong or random click and you can tumble head over heels into a glorious pocket of suburban Illinois high school life where girls named Nikki exult over a JV tennis match and rage against the unfairness of the yearbook staff being blamed for drinking on school property. Diaries provide the same sort of public self-expression as favorite songs—the out-of-the-moment moment, advance nostalgia, aching for something you haven't lost yet or maybe haven't yet had to begin. There's an irresistible questing in all of the journals—the frustrations of suburban reality enlivened by an injection of head-in-the-clouds romance.

"Everybody uses the site differently," says its bemused founder, Fitzpatrick. "Some people don't write personal thoughts, just their day-to-day boring activities. Some use it as a chat forum. But some do spill everything. I guess they find it easier to talk to everybody indirectly than one person directly."

People as old as fifty-five have livejournals, as do many web-savvy professionals in their thirties and forties. But most dedicated adult internet journalers graduate to the more malleable (and less centralized) services like Blogger and Pitas. LiveJournal has become the domain of the young: at the beginning of 2003, the site had well over 800,000 registered journals (with new ones added at the rate of one thousand–plus per day), with diarists living everywhere from Albany to Afghanistan. A vast majority of the journals were created by people between the ages of fifteen and twenty-three, with the largest spikes in usership among seventeen and eighteen-year-olds. This schism is both relevant and obvious.

Livejournals represent the truest and easiest realization of the essential teenage (and artistic) tenet of the importance of a "room of one's own," and yet the framework of the website is enough to make each individual room interconnected into a motel mosaic of richly felt lives. While other youth-targeted sites exist (including the venerable Diaryland.com and recent knockoffs Ujournal and Deadjournal), in many ways what Fitzpatrick unwittingly created, with its clunky but charming design and inherent mutability and connectiveness, was the ideal tool for modern teenagehood—the most sustainable and meaningful realization of the emo aesthetic. LiveJournal is at once a vehicle for vital self-definition and vigorous communication. Much as Vagrant Records (and others) rewired punk values for the mainstream, diary websites reimagine the hoary teenage trope of the diary for the public at large. Now every young person is given the tools to write their own story—and nearly every one of them who has sustained access to the computer does so. This is not a fringe thing—livejournals are now an essential part of youth culture in America.

For adults, the diary is a private object, a tangible book to be locked away with a heart-shaped key and hidden under the pillow. For them, the internet represents all that is amorphous, gigantic, and frightening about our violently public modern life. For young people, livejournals represent the almost thoughtless collusion between public and private, between individuals and a group, between the real world and the computer screen, and, yes, between resistance and community.

TV, movies, and, more than occasionally, real life have taught us that diaries are very often like the gun in the first act—it's gonna go off before anything's over. On some level, diaries are kept because we want them to be discovered. Anything truly private—self-denyingly, absolutely, terrifying private—isn't something that most people would write down and then hide under their pillow. Usually, what we write is what we wish we could say to others, but can't. The diary is often imagined as a person, as the ideal confidante. The phenomenon of the public diary is the perfect inverse of this. It maintains a whiff of privacy, so self-indulgence isn't just allowed, it's encouraged, but it also gets results.

You're writing to yourself, writing the words you wish you could communicate but, in this case, you get it both ways. The subject of your angst can see inside your mind—read your thoughts, as it were. You get to have your gun in the first act, have it go off in the third, and then leisurely hold it while it smokes (and possibly you do too) for the rest of the night.

"I make fun of livejournals, but of course everybody has one and I read them," says Kate Flannery. "The way I look at them is the same way why I think kids go on the internet at all. You lead this limiting life in your small town, but you can have an LJ and every detail of your life is suddenly of interest to someone else. It's totally voyeuristic but with a tremendous draw. Just hearing what someone had for lunch is interesting on their LJ. And that's what punk is—feeling different from someone else, feeling unique and special. Plus it's so much fun to put a counter on your LJ to see how many creepy weirdos read about what you did last night at a party."

If a Dashboard Confessional song proudly identifies itself as a "trophy display of bruises," any randomly chosen livejournal is a half-filled trophy case, one that gains fresh new bruises daily and in real time. Emo songs are idealized and romanticized versions of youth, sadness, relationships, and loss that resonate with a large group of young people, but part of their appeal is their specificity to the songwriter who crafted them. Going online and reading people's diaries is shockingly intimate and immediate, and, for some, too corny for words. But each diary is a singer and each entry a nuanced (or intentionally abrasive) song. And, more important, each entry is *true*—or at least emotionally true, which is what counts these days anyway. When the room full of young people sing along with Chris Carrabba's deeply personal lyrics, each one is working through something entirely specific in their own heads separate and distinct from what Carrabba himself intended. Livejournal gives each fan a chance to be his or her own artist, gives voice to the voiceless long after the concerts or CDs have ended. If Carrabba raises seemingly insignificant problems to global-level events, livejournals are able to do so in a far more compelling and universal way, because online, amongst peers, moral relativism rules. If you say life is hard, go ahead and say it.

This is the venue for it, this is the language. Happy public faces are allowed to be unhappy in front of a completely refigured public. Home problems are communicated in the visceral way they are felt. As one girl writes:

> i heard my parents talking last night about how they should just give up on me or something. what the hell. i know i can't listen to them because it won't get me anywhere in life. i should just not listen and use it as fuel to prove them wrong, but i don't have enough energy. it's too discouraging that everytime i get a good score on a test or do good at SOMETHING all i get is "oh, that was mediocre" and that just cuts down on what i think of myself. do my parents know that they've made me into one of the least confident people alive? that i'm constantly doubting myself compared to other kids and especially my friends? no. they don't know. do they know that i could go get drunk and smoke weed and have sex every weekend and they wouldn't know, but i don't because i respect myself more than that? no, they don't know. i haven't been eating sleeping or thinking right. and i bet my dad's going to come yell at me now. my parents don't know shit about me and they think they do that's what annoys me the most.

No one knows, she writes, no one knows. But I found her words— and so did hundreds of other people. Another high school girl writes:

> I got pissed off at my mom the other day. She put me down . . . I felt stupid. Then she said I was grounded from the computer, walked out to go to the store and slammed the door. I grabbed my pot of lip balm and threw it at the coffee table in the middle of the living room. I was still mad so I punched my closet door (a mirror), a few times. I didn't want to look at myself. I was crying. I got a migraine. My eyes and cheeks burned. By what she

said, she was making sure I knew I was a failure. I know
it now. I am sorry for that. I wanted to kill myself from
the pressure she was putting on me. I stared at myself in
the mirror and spit on it, and I hate it. I hated myself.
I shoved the scissors and my pocket knife under my mat-
tress. I think they are still there.

She makes me so mad! She makes me feel like shit about
myself! I want to leave . . . I want to go. I want to fly
away and be with Gerald*. I was Rebecca* when I was at
Gerald's. Now I am just the girl they want me to be.

I am so lonely without him. It hurts. I wish I still had
my Pocket Pikachu.

Livejournal entries are, at once, solipsistic, dreamy, outrageous, impenetrable, obvious, cloying, monotonous, engaging, hilarious, lovelorn, and
rude. They are minute by minute. There is no shyness—there is no time.
Contradictory feelings are piled up on top of one another (livejournals
update from the top down) like Lincoln Logs and no one ever looks back.
This is how life, especially young life, works.

In addition to diary-style updates, endless questionnaires pass from
journal to journal like viruses, infecting one and then spreading throughout that journaler's friends and peers before moving on. Questionnaires
most often focus on the typical, age-appropriate obsessions—sex and
music—with questions rarely straying from the "What song are you listening to right now?" "Have you ever done any drugs?" "Who was the
last person you kissed?" axis. But they are almost always filled out in full
by everyone, blamed on a nonspecific combination of boredom and peer
pressure. Appearing as they do in pretty much *all* journals with an undeniable regularity, the questionnaires serve a larger purpose as dipstick
checks of selfhood. When teenagers fill them out at four in the morning
while stifling yawns they might not realize that these are progress
reports, diagnostics on all the important maturity categories, as well as a
handy line-by-line way to compare yourself to friends and strangers and,
conversely, to present yourself (as currently constituted) to them.

Similar to questionnaires but perhaps less telling are the infinite polls or tests floating in the endless web of the internet. Each of these is a brilliant time-waster—at the end of a glaring unsubtle set of questions, the poll informs you what John Cusack film character you are, or what "hipster" underground band you are, or which '80s Saturday morning cartoon character you are. The polls are far-ranging in subject matter, topicality, and intelligence, but people are mad for them just the same. Completing a poll gives you an illustrated boxy icon to place in your journal and another handy compare-and-contrast flag for your friends and random lurkers. In one of the more telling stats of this book-writing process, I—unlike many of my subjects—registered as a paltry 16-percent emo, or "Anti-Emo," in the exceedingly popular "How Emo Are You?" poll.

For some, livejournals provide the spark of celebrity that many young people feel they deserve. It's the perfect venue for your ongoing one-woman show, where words are written like knives—just to see how deeply they can cut—and truth is adaptable. For others, the ability to write a daily account of events is not about documenting the highs and lows, but rather, restoring agency over your own life. If you are picked on at school, or your best friend made out with your long-term crush, these events can be reformed and reshaped in your journal. Pushed to the fringe in reality, online you are allowed to reassert primacy over your own narrative, to once again become the protagonist in your own story.

In fact, it was on one person's journal that I found the most credible explanation for the proliferation of livejournals—and also a fairly good argument for their existence (although I would argue that number nine would be "post in your livejournal and then return to step number one"):

> How To Have A Nervous Breakdown:
>
> 1: Think about everything going badly in your life (re: relationships, grades, hormonal imbalances, bends in your neck)

```
2: Multiply it by 5

3: Start hyperventilating and slowly begin to cry
between breaths

4: Realize that your teenaged years are supposed
to be the greatest years of your life

5: Think about the fact you'll be dead soon

6: Scream, Throw Things, Shake crying

7: Eat a comfort food

8: Pat yourself on the back, you've achieved your
nervous breakdown
```

I found Lauren's diary while browsing amongst those that listed Dashboard Confessional as a main interest. Her writing was so rich with emotions, physicalized and immediate, it was almost impossible to read through—but even more impossible to turn away from. When I stumbled upon her, she was sorting through the detritus of a pre–junior year summer that for me had passed in a brief, air-conditioned hum, but for her was dramatically lived and died on a daily basis. There was love and sexual fumblings, friendships forming and collapsing, family changes, and school apprehensions and excitements—often all within the same day and sometimes within the same entry. Occasionally, entries would be given the titles of Dashboard Confessional songs, as if that in some way made them more real—a first-kiss reflection was titled "Hands Down," a dark night of psychological angst was headlined "This Bitter Pill." Sometimes events would be described not with Lauren's own words, but with song lyrics meticulously typed out in full. (This is a frequent occurence in livejournals. Often the line between fact and fiction is blurred at will—"life is just so funny but why did *Dawson's Creek* have to be so sad?" wrote one young journaler.) Rather than diluting the songs' power, these appropriations enlivened the lyrics and teased out the emotions behind them. Once they were captured on disc, the moment was immutable. Here, in palpable breathing teenage confusion, was how emo is lived in America, from moment to moment, from night to night. The songs were starting places and bookmarks. The feelings existed in the peaks and valleys between.

As the school year approached, Lauren's feelings swung high and low—often days apart, but neither more real than the other.

10:02 pm—sad.

I've been lying on my bathroom floor crying, and trying to figure out why. my day hasn't been terrible, but it's been bad.

i wish there was something i could do that would make me feel beautiful. i want to be beautiful.

my life isn't as hard as some. but for some reason, it is absolutely exhausting for me to wake up in the morning and go to sleep at night. honestly, i'm sick of LIFE, i'm tired of taking my pills. i'm tired of being hungry and having to eat, being thirsty and having to drink, and being tired and sleeping. i'm tired of laughing at stupid jokes and singing to stupid songs.

i'm frustrated and sinking into once-every-two-weeks depressive stage. i'm tired of knowing this is coming but not being able to prevent it. why why why why why.

This entry is followed by:

```
1:26 pm--she always wears blue                    ⬚

i'm falling in love . . . with life :)

i've found that a certain someone does that to
me.

now i want more summer . . . more soccer fields
and sneaking out and dashboard songs and video
games and 'walks to remember' and making out,
long drives and brown eyes and guys that just
don't quite fit in.


we're like one big dashboard confessional song.
:D
```

I contacted Lauren via instant message a few months later. The feeling of actually talking to someone (or at least electronically communicating with them) after a long period of reading their diary is as disconcerting and slightly creepy as one might imagine. Livejournals—like Makeoutclub, like the internet itself—don't work well as one-way mediums. One must give as good as one gets, or else the scales of expectation and perception are permanently out of whack.

Lauren describes being a seventeen-year-old in Indiana as "the most boring age alive." Why? "Because we can drive, but where to?"

"I keep my livejournal because it gives me an audience," she says. "It's nice to see other people's reactions to my opinions and answers to my questions. I also feel that I've made a lot of friends through livejournal and we depend on each other's lives. The connections are made randomly—you stumble upon someone's journal, comment, they go to yours, comment, and suddenly you've developed a sort of relationship and you need their words. It's like when you come home from school and your friend calls and she says 'How was your day?' But in livejournal, we actually do care how your day was."

I ask her how else these relationships differ from those in her real life.

"My real-life best friend knows a lot about me—we share inside jokes, go places together," she says. "But my friends on LiveJournal, they know me much better. They see my insight and understand what I can say online and not out loud."

How are you different online?

"In real life, I'm very loud and goofy. I tend to hide emotions well, so to others I am rarely sad or depressed. Online, I can shock people with my hardcore feelings—depression, suicide, love, sex—and my dirty mouth."

I ask Lauren how LiveJournal has changed her and her world.

"Simply put, LiveJournal is everyone," she says. "There's nothing you can't see there. I know people from all over the U.S. and all over the world. They teach me about life. I'm in a community about girls in psychiatric therapy, which is an eye-opener for those that think they have it bad. LiveJournal has given me so much in the way of relationships, philosophy, and advice."

There was a period in the fall when Lauren quit her livejournal. She began by thanking her new friends:

i once met someone very special online; he imed me because he had heard I had a bad day. i didn't know him, but i poured my heart out to him, and he helped me more than anyone has. i had one of the worst days of my life about a week later, and he was the first person i called. i can't tell you how hard i was crying . . . we had never talked on the phone before, never met, but i called him because i knew, and he knew, and now we both know. he listened to me hiccup, and stayed up late to play the guitar for me, and i cried even more, but i never let him hear.

that's when you know you've met someone who was born with your heart.

and you, i love you, and thank you for getting me through that. i wouldn't have made it without you.

She then segued into saying that she had cut her hair and it was time for more changes—so no more journal. What followed that post was fascinating. Even though Lauren had stopped updating the main page, the comments beneath that last entry grew and multiplied. One by one, friends, and then lurkers and total strangers, posted to bemoan Lauren's absence, and to thank her for her journal. People from all over the world who had never before revealed themselves to her went public and proclaimed how much Lauren's words had meant to them, helped them, inspired them. Needless to say, Lauren soon returned to her livejournal.

"It was an amazing feeling," she says of that time. "I had no idea I touched so many people but it made me feel like I was helping someone and it made me feel like I wanted to help some more. I'm not sure why my writing is so important. I appreciate life, I guess, and it shows."

In a natural, unassuming way, Lauren had become a Dashboard Confessional all her own. Her own deeply personal words had an effect on a legion of like-minded strangers, but this time there was no stage, and she needed the encouragement and presence of her fans as much as they needed her words. Peer-to-peer support, emotional honesty, and a built-in, limitless network to draw on—all of the staples of punk, reconfigured to a new and vital medium.

Being a teenager in America at the dawn of the twenty-first century is—as it always is—to be confused, to be supercharged, to be disenfranchised, to be desperate for *something*. It is also, as always, about being in love with love, and obsessed with finding it buried within each and every minute. Teenage years are eternally twilight because it's the first time in life when we realize and understand time—that it passes, that things change, that you and everyone else won't be this way forever. It is advance nostalgia—the contradictory wish for something more and for nothing else. When teenagers read each other's livejournals, it's like listening to a Saves the Day song—watching familiar emotions trapped in amber, justifying your own feelings, and expanding your horizons—a feeling both safe and widening. For someone whose teenage years are past them, reading these journals is an act of recognition. Reading about first love, about first heartbreak, in the genuine, heightened, and wonderfully self-important language of the person experiencing them, someone who honestly has no idea of perspective, of balance, of what's to come, can be painful but intoxicating, an empathetic entertainment far greater than any mutant combination of Salinger and the WB network could produce. It's like a thirty-year-old listening to a Jawbreaker song, except the lost youth isn't his anymore—it's everyone's.

At the dawn of her sophomore year in high school, Mandy* took a moment and perfectly captured all of this. It may not be rocket science and it may not be Rites of Spring, but it's pretty right on:

I just ended the biggest therapy session . . .

I finally realized how much, we are all growing up and I can't believe it. We've come such a long way since the junior high days and even the freshman year days. We've matured . . . we've been hurt . . . we've been in love . . . we're discovering ourselves and who we are.

I'm sitting here bawling my eyes out and I have no idea why. I'm not sad . . . reliving all those past moments tonight just made me want to cry for some reason. Actually talking about some of the things that have happened just brought something out of me that never surfaced before.

I first met Henry* when I was surfing the messageboards on Make-outclub on the last Tuesday in July. After reading through the posts, I clicked on his name to get a look at his profile. He seemed like a totally familiar type: a bit on the heavy side (judging from his picture), young-looking face, serious-looking eyes. His listed website was a livejournal, so I clicked on that too. His livejournal username (and email address) hinted at more traditional, indie-leaning tastes. I learned from the user profile page that Henry lived in Arizona and was sixteen years old.

The current post in his journal began with the words, "Let me just sort things out." It read,

> Kara* got back into town last night. This event magnified things one million percent. While she was gone on her trip, she didn't really exist. She was a figment of my imagination, someone who had once been. Something that was always in the back of my mind, but wasn't quite tangible. When I saw Kara's screen name appear on my buddy list, time stopped. I looked three or four times, to see if it was real. I burst into tears. She is real, she does exist. After the sobbing stopped, I went to the bathroom to look in the mirror. I looked myself over for quite a few minutes. I talked to the boy in the mirror, I asked him many things. I asked him why this had to happen to me, why did I have to fall for this Kara girl? I looked at a picture of Kara that I had saved on my computer, kissed my two fingers, and placed them on her picture. I stared at that picture, long and hard, and I had the most overwhelming feelings flowing through my body, and I broke down.
>
> And that's how I feel . . . this is me.

This is heady stuff. Henry is in love with someone called Kara and his clearly unedited, unself-conscious purge of his feelings for her is, quite possibly, the most emo thing I've ever encountered.

Now, this is no time or place to get judgmental. My own writing at age sixteen was ten times as wrought, romantic, and self-exploring. Yours probably was, too. The difference is that I would never, ever, ever have shared those feelings with anyone. The writing I did—especially about girls—was for me and me alone. There were times when I wanted to express myself to others—desperately. Instead, in those moments, I would curl up with what I had written and read it again and again. My thoughts were what I wanted to hear—I was the only person I could trust. Sixteen-year-old Henry has no such concern—he goes for it. He puts himself out there for strangers and passersby to read. And read they did—after posting that missive, two comments (one anonymous and one not) appeared, both apparently from girls, both of whom said that reading what Henry had written had made them cry. There was no judgment, just a transfer of feelings.

After I caught up on Henry and Kara's tortured relationship, I met their friends. First up was Francine* who spent a week at Bible camp drinking and daydreaming about sex. She takes diet pills, is 5'1", thinks she's fat, and has pizza for breakfast. (Henry posted once to tell Francine that she is so cute and she shouldn't worry. This meant a lot to her. Maybe *they* should date?) Trevor* is sixteen, watches *Amelie* every day, and cries with loneliness every time he gets to the part at the end when Amelie and Nino look at each other and discover their perfect love. It seems like he has tons of friends, and music and movies to be involved with, but says he's bored all the time. All of these people have taken the same quiz in the past week, but Bonnie* is the only one who admits to having smoked and taken drugs in the past month (everyone has had a drink); no one claims knowledge of erogenous zones. Bonnie has friends galore and a posse. Her diary reads like a virtual suburban version of *One Crazy Summer*. Every night is the last night on earth and sex and love are both impossible but eminently desirable. She's obsessed with the idea that no summer will ever be as good as this one.

Over the next few weeks and months I became quite familiar with Henry and Kara in Arizona—the gentle put-downs, his inability to accept her just as a friend, the drama, the friends weighing in, the scandals, the breakdowns. Eventually—and perhaps inevitably—Kara caved and the two were a couple. Henry's posts reached ecstatic highs. It was amazing to watch this relationship play out in real time in front of me— the cut-and-pasted IM conversations, the cryptic comments chock full of emoticons heavy with meaning. It was familiar, both in its intensity and abandon, from my own high school memories, but this time I could read both sides of it. (Him: "friday night donnie darko at Kara's house, i can honestly say i have no clue what happened during that movie, but it was definitely playing. I love everyone and everything right now, nothing could be more perfect;" Her: "I enjoyed donnie darko wayyyy too much tonight.") And despite her shaky emotional standing, Kara won out every time. Just as on the Makeoutclub.com boards, online the women have the answers, the boys are revealed as bumblers. Despite Henry's false bravado, you could taste his cottony, nervous mouth through the screen, his sweaty, desperate palms. Has it changed relations between the genders to have such unlimited access to people's innermost thoughts? To realize how obsessed they are with sex too? That simple hugs mean that much? That every move is analyzed and broken down later? That she's awake at 4 A.M. too . . . ?

Then, it happened. It had only been about three weeks, but that's a lifetime in high school and online. It was sudden, it was awkward, and it was messy. It was over. And the thing is, I could see it coming. There was some vagueness in Kara's postings starting the week before—she was addressing entries to mysterious people, fluctuating wildly from giddy to morose. Poor Henry was hopeless. He would comment on her posts, asking who she was talking about, trying to play it cool. As soon as I saw his post from the weekend, I knew it was over: "vagueness scares me." He had tried calling her cell phone and had been told that she was at Chili's with her family. She'd call him back. She didn't sound the same. She never called. When it all went down on Monday evening, with Henry crying, desperately trying to fall asleep, and wondering if anything could ever feel OK again, I had a catch in my throat. Because I've been there—been the awkward, too-serious suitor, calling too much then kicking myself for picking up the phone again. The one with the full-length romance scripted in my head only to find out I didn't even get past the opening credits. For my often cynical generation livejournals are Cheever's "Enormous Radio"—an illicit glimpse of what's going on behind other doors, in other cities, in other lives. Do we want to be entertained or do we want to connect? Either way, Hollywood doesn't stand a chance.

The romance I had watched wasn't entertainment created solely for me, though; this was real. I only got to share in it. Part of me wished I could call young Henry up, tell him it would get better; email Kara, let her know that Henry feels badly about his anger, that he's mostly just embarrassed and frustrated. But the beauty of this is that they'll figure it out. He'll be OK. It's going to suck for a while, but he'll make it. She'll move on. That's what being a teenager is about too: fucking up for the first time and learning what it feels like and then learning (or choosing not to learn) from that.

Will these journals still exist years from now? Will Henry go back, reread some of his reaction to Kara dumping him—the furious anger, the lashing out, the name-calling, the snide bitterness—and be mortified? Will he realize how hard all of this was for her—how the world really isn't lined up against him when he's sad and venerating him when he's happy? Will his reaction be like Chris Ryan listening to the Promise Ring in his twenties, or Blake Schwartzenbach listening to the songs he wrote a decade ago and cringing? Or will the internet swallow up these thoughts too, making them even more ideal—solid, but transient—there when we need them and need them to be seen, but gone, eventually, when even the scars have healed.

I asked Lauren if she ever regretted any of the words she had written in her livejournal—well aware that in my few months of observation, she had already declared her undying love for three different boys.

"Absolutely not," she typed back instantly. "I do not believe in regret. And I would never regret my own feelings."

After all, this too is emo and this too is about disappointment. Not in a negative sense, because what comes next can be just as thrilling. The bruise left by a botched relationship is deeper and darker than the result of a favorite band selling out or moving on—the act of reading diaries instead of lyric sheets raises the stakes immeasurably. And yet, and yet. It's about young people finding themselves in public and private—potentially embarrassing themselves, but learning either way. Livejournals flatten the landscape, make everyone equals. It's like a giant counterculture sequel to the popular online life simulation game "The Sims"—except with real hearts on the line and real tears on the keyboard.

The hypertime of the internet may supply a constant cycle of fresh emotions to each microgeneration of teenagers, but nothing—*nothing*—will ever remove the johnny-come-lately sneer of opinionated youth.

"I'm not old school by any stretch," says Kate Flannery. "I'm only twenty-one. But I went through *hell* to get to where I am today—to build up my record collection to this point. I got beat up. I got made fun of. And now all of these kids have to do is point and click and suddenly here's cool bands you can listen to. And you don't have to build a personality for yourself because it's already all there. When you would go to a show in 1995, you knew the kids there knew their stuff and everyone had gone through the same thing to get to that point. There was a community and a bond. Now—now you don't have to go through anything. So how can those kids possibly appreciate it like we did?"

I point out that she sounds like punk rockers a decade her senior decrying the death of the 7-inch single, and she backs down a bit.

"There are benefits too." She sighs. "The fact that, to some of these kids online, it's cool to be vegetarian, or feminist, or say you're into punk. I guess if you're passionate, you're passionate, and that's cool."

I ask her if she thinks livejournals herald a major change in teenage life.

"Oh definitely," she says. "Definitely. And, at the end of the day, I guess it's good. Because so much of teenage life is internal and that's clearly not the case anymore. Because not just punk kids have livejournals. The normal ones do, too. Half the bad stuff about being a teenager can be traced back to 'no one else feels the way I do, no one else can know what it's like.' But clearly everyone *does* know, because now you can read what they've written."

The truth is, a lot of what one can find in LiveJournal is absolutely "fake." Created drama, performed feuds, self-concious kindness—all of it is present in nearly every journal. There are some who have raised the daily entry to an art form all its own, such as former Makeoutclub diva Jeralyn Mason, whose livejournal became required reading for many when she moved to New York City to attend school. Each entry was oozing with adventure, with music, with sex, nightlife, cheap cigarettes, and even cheaper vodka—and people tuned into it with the same voyeuristic glee that causes millions to tune into reality shows on television. "Livejournals are the perfect way to keep in touch with internet friends," she says. "All it takes is a click and you know what's going on. Of course, that creates a lack of *real* contact and that seems to lead to way too much drama. I get spotted in clubs and all sorts of people write about me online. That's why I had to close my journal recently—I have to learn to be more careful."

In teenage life, in emo music, and on the web, issues of "fake" and "real" mean less than curfews. Honest or not, seeing people as they most want to be seen oftentimes only highlights the cracks in the veneer, the false cheeriness, the desperation. For proof, just go to any punk-rock show, anytime, anywhere—check the makeup, the outfits, the sneers, the *trying.* You can't hide yourself online because the posts add up, the days begin to run faster and faster, and a bigger picture emerges. Even at the most extreme and gaudy corners of LiveJournal.com this holds true. Maybe not all of it happened; maybe some of it was for effect. It's not "real," per se, but teenagers have enough that's real in their lives. It's close enough. People get what they want out of livejournals—if they can't find it, there's always one million more places to look.

Near the end of 2002, a musician named Scott Windsor released his second album under the name The Lyndsay Diaries. The album, *The Tops of the Trees Are on Fire,* came packaged with somber production notes, likening Windsor's solo acoustic songs to Dashboard Confessional. There was also a promotional baseball card that featured Windsor looking devastated, clutching his guitar. The songs on the record were flimsy little things, half-baked sentiments and gauzy lyrics about sad days and sad girls. Windsor's first album was called *Remember the Memories,* and his second included a nostalgia-soaked swoon entitled "Mixtapes and Memories." Windsor is twenty-one years old.

The Lyndsay Diaries began in a tragic accident. Windsor was breezing through high school, drumming in a heavy metal band, when he was involved in a car crash that left his best friend paralyzed. Overcome, Windsor wrote a song for his friend that made up what it lacked in subtlety ("I just keep on crying . . . remember those games we used to play in kindergarten?") with hushed, almost unbearable solemnity. An upstart emo label in California, The Militia Group, somehow got ahold of the song and instantly offered Windsor—who had yet to write a second song—a three-album deal. The name of Windsor's "band" refers to a quiet girl who Windsor had dreamed about in college—one who was popular on the outside, but, he imagined, would be much different if only people could see her inner self, her diary.

In effect, The Lyndsay Diaries is the first homegrown post-Dashboard, post-internet emo act. The business has accelerated to the degree that a breaking act such as Dashboard has a (gallingly earnest) imitator a matter of months into his career, to the degree that an unassuming college student with some pain in his life and a penchant for spelling it out can get a multialbum deal.

When I met Windsor in the fall of 2002 I was intent on finding out *why*. He was soft-spoken with a gentle twang redolent of the South (where he went to college) and the Midwest (where he was born). He seemed bashful, overwhelmed, and a bit out of place. We sat and spoke in the cramped din of CBGB's—where all of this emo business began for me, months ago.

"I'm a super nostalgic person," he said. "I'm always thinking of the past. I went through a couple of years where I was going through a lot of stuff, and to cope with things I put myself in different positions from the past when things were good. It's weird, though, how we turn memories around to make them a lot better than they really were."

Windsor talked haltingly about how he thought he didn't have anything to write about at first, and then turned one winter vacation's ennui into his first album. "I usually write stuff down right as it happens," he said. "I just jot it all down in a notebook and then I'll go back over it and form it into songs."

"So, it's your diary," I said.

"No, my thoughts. Well, kinda like my diaries, yeah." He laughed.

I asked him if he had a livejournal. He rolled his eyes.

"Oh, no. I actually don't like livejournals. When I was in school everyone had them. We'd all hang out at night and then everyone would just go home and post what happened in their livejournals, and then respond and have fights on there. If I had one, I wouldn't let anyone see it. It's the stupidest thing in the world. I was like, who cares, we're twenty years old." He laughed again.

"But, that's exactly what you *do* do with your songs," I protested.

"No," he said. "People write stuff on livejournals because they *know* people are going to be reading it. I try not to do that with my songs."

I mentioned that his idea of "Lyndsay" having a secret self seems almost anachronistic in this day and age—when it seems very likely that he *could* have read her diary.

"Naw," he said, shuffling his feet. "Only if you could read what she didn't want anyone else to see could you understand the person. I mean, it's not like you could read her livejournal!" He laughed loudly.

These days, though, you really can do just that. As Windsor makes a bid for his weepy indulgences to become the next iteration of emo, he is surprisingly ignorant of both his audience and their terrain. With the amount of media open to them, the tools for self-expression that are piped into and out of their bedrooms, kids don't necessarily need Lyndsay's diaries or even Scott Windsor's. Now, they can have their own.

"Obviously I don't know what it was like before my time," Windsor said to me before he sound-checked, "but it just seems like kids go through a lot these days and need an outlet or something to relate to. I definitely think there's a need for it."

There certainly is, but he doesn't fill it—and neither do the legions of upstarts and imitators crowding the rosters of cash-starved major labels. Livejournals and their ilk are the ultimate expression of emo DIYism. No need to start a band to express your feelings and no need to parrot bands that come close. Who needs imitations when we have the real thing? Out of the never-ending, burst-and-bloom cycle of emo—impossible highs and hopes and inevitable disappointment—it is the peer-driven hypertime of the internet that offers not only a way out, but a way forward: a medium that straddles the basement and the stadium, the individual and the community.

At the end of the teenage years, it becomes clear that there is no such thing as an emo artist—only emo songs, albums, or moments. Dashboard Confessional opened people's ears, but it's the internet that stitched their hearts together. Fake or real, heightened or bummed out, no one will deny that music can save lives. But in 1,001 very real ways, the web can too. Just ask someone I ran into online one hot August night. Someone named Emily—a fifteen-year-old girl in the rural south with a tough life, a prescient screenname, and an entire world that couldn't have existed for her just five years before.

> EMO IS NOT A TREND: I went to a private school and I didn't really have any friends. I was stuck between trying to fit in and giving up on fitting in. Truth is I really didn't know much about music genres and what I liked just then.

AGREENWALD: why did you move and when did you do it?

EMO IS NOT A TREND: Well I had a bit of an abusive childhood, and I was the fat ugly kid in class until high school. By the time I got to 9th grade I was pretty paranoid about nobody liking me, et cetera. I did get quite a few friends, actually, but I was ignorant and took them for granted during the summer because they didn't talk to me much. My best friend Nina*–the one who introduced me to emo bands–seemed to think that I didn't like her, and I thought Nina didn't like me, so we didn't talk either. That brought me down real hard. And I live with my grandparents, and they hated where we were living. So one day I was like I don't need to stay here, we can move. And I think it happened about a week and a couple days ago.

AGREENWALD: so is it safe to say that your music is helping you out a lot these days?

EMO IS NOT A TREND: Music has always helped me out. Nina and I are a lot alike, and the first thing we found out about each other was that were it not for music we'd probably both either be stuck in a crisis center or dead by now. I rely a lot on music to get me through the day. When I get home from school the only things I do are go online and listen to music.

AGREENWALD: what do you do online, mostly?

EMO IS NOT A TREND: Well first I check my e-mail..cause usually I have comments from one of my journals, and I talk to people online, and update my journals, and go to sites like emotionalpunk.com and read the news, and of course dashboardconfessional.com..I just pass the day along, because there's a baby. I lived with my grandparents until I was 5 and my father got remarried to a woman who didn't like me much. She found every excuse possible to beat or whip me. Sometimes she used her hand, sometimes a belt, a two-by-four, a palmetto stem..whatever was handy. I remember once she said she was going to spank me for every time I had ever lied to her, and she told me if I winced or cried she'd do it more. So she did that for maybe 20 minutes. And sometimes she'd make me stand with my nose to a wall for 8–10 hours at a time without feeding me and I couldn't sit down or make any noises, and she'd sneak up behind me and hit me. Grandma says that when I was younger I used to say that I was afraid my half-brother was going to come and lift my covers and do bad things to me. Anyways we lived in a really nasty trailor at first with holes and bugs and stuff, and eventually we got a better house. I lived 2 hours from school and 1 hour from a convenience store. My dad hunted and we had stuff like wild boar and alligator tail for supper. I had to get up at 5:30 to catch the bus. Anyway, my dad was a paranoid schizophrenic but he didn't take his medication. And I guess one day he just snapped or something because my grandma got angry and took me home with her. I lived with her until I was 11, when she wanted to move to Seattle, WA. But we had to have permission from my dad and he denied it. After court we started visitation and I had decided to move back with them because they were being really nice to me. Then my dad died in a car wreck. So I went back to living with my grandparents. My grandma used to be really strict and protective and unfair because my mom wasn't exactly the best child. She died from an overdose of cocaine. So Grandma was pretty bad, and I was rebellious and angry and depressed. It got to the point (in about 6th grade) where I was furiously angry at everything, and then in seventh grade I became suicidal. I wrote poems and songs about killing myself. Towards the end of 8 grade I started actually cutting my arms and stuff. I started doing that on a regular basis and eventually Grandma figured out that it wasn't the cat that was doing that to me. So she stuck me in therapy and I was just kinda mellow about it. It's gotten to the point now where I'm just pretty much like yeah, things really suck but I just gotta deal with that. But I still get really depressed a lot and hit mood swings, and I still cut myself sometimes. I probably have about 60 scars on my body now.

AGREENWALD: that's an incredible story. i'm so sorry you've had to go through so much at such a young age.

EMO IS NOT A TREND: I try not to pity myself. There are people who have it much worse than me.

AGREENWALD: but it sounds like you're doing ok, like you said earlier: food, music, and soda to get you through the day, right?

EMO IS NOT A TREND: Yeah, that and internet..I can't believe I forgot internet. Internet is like my blood.

AGREENWALD: what do you think your life would be like if you didn't have the internet?

EMO IS NOT A TREND: I assure you I wouldn't be here were it not for the internet. Internet and music, they kept me alive. In seventh and eighth grade I had no friends so I relied on my internet buddies to cheer me up. I've been tinkering on the computer since I was 3, and I like to call myself a geek. I could teach half the computer classes I'm in. But I really started relying on the internet in seventh grade probably, because that was when I started getting suicidal.

AGREENWALD: how did you rely on it then?

EMO IS NOT A TREND: I got an online journal then. Live Journal, actually. And I wrote everything down in there. Poems, songs, emotions I was feeling—I wrote it all, and that really helped. And then my internet friends read it, and talked to me about stuff, and a lot of them could relate to everything I was saying. And that really helped, to have someone like me to talk to. No one in that private school was like me at all. I had no one to talk to. I became an internet junkie, because it was my escape. My grandma still calls me a fantasy freak. And I am, really. Because most times, fantasy is all I have.

AGREENWALD: that's amazing that livejournal could help you so much.

EMO IS NOT A TREND: It was a release, somewhere where I could let everything out so I didn't have to keep it all inside.

AGREENWALD: and the weird thing about it is, even though it's anonymous, people can be so supportive.

EMO IS NOT A TREND: That's true. When you've been through shit, I think that tunes you into other people's emotions and problems. It gives you insight—it makes you want to help them. I have so many friends that I met online. There are a few real important ones though. Like Ned*. I've been talking to him since the middle of eighth grade. He's always been there. And Tommy*, he's had it worse than I have. We're good friends. And Greg*, who lives in Hawaii, is always cheerful and cheers me up. There's a lot of them, and they all mean a lot to me. Because they have always done their best to help me, and that means a lot to me. It's like fans supporting a band..it keeps everything moving along smoothly.

AGREENWALD: but it seems so much more intimate and, in many ways, important—because you're all fans of each other.

EMO IS NOT A TREND: Yeah it's important, because you have direct contact. But still . . . Life is just a bunch of fans, really..fans of other people, fans of bands..everyone keeps everyone else going.

ACKNOWLEDGMENTS

First and foremost, I am massively indebted to my agent, Jim Fitzgerald, for believing in me and in this project long before I was able to do either. In every sense, this book would have been impossible without his tireless help and unwavering vision.

Similar thanks are due to my colleague and friend, Marc Spitz, for introducing me to Jim in the first place—and for listening to my stress and worry for nearly two years. Thanks also to Surie Rudoff for her able legal advice, my editor, Michael Connor, and all at St. Martin's Press.

I would be nowhere—personally or professionally—without the constant presence, encouragement, and good-natured mocking of my friends Chris Ryan, Matt Jolly, Sean Howe, and Lara Cohen.

Thank you to Andy Gensler, Dave Moodie, Ron Richardson, and Greg Milner for giving me my professional start. Thanks also to all of my friends, colleagues, and family at *Spin,* especially Jon Dolan, Alex Pappademas, Chuck Klosterman, Charles Aaron, Sia Michel, Tracey Pepper, Sarah Lewitinn, Caryn Ganz, Dave Itzkoff, Maureen Callahan, Kate Carrington, Adrienne D'Amato, William Van Meter, and Andrew Beaujon. A giant thanks and shout-out to the ghost of Spin.com, and my friends Beth Wawerna, Mike Hauswirth, and Julie Ann Pietrangelo.

Chris Carrabba made himself open and available to me from the earliest imaginings of the book—and trusted in my ability to tell this story when I was still wracked with doubt. I owe an enormous amount to his generosity, as well as to the entire extended Carrabba and Dashboard Confessional families.

Certain people went above beyond the call of any reasonable duty to help with the writing and research of this book—for that, I am eternally grateful to them: Brian Bumbery; Carrie Klein, Steve Martin, Amanda Pitts, and Laura Eldeiry at Nasty Little Man PR; Kathi Haruch; Jessica

Hopper; Rich Egan, Jon Cohen, Ryan Quigley, Tricia McNulty, and all at Vagrant/Hard 8; Mike Schoenbeck, Scott Schoenbeck, Johnny Leffler, Mike Marsh, and the rest of the Dashboard touring crew; Jessie Tappis; Darren Walters and Tim Owen at Jade Tree Records; Jim Adkins, Tom Linton, Rich Burch, and Zach Lind of Jimmy Eat World; Michele Fleischli and SAM; Rick Marino and the rest of the Jimmy Eat World touring crew; Luke Wood; Geoff Rickly; Adam Lazzara, John Nolan, and Taking Back Sunday; Kate Flannery; Gibby Miller; Sarah Cairns; Jeralyn Mason; Alex Coletti; Jenny Toomey; Tristin Laughter; Anna Hillinger, Richard Reines, Stefanie Reines, The Starting Line, and all at Drive-Thru Records; Travis Morrison; Ben Holtzman and Joe Carroll; Jonathan Poneman, Chris Jacobs, and Steve Manning at Sub Pop Records; Ben Goldberg and Nils Bernstein at Matador Records; Victory Records; Jason Gnewikow; Nikki Evenson and Rachel Everson in Texas; Priya Motaparthy; Angela Cheng; Lauren Panepinto; Hilary Okun; John Szuch; Amy Pickering at Dischord; Jolie Lindholm; Brad Fitzpatick; Andrew Smales; Chomsky (the band); Neal, Ellen, Emily, and Noonie Bien; Robert Vickers; and Chris Baty.

A special thanks to all of the "kids"—those who spoke with me on the record and shared their thoughts with me off of it. Those I met standing on lines in New York, Arizona, Florida, California, and Texas and those I met online. Thanks to those who shared their words and hopes and fears with me—whether they knew I was reading them or not. Ian Bauer, Howie Kussoy, Anthony Lombardi, Justin Bolobanic, Whitney Borup, Keith Colleluori, Lauren, Jesse, Iris, Connie, Melissa, Danielle, and all of the rest: this book is nothing without you.

Thanks to my father, Michael Greenwald, for having the exact right amount of confidence in me and to my mother, Anne Greenwald, for having the exact right amount of (loving) doubt.

Thanks to my grandmother, Sylvia Greenwald.

And one more thank you to Rachel Bien, even though it could never possibly suffice. Thank you for being my best friend and anchor throughout all of this. For putting up with me even when you shouldn't have, I will be forever grateful. I will also consider cleaning my office.

In memory of my cousins: Amanda Davis, James Davis, and Francie Davis.

And finally: thank *you!*

INDEX

Note: A fictitious name is denoted by an asterisk.